Lost Among the Baining

Lost Among the Baining

Adventure, Marriage, and Other Fieldwork

Gail Pool

University of Missouri Press
COLUMBIA

Copyright © 2015 by
The Curators of the University of Missouri
University of Missouri Press, Columbia, Missouri 65201
Printed and bound in the United States of America
All rights reserved
5 4 3 2 1   19 18 17 16 15

ISBN: 978-0-8262-2051-6
Library of Congress Control Number: 2015940297

∞™ This paper meets the requirements of the
American National Standard for Permanence of Paper
for Printed Library Materials, Z39.48, 1984.

Typesetter: K. Lee Design & Graphics
Typeface: Adobe Caslon Pro

For Zach and Alex

What am I doing here?

—Arthur Rimbaud, writing home from Ethiopia

Contents

Prologue   xi

PART 1   *Lost in New Guinea*

1   Starting Points   3
2   Points of Departure   13
3   Niu Guinea   25
4   Pig Food   40
5   Taro and Gin   57
6   Moving Day   73
7   Jungle Boots   84
8   "Our Fathers Never Told Us"   98
9   A Time of Rain   113
10   Masks   127

PART 2   *Lost in America*

11   The Story of a Lifetime: Part 1   151
12   The Story of a Lifetime: Part 2   164
13   The Story of a Lifetime: Part 3   176
14   The Story of a Lifetime: Part 4   188

PART 3 *Well, This Is History*

15	Testing the Water	201
16	Wading In	210
17	Many Rivers to Cross	222
18	The River of Death	235
19	Back Eddy	245
20	Unexpected Currents	261
21	Across	270

Prologue

I think it was only in the Port Moresby airport, while scanning the baggage regulations—*No spears! No arrows!*—that I truly believed we were going back to New Guinea. It should not have come as a surprise. We had been planning the trip for months. But it had taken such a long time to get there. Almost forty years.

In 1969 through 1970, my husband and I lived in New Britain, in what was then the Territory of Papua and New Guinea, doing fieldwork among the Baining people. Jeremy was an anthropology student at the time, gathering data for his doctoral thesis. I was an aspiring writer.

The trip was a fiasco, both professionally and personally. On returning home, I believed, with young passion, that it had ruined our lives. Jeremy left the field of anthropology altogether. My own early account of the trip began bleakly: "There was nothing redeemable in this experience." Not surprisingly, that manuscript did not go far.

But the experience was extraordinary, and it never lost its hold. It was always there, lurking just below the surface of our lives. Socially, with friends, or at the gatherings we would infrequently and reluctantly attend, we would suddenly find ourselves calling up the anecdotes we knew would entertain: our tales of eating bats, of fighting horned beetles, of confronting slimy logs spanning rivers, and, of course, of the enigmatic people we had lived with, whom we could neither understand nor forget. We felt guilty indulging in these tales. They seemed such an easy way to instantly become Interesting People. But neither of us excelled at small talk, we were aware that in company we seemed dull, and there it was, these tales made us Interesting People—we would seldom resist.

Privately, the experience was darker. Emotions were always smoldering like the fires in the great New Britain volcano Tavurvur, ready to burst forth in flames and burning lava. We would be discussing something—it might be something trivial, like what to have for dinner, or it might be something large, like work, or our relationship, or our son—and we would suddenly find ourselves locked in a deadly embrace, edging ever closer toward the crater's molten heat until we were battling on the rim, as if fighting for our lives. It felt primal. It could get physical. It was fortunate that I didn't have my bush knife or Jeremy his New Guinea shotgun close at hand.

As the experience evolved, as the tragedy came to seem a melodrama of marital discord set in the bush and then a comic coming-of-age story in the jungle and finally all of these at once, the battles tempered. But they didn't end. We would still find ourselves glowering at each other across a room, our bodies taut, debating nothing more than a single word—*ambition*—and nothing less than the nature, the conduct, the very point of life. The same battle, born among the Baining and never resolved, pulling us apart but also binding us together: How could we separate? Who else would ever understand? In going to New Guinea, we had embarked on a journey that wouldn't end.

In the decades that followed, I tried to write about the experience many times, digging up my journals, still redolent of jungle rot, trying to hack my way through the bush. But nothing really worked. Either I couldn't penetrate the jungle, or I couldn't find my way out.

I sometimes wondered whether going back would make a difference. "Closure" may be a cliché, but like most clichés it is based on something real. Sometimes you can manage to embrace the past, or let it go.

Yet it seemed that if we couldn't come home, neither could we return. I would suggest it from time to time, but I don't think I ever meant it and we never seriously considered it. It's true that for many years, we hadn't the money: Boston to New Guinea is an expensive trip. We hadn't time: we were working hard, Jeremy couldn't take off the month we thought we would need, I had teaching schedules and writing deadlines.

And then Australians we knew said that since independence in 1975, New Guinea had grown terribly dangerous: one reported that he had been mugged at gunpoint, and we promptly added "unsafe" to our list of reasons for not going. But we knew that he was talking about Port Moresby, always a rough town, ranked by the *Economist* in 2004 as the worst capital city in the world to live in. We felt pretty sure that our own destination would be safe. We were certainly afraid of returning, but our fear had nothing to do with muggings. If we went back, would we meet that sorry young couple in the bush? Would we once again become them? And if we did find closure, what else might come to an end? Perhaps this ancient paste was all that held the two of us in place.

But then, in 2008, a major conference on antiquarian maps—Jeremy's new field—was scheduled for Wellington, New Zealand, and he said that he wanted to attend. He had always dreamed of going to New Zealand; he had heard that it was dramatically wild and rugged, the kind of terrain he loved. He wanted to see the Southern Cross. In general, I would go along to these meetings, although I had no particular involvement with maps. But most had taken place in European cities—easy trips to places that I loved: Florence, Amsterdam, London. I didn't doubt that New Zealand would be beautiful, but I wasn't especially drawn to it, and this seemed a long way to travel for a very mild interest.

Unless—since we would be in that part of the world . . .

We took this slowly, edging our way around the rim of the volcano. We discussed it for several months, skirting any embers and keeping to cool and solid ground. We talked about time and money. We considered health and age. We questioned whether a short trip would be worth it. We pondered what to do with the dog.

We talked to family and friends, who responded in amusingly disparate ways. "Wonderful!" they might say. "Amazing!" Or, "Really? But wasn't that the worst year of your life?"

"It's always disappointing going back," said a colleague.

Always? I thought not. But you had to be prepared for what you might find. The Baining youngsters might be carrying cell phones these days. There might be satellite dishes outside the huts. There might be highways, smog, noise. Loggers might have stripped the rain forest; miners might have gouged out the mountains. New Britain's beloved capital, Rabaul, always so lushly *there*, was already half gone, buried since 1994 in Tavurvur's ash. So many people we had known would have died. Would anyone even know who we were: Kusaiki and Iara, those two white youngsters who had lived in these mountains so many years ago?

Yet even as we talked and brooded, I think we knew from the first that we would go. The very idea of it filled us with a nostalgia we had never felt before. The intensity of my longing took me by surprise. I just wanted to be there. I wanted to bake in that heat, to smell the *kunai* grass, to hear the raucous cry of the *koki*, to taste taro. I wanted to meet the Baining again. I wanted to reenter that past so vivid it always seemed to be alive, unfolding right now, bound forever in the present tense. I wanted to lay those young ghosts to rest. It was time.

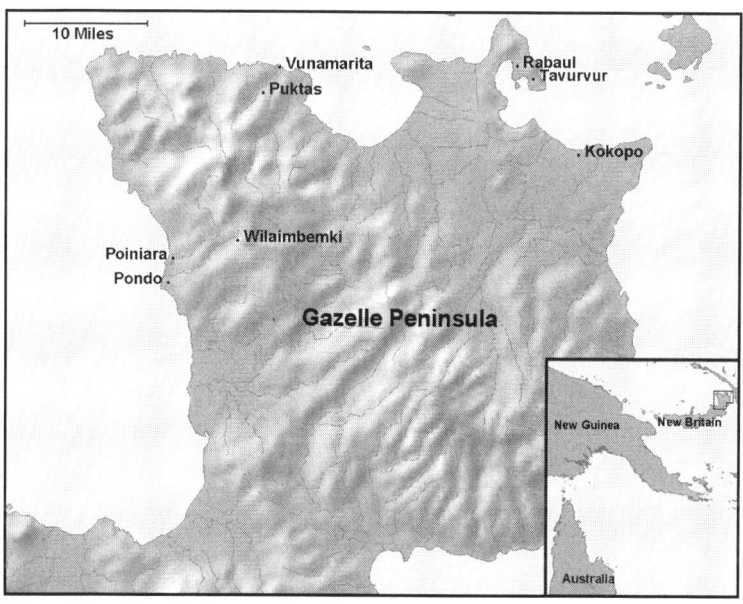

Map of the Gazelle Peninsula of New Britain

Lost Among the Baining

PART 1

Lost in New Guinea

1

Starting Points

It is the fall of 1967, and Jeremy and I are living in London. We are renting a row-house flat on Clifton Hill, between tony St. John's Wood and gritty Kilburn, on the 159 bus route that takes us everywhere. The flat is large and not too shabbily furnished but damp in its basement setting. A frog lives just outside our window, in the cellar, and a cat comes to visit almost daily, a beautiful black creature we pamper with treats. "No pets," says our landlady, Mrs. B., who lives upstairs and watches us closely. (Students! She has inventoried every cup.) "It isn't ours!" we say—every time—hoping that the cat purring on the sofa will distract her from the illegal paraffin heater in the corner of the room. She eyes us sternly, but perhaps she feels maternal—we look so very young; she never throws us out.

We have come to London from Cambridge, Massachusetts, just months after graduating college and one year after getting married. Harvard undergraduates do not often marry in 1966, and we take our families by surprise. "And you swore you wouldn't marry till you were thirty!" "Marry now and statistics show you'll be divorced within ten years!" This last from Jeremy's father, ever the academic, who has now guaranteed that we will stay together at least a decade, if only to prove him wrong.

I myself feel terribly shrewd to have married at the start of senior year, avoiding the postgraduation nuptials cliché. I am convinced that starting out together as students has set us on an equal footing and saved me from the housewife syndrome. I have somehow failed to notice that I have simply become a housewife one year early. Nor have I noticed that being students together has nurtured a fierce sense of competition, which sprang to life in Cambridge, has thrived in London, and will bloom with lush vigor in the rain forest of New Guinea, when we have no one to compete with but each other.

Jeremy is twenty-two years old. He is tall and very thin with gray eyes and a dimple that emerges when he jokes, which is often. He's so quiet it can take a while to realize how smart he is; so apparently low-key you wouldn't know that while he hates to fight, he loves to win; and so modest you might easily miss his ambition. But he was one of the stars of Harvard's Social Relations Department, where cultural anthropology was housed; his two-hundred-page thesis earned him a summa; and he is clearly headed for academia where, like his father, mother, and brother, he feels at home. He is now studying anthropology at the London School of Economics, with fieldwork for his doctoral dissertation to start next year.

I am twenty-one. I am small and slim with thick dark hair that I wear in a braid to one side. I'm prone to discontent except when I joke, which is often. I'm so quiet it's easy to miss the fact that I'm intense, and so polite you'd never guess that at home I'm generally up for a fight. But in truth, although I don't yet know it, I hate to win.

I am not headed for academia if I can help it. It might appear that my classics degree has prepared me practically for little else.

But this is not how I see it. I see myself as pragmatic, someone who plans ahead, and I too am ambitious: ancient Greek, I am certain, has prepared me to be a writer. While Jeremy attends classes, I tutor Latin and work diligently on a curious little novel about a young man who finds himself literally disappearing. I give remarkably little thought to what, if anything, this story might imply.

We are living in London because we fell in love with the city on our three-month trip through Europe the summer of our junior year: the American Grand Tour rendered not so grand on five dollars a day. We are also in London to escape family: my own in New York City, which includes a seriously unbalanced sister whose notes to me might read, in full: "Dear Gail: Fuck you! Love, Lynne"; and Jeremy's father in Cambridge, a political scientist at the Massachusetts Institute of Technology who sits on the wrong side of the Vietnam War teach-ins and has inspired students to wear buttons that read "Shoot Pool!"

This is the sixties: we are also in London because we have grave problems with our country. I have been actively involved with civil rights, doing voter registration in Birmingham, Alabama, in the summer of 1965. We have both protested the war, and the chance of being drafted to fight a battle that we believe Americans should not be fighting shadows Jeremy and every young man we know. Although this will change in the course of the year—as I follow the upheavals back home and feel myself intensely, indelibly American—when we leave the United States, I am not at all sure that I want to return.

We live student lives, at once earnest and impulsive. We debate world problems, we discuss Deep Issues, we read. We walk the city, we go to films, we go to more films, we booze with friends.

We travel, poorly and poor, falling ill in Paris, running out of money in the Loire Valley, behaving badly in the great museums of Amsterdam with friends, art students no less.

One trip we take posts a warning that I curiously ignore. In the summer of 1968, we travel to Norway, where Jeremy lived for one year as a boy. We visit Oslo, but what he most wants is to hike in the Jotunheim mountains. It is a family tradition: his grandfather took his father, his father took him and his brother, and now he wants to go with me.

On this trip I make two discoveries. The first, really, I already know but have refused to acknowledge: I am not an outdoors person. I am urban, a city girl, a New Yorker to the bone. My idea of an outdoor excursion is having coffee at a sidewalk café in Greenwich Village. I do not get the point of hiking, I do not enjoy it, and I do not do it well.

The second discovery, however, comes as a surprise, although I don't understand how this can be. We are crossing Besseggen, the ridge made famous by Ibsen's Peer Gynt, who claimed to have crossed it riding a wild reindeer. The ridge is narrow, with a drop hundreds of meters down on either side. "Look at that view!" exclaims Jeremy, and indeed it is a stunning view. In fact, I am so stunned that I can focus only on my feet, which do not move. How can I not have known that I am seriously acrophobic? I have no memory of this phobia. Is it new? I am utterly, unbearably terrified of heights.

On the whole, this little jaunt does not bode well for fieldwork, which will take place in one jungle or another, which will no doubt require hiking, which will probably involve heights, and which looms just ahead. But with youthful insouciance, I do not take any of this in.

―――――

Fieldwork. This has been in the cards since I first met Jeremy, and by now I know all about it, secondhand. In 1968 fieldwork is the cornerstone of anthropology, the heart of it, the centerpiece, the main attraction, the Grand Thing. Anthropology departments send graduate students, armed with notebooks, cameras, and tape recorders, to live for some eighteen months among a so-called primitive tribe. The texts of the discipline are based on the fieldwork of earlier practitioners—Franz Boas, Bronislaw Malinowski, Sir Edward Evan Evans-Pritchard, Margaret Mead—and students are expected to do original work of their own.

In time, this concept will expand. In time, anthropology students may settle almost anywhere: in urban neighborhoods, in fishing villages, even in companies to study corporate culture—in the eighties an anthropologist will pop up in the company where Jeremy works, and he himself will become an informant.

But in the sixties, such areas of study are left to sociology: anthropology takes on the "primitive." And though already this word *primitive*—so pejorative, so indefinable, so imperialist, so arrogant—is coming to be shunned, the concept of it thrives. Within the circle of anthropologists, stories abound: of rude living, hardships, and mud; of strange ways and gross misunderstandings. At one gathering, we hear about a bishop in some far-off land visiting a local Mass where suddenly onstage before him a villager kneels, and, to the priest's horror, they chop off the fellow's head! An apocryphal tale, no doubt—or maybe not—and told with great hilarity. I too laugh, and nod, transfixed.

The first challenge for the anthropology student is finding a society in which to perch. The ideal is a group that has had as little contact as possible with outsiders who inevitably—whether by actively proselytizing or by virtue of just being, so differently, *there*—will have altered, or "corrupted," the traditional culture.

By 1968 anthropologists do not expect to find an untouched culture, however much they may dream of it: Western civilizations have long since been sending out their explorers, their missionaries, their patrol officers, their developers, and, of course, their anthropologists. They have been transporting their diseases and addictions. They have been exporting their goods. Above all, perhaps, there are those goods. Even without the actual arrival of outsiders, goods make their impact: a village that has never seen a white person will nonetheless be altered by the advent of metal knives.

The question then is not of purity but of degree: How much of the traditional culture remains? And just how choosy can a student be, when contact has spread, anthropologists have multiplied, and traditional societies have diminished in number and in size?

Often, in making their choices, students go to the region where their thesis advisers worked: information is more personally available, contacts more likely to be at hand. Jeremy's adviser went to New Guinea, New Guinea rituals have sparked Jeremy's interest, and he decides on New Guinea.

This is fine by me. At this point, I do not even know where New Guinea is.

Once Jeremy begins actively searching, his adviser steps in to help. He is a big, compassionate man, somehow at once brooding and jovial, who has been through this himself and has our welfare in mind. He recommends the Bariai of New Britain, a group he describes as friendly, ritual oriented, and situated on the coast, a good location for culture-shocked young anthropologists who might be in need of a break.

We promptly visit the British Museum and read missionary descriptions of the Bariai and their language ("I circumcise, you circumcise, he/she/it circumcises"). Jeremy sends out queries. We grow excited as the trip grows real.

But soon a stern letter arrives from an anthropology professor, warning Jeremy to cease and desist: these are "his people," he says.

"*His* people!" we laugh at the colonial hauteur. "Academics!" we shake our heads. But protocol demands that Jeremy withdraw.

No matter. Another name comes quickly to the fore: "Well, there are the Baining," someone says. They pronounce it "*Byning.*" Just a name. We learn only that these people live in the mountains of New Britain, the largest island in the Bismarck Archipelago, which is part of the Territory of Papua and New Guinea. (By now I have looked at a map.) Are they also "taken"? Warily, Jeremy puts out feelers, and a professor at the Australian National University (ANU) in Canberra responds.

No, she informs us, no one is working among the Baining—several projected Baining field trips have for various reasons fallen through. In fact, no anthropologist has visited these people since 1928, when Gregory Bateson was there, and he considered his field trip a terrible failure and wrote essentially nothing about it.

Indeed, she says, someone should take this on: it seems to her urgent that these people be studied before their culture disappears. She feels guilty that she herself hasn't gone, but several things have interfered, including a weak knee that is a handicap in such rugged mountain terrain.

About the Baining themselves, she can tell us nothing, but she believes that Baining ritual is still going on in remote mountain villages. She suggests that we write to Bateson. Perhaps he will explain the difficulties he had? Share his notes? Almost as a postscript, she adds that colleagues have pressed her to warn us that the people are "ugly and dirty." (Clearly, political correctness has yet to arrive.)

This is not what you would call an auspicious introduction. Gregory Bateson is an eminent former anthropologist and a prolific writer, the author of *Naven*, a classic in the field and one of Jeremy's favorite books. What made this Baining trip so very awful that he wrote nothing about it? Why in all these years has no other anthropologist visited these people? Why have so many prospective field trips fallen through?

Obviously, for me, the Bainings' locale isn't suitable at all. Rugged terrain: I can barely hike in Central Park. Mountains: I am acrophobic. The villages are remote; we will be isolated, miles from a break. Are the people really "ugly and dirty"? We agree that it doesn't sound promising. In truth, both of us are thrilled.

Still, we do not make a commitment, though neither of us really doubts that we have both made up our minds. Jeremy writes to Bateson, and we return to the British Museum, to poke around.

The picture, as we color it in, does not grow prettier. We learn that the interior of the Gazelle Peninsula, where the Baining live, is indeed rugged territory. Getting in and out will be difficult in the best conditions, probably impossible in the rainy season, when the rivers will flood. We will have to take in ample supplies and set up for the long haul. Breaks will most certainly be infrequent, medical help out of reach. We will need to stay fit and healthy for safety and even survival.

As for the Baining, we can learn almost nothing. Little is known about the language beyond the fact that it is neither Melanesian nor related to the surrounding languages, and it is difficult to learn. We do discover that the Baining have two claims to fame: The first is the massacre, in 1904, of an entire mission station—fathers, brothers, and nuns. A dramatic assault, apparently anomalous for what appears to be a peaceful people, and never fully understood. The second is the Baining rituals, involving both a fire dance and a spear dance and extraordinary "masks," elaborate and eerie painted structures, some worn on the head, others carried. No one has described these rituals in detail or knows what they are for.

As we take all of this in, the aura of myth and mystery, challenge and fantasy strengthens. And then we hear from Gregory Bateson.

"It is now 40 years since I saw [the Baining]," he writes, "and your letter reminds me of a most miserable and frustrating period of my life."

He describes the Baining as "monstrously difficult to work with," "very shy and frightened," a nearly forest-dwelling people who seemed inherently depressed when living in houses and happiest wandering in the bush. To his amazement, he says, their main topic of conversation was taro, their main interest geometric designs they might use for their masks. Their language, he adds, is "abominable," and he complains that a main problem seems to be the way they speak it.

Reading this letter, we laugh out loud. What are we to make of it? Can he really be saying that the Baining don't speak their language well? This is Gregory Bateson. Clearly, he had a bad trip. As he says, it was his first field trip, he was very young, and though he thought that "the then fashionable controversies" in anthropology were "all nonsense," he did not know how to think about "other aspects." All the same, he seems to have responded with incredible force to these people.

"My feeling about them," he writes, "no doubt caused by my own failure to make any sense of them, is that they live in a tragic atmosphere. Almost wild animals who had been eaten and domesticated or enslaved by the coastal people for hundreds of years, and somehow knew that their species was doomed."

Doomed! By now we are giddy. Massacres, fire dances, rugged mountains, uncrossable rivers, isolation, the risk of illness—even death!—and a doomed and tragic people. How can we resist?

Jeremy's adviser grows concerned. He doesn't like the sound of this at all. It will be hard, he says, harder than we know. He warns us not to underestimate the physical impact of such rough conditions. He warns us not to underestimate the psychological impact of isolation. He warns us not to underestimate the trials of working in a difficult culture.

"We can find another society," he says—repeatedly. "You don't have to do this!"

But he is wrong. We do. *We* will solve the mystery of the Baining. *We* will break this strange curse of exclusion. *We* will succeed where others have failed.

2

Points of Departure

Planning a trip to the Baining Mountains, we quickly learn, is not like planning a trip to Italy or France. There is no Michelin Guide with recommendations for the best restaurants, the best routes, the sights that will be *vaut le détour*. There aren't any restaurants. There are no routes—there aren't any roads! And there have been no professional travelers—or tourists—to evaluate the sights and pass their opinions on. A few stragglers have no doubt wandered through, strays from the plantations. But for the most part, the only outsiders in the region have been missionaries counting souls, patrol officers counting bodies, and one anthropologist, counting the days until he could leave.

This is not a trip for people who need to know beforehand what they will find.

At a distance, Jeremy and I cannot gauge exactly where we will be going. The maps of New Guinea we have do not show where tiny Baining villages are. And this is 1968: no Google Earth! It is not that this is uncharted territory. Somewhere there are detailed military maps: New Guinea was a battleground in World War II, and there was major fighting in New Britain, in just the area where we are headed. In Rabaul the Japanese and the Australians struggled for control of Simpson Harbor, the best deep-sea port in the South Pacific.

Somewhere too there may be more recent maps drawn up by the Australians, who are now in charge of the Territory, a United Nations protectorate. But these maps are not readily available in our part of the world. To see them, we will have to wait until we reach New Guinea.

What then can we learn in London? Not much. Mainly what we can find in the writings of some German Catholic missionaries who have worked in the region for decades, most notably the articles of Father Rascher, one of the nine religious massacred by the Baining at the St. Paul Mission in 1904.

Unfortunately, if not too surprisingly, these German missionaries have written in German, a language that neither Jeremy nor I know. Undaunted, we trundle off to the British Museum daily, pocket dictionary in hand, and work away at the yellowing texts. There we are, two anonymous spirits proud to join the famous shades in the Reading Room—Karl Marx! Virginia Woolf! Oscar Wilde! Hunching forward over the table, diligent as ants, we carry morsels of information to our notepads.

How much of what we gather can be called "information" is debatable, and we treat these efforts with wry humor. After all, we are reading about Baining customs, thoughts, and language as filtered through the cockeyed worldview of the Society of the Missionaries of the Sacred Heart and rendered in a language at once foreign to the Baining and to us. Who can say what strange configurations will emerge from this process? The year 1900 is in any case a long time ago: anything we read, even if it was accurate to start with, is likely to be outdated, a record of beliefs and rituals long gone, extinguished perhaps by the missionaries themselves.

Still, we take what we can. We copy out a cycle of Baining tales about a folk hero called Hrini. We have our first glimpse of the Baining language, that tongue we will hear—have already heard—so maligned as "difficult," "abominably difficult," and just plain "abominable" by various non-Baining who have never managed to learn it. Most striking, at first glance, is the Baining inflection of nouns according to shape. A piece of wood, *amung*, becomes *amungom*, if it is short and round; *amungingl*, if it is long and thin; *amungring*, if it is flat; and *amungini*, if it is small. This seems utterly strange to me, and delightful.

For myself, I do not doubt for a moment that I will learn to speak Baining. Despite my halting French, my half-baked Norwegian, my inability to speak a sentence of Latin or ancient Greek, I continue to believe that I am "good at languages." In any case, this will be different. This will be immersion. Like a child, I will hear and repeat.

But first, we are told, if we are to communicate with the Baining at all—or even reach the Baining villages—we will have to learn Pidgin English, the lingua franca of New Guinea. And we are advised to learn it at once, before leaving London, so we will be able to cope as soon as we arrive. We head for the Language Lab.

Pidgin English, it turns out, has evolved in a country with more than eight hundred languages as a means for New Guinea tribes to communicate not only with the European tribes that have at various times invaded their land, but also—in recent times—with each other. Sometimes called New Guinea Pidgin, or simply Pidgin, or Neo-Melanesian, or Tok Pisin (the name that will eventually catch on), it is a language with a Melanesian structure and largely English-based vocabulary, with some German and other influences tossed in.

When I first look at the exercise books, I confess my reaction is mixed. The vocabulary is wonderfully colorful. "Hair," I discover, is *gras*, and "mustache" is *mausgras*, *maus* being the word for "mouth." Mouth grass! *Asples bilong mi* means "my hometown": *ples*, of course, is "place," and *as* is, well, "seat." *Bilong* is a possessive that appears everywhere. My favorite expression is "*mixmasta bilong Jesus*"—Jesus's mixmaster—"helicopter"!

But I have trouble seeing Pidgin English as a real language. When I read that "I'm going now" is *Mi go nau*—which I pronounce slowly, *à l'anglais*, "Me go now"—I can only laugh. Surely, this is baby talk. This is Tarzan-speak. I feel embarrassed for this language.

But then I listen to the tapes recorded by native speakers at normal speaking speed, and I gain some respect. Baby talk indeed: I cannot understand a word.

Most days then, Jeremy and I work together, and as we make our way to the British Museum or the Language Lab, holding hands as we walk through Holborn or Bloomsbury Square, a sense of togetherness prevails. To outsiders, we seem joined at the hip, and I start to fear that we're joining at the hip: Siamese twins who do not know where one leaves off and the other begins.

Evenings, back home, I feel the strain. Here I am, reading about the Baining, transcribing stories about Hrini, studying Pidgin English. But this is Jeremy's fieldwork, not mine. It is not at all clear to me what my role in this enterprise will be.

"What will I do there?" I'll say, as we linger over coffee after dinner.

"What do you mean, what will you do there? You'll be there," he'll reply.

"Be there!" I'll scoff, doing my best to saturate the phrase with scorn. Does he think that this isn't an issue? Is this really not an issue? We will gnaw on this all night. We will gnaw on this for years: life versus work, experience versus achievement, being versus doing, and, most basically, *you versus me*.

It is not that I don't believe in experience, or "being there," as Jeremy has put it. I do. This is the sixties, after all, and I am very much a child of my time. I long for experience; I value it over information. When I travel, I do not study books beforehand—I am *there*, certain that I'm absorbing the essence of places, as if by osmosis. I take great pride in being open: if Jeremy simply said, "Let's spend a year in New Guinea," I am sure that I would see it as a grand adventure and agree to it at once.

But this is not what we have.

"*You* aren't going to just *be there*," I say.

I remind him that he is getting a degree, that he is seeing to his career, that he is *gaining a foothold on his future*. I too feel the lure of this path. After all, I attended Hunter College High School: all girls, all academics, all competition all the time. I too have my Harvard degree. I too have been taught—and taught well—not to simply *be* but to achieve.

And in fact, I am wildly ambitious. I want to be a writer. Visions of greatness dance in my head. But as yet, apart from high school poems, I have published nothing. How do I know that I'm really a writer? How can I put my career on hold before I even have it? I am twenty-two years old, and I feel that I am running out of time.

The idea that I might write about New Guinea does not occur to me at all. I know fiction and poetry. I know Greek drama and epic. I have never read travel literature; I have never read the work of Freya Stark, or Eric Newby, or Isabella Bird; and at this point, I do not even know that the genre exists. And then, this is fieldwork, not travel, and so far as I know, books about fieldwork are monographs, academic books: anthropology. As I see it, for a year and a half, I will write nothing at all. And if Jeremy is working, and I am not, I know I will be viewed as "just a wife."

Just a wife! This fills me with dread. There is nothing in the world I want less than to be *just a wife.*

Clearly, I need a project of my own.

At first I think that I will go into anthropology myself. This makes sense in many ways. We have already heard from Margaret Mead—as it happens, Gregory Bateson's former wife—who has written a sharp, almost scolding letter, telling Jeremy that if he plans to study "the ritual expression of opposition between the sexes," which is his thesis topic, he must have a woman sharing the research: the Baining women, she is absolutely certain, will speak openly only to another woman. Presumably, that would be me.

But I have no intention of being a "helpmeet"—a word I associate uncomfortably with "sweetmeat"—one of those women who do half the work and are mentioned only in the acknowledgments. No, if I am going to do anthropological work, I will have a thesis and degree of my own.

At this point, with fieldwork imminent, it is too late to apply to a PhD program or even to register for courses. But I do not see this as a problem. My plan is to get a degree in reverse, gathering data while in the field and doing the course work after we return. It doesn't bother me that I have no training. With my learning-by-osmosis philosophy, I put little stock in training, and I am sure that I can learn what methodology I need by reading appropriate texts.

"Can you make up a list?" I ask Jeremy, and I promptly set about reading some extraordinary books.

But while I love the sure elegance of Evans-Pritchard explicating his concept of magic among the Azande and the clever insight of Bateson's schismogenesis, a theory of competitive relationships that I immediately apply to my marriage, I find that anthropology is not for me. It is a field where theory is on the rise: Levi-Strauss is ascending to his throne. And already I feel a growing distrust of theory, a skepticism toward generalizations, and rules, and universals, an antitheory theory that will so flourish in the perfect conditions of Baining society, it will take hold of me for life.

By now, though, with all this reading, I have used up what little time I had. Soon we will be leaving, and I still have no Project of My Own. As the time for our departure draws near, my quest grows increasingly frantic. "Perhaps I will collect myths," I say. Or, "I think I'll do a photographic essay." Or, "What I would really like is to study children's acquisition of language." I form no plan for what I will do with my collection of myths, I barely learn to master the complex Nikon camera that we have bought for the trip, and if I opened a single book to explore children's acquisition of language, it would occur to me that this field is no less academic or theoretical than anthropology itself. But each of these ideas sounds exciting and makes me feel I have direction for a while, until I decide that for some reason it won't do and I turn again to one of the others. My lazy Susan of possibility spins.

Sometimes, out of frustration—with my own indecision or with Jeremy's lack of concern—I will say, "You know what? I'm not going!" This triggers an alternative script to our postprandial fight. But this battle, though intense, is brief, the premise is so disingenuous. If Jeremy is going, I wouldn't miss this for the world.

In the spring of 1969, we pack up our meager belongings, ship them to family for storage, and set off for New Guinea. We are taking the western route. First, to the States, to visit family. Next to Hawaii, to visit Gregory Bateson. And finally to Canberra, to the Australian National University, to visit anthropologists who have done fieldwork in New Guinea.

We are both excited to be finally on our way. But we both feel anxious as well. Jeremy, for the flying time ahead—he is not an aerophile, and we have many plane hours ahead—and perhaps about his work, though this is not something he would discuss or even acknowledge. I, for my dilemma, still unresolved: I have no Project of My Own. I imagine everyone we meet on our three-part journey asking what I will be doing in the field and sizing me up as *just a wife* tagging along.

As it turns out, on the first leg of our journey, visiting family, my fears prove entirely unfounded. My own parents are not overly concerned about my career. They seem mainly worried that I will be eaten. As we sit around the table after dinner, Michael Rockefeller's name hangs in the air. What actually happened to him? they ask. And where actually was he? And where actually are you going? My parents are in any case old-fashioned enough to believe that a wife should follow her husband anywhere, even to the ends of the earth, although they never expected me to take this quite so literally.

Nor are Jeremy's parents especially concerned about my career. As I should have expected, they are focused on their son. I am merely an afterthought. If anything, his mother has praise. She certainly doesn't believe that a wife should follow her husband to the ends of the earth, sacrificing career and a comfortable life: she left her own spouse some time back. But it is a different matter when the husband in question is her son. She thinks it sounds exactly right that I will live in a hut with an outhouse, dine on tubers, and give up my work for the sake of his career.

———

The second stage of our journey, meeting Gregory Bateson in Hawaii, does not prove problematic either—not, at least, for me. A tall, angular man with a shock of white hair, Bateson seems kindly and impressive as he greets us, filling up the doorway of his small house. He welcomes the two of us together—he may even assume that I am an anthropologist too. And though I am too self-absorbed to consider it, it isn't likely that he cares. His mind is on other things.

"After forty years, I still get depressed when I think about the Baining," he says as he invites us into the house, even before we have sat down. Exactly as he said in his letter. He considers his Baining fieldwork a wretched failure. And here we are, wafting in like an ill wind, stirring up bad memories.

He talks with us through the afternoon, he takes us to dinner with his wife and baby, he talks some more in the evening. He describes trying to learn the "abominable" Baining language: "Everyone seemed to speak in their own personal dialect," he says. He describes simply trying to find people to talk to: "I was always scrambling through the bush," he smiles sadly. "They always seemed to be disappearing." He describes trying to relate to people who talked mainly about taro, if they talked at all: "*Taro!*" he says, as if he still can't believe that anyone could take such an interest in taro. "It was high praise if you told a woman her taro was as white as an egg," he says. He talks of struggling to make sense of their culture, and again he mentions failure. The word hovers in the room.

Years later people will say that Bateson shaped attitudes about the Baining by suggesting that their culture and social structure could not be studied. And no doubt as we sit there listening, he is shaping our own. But this is not in fact what he tells us on this visit. What he says is, "This is not the place to go for a first field trip. Go somewhere else first—prove you can do fieldwork. Because the Baining society and culture have so little structure, as an inexperienced anthropologist you will feel that you're missing something—or perhaps everything. And if you write up what you find, others will also feel that you did indeed miss something, or perhaps everything." The first-time anthropologist, he says, will not be believed.

Is Bateson worried that we will succeed where he has failed? At twenty-two, I am too innocent even to imagine this. An imposing figure with an imposing career, he seems to me genuinely concerned that we should not repeat an experience that left him feeling so defeated. He seems concerned about *us*. It is for our sake he thinks we should go elsewhere. But he is old enough to know that we are too young to heed his advice.

Visiting Bateson draws us together—once again we feel unified in taking on the challenge of the Baining—and at this point, I want to go straight to the field. I have no desire to visit the Australian National University in Canberra. I expect I will be uncomfortable among the anthropologists, who I am certain will view me as *just a wife*, and antiacademic as I am, I think the visit will be of little use. As I see it, we had to visit family, we wanted to talk with Bateson, but this stop is optional and superfluous.

Jeremy does not agree. Meticulous in his work, he does not want to miss a thing. He feels that at best he will learn something about the Baining, and if nothing else he will get advice about doing fieldwork in New Guinea from people who have actually been there.

But neither proves to be true. No one at ANU knows anything about the Baining. It is true some people have worked close by, but "close by," we learn, means little in New Guinea, where communication is blocked by mountains and does not extend ten miles. All they can offer us is hearsay, and we suspect that what they have heard has been negative: although people try to be encouraging, they do not seem overly optimistic about our trip. "You will never learn Baining in a year and a half," one linguist tells us outright: the language is known to be difficult, and the Baining are known to be uncooperative. *Uncooperative*: this is an adjective we will hear applied to the Baining so often it will come to seem like a Homeric epithet.

We do acquire some books that we hope will be useful. These include the linguist's contribution, a book on learning an unwritten language, and a slender volume on tropical diseases and their symptoms that will become our favorite reading. ("Do you think my tongue looks prickly?" "Are my gums slightly green?" "*This gland!*" "*My ear!*" "*WTF is this spot?*") We also pick up a standard list of "What to Take to the Field," a reminder of summer camps past. This curious log includes a toasting fork, tea towels, and three ties.

For me, the ANU experience is just as bad as I feared, and though everyone is exceedingly friendly, I do not behave well. I let Jeremy know that I hate Canberra. "A planned city," I sneer. I complain about the cold: it is autumn in Australia, and I long for the tropics. I cannot bear how everyone asks me what I will do in the field. At a party given for us by a welcoming young couple, as I circulate, wine in hand, I tell one person that I plan to collect myths, another that I will do a photographic essay, and a third that I intend to focus on language acquisition. I imagine these people conferring later and concluding that I am mad.

I see myself as so self-aware. And it's true, I perceive my hostility, my insecurity, my frustration with the role I have been asked to play, and my inability either to refuse it or to play it well.

Yet I understand so little, although it is right there in front of my nose. Between being and doing, there is no debate at all.

One day not long before we leave, we are having coffee in the faculty room with the anthropologists, and all I can think about is how very ordinary these people are. How narrow. How *academic*. They have been In the Field. They have experienced Other Worlds. But who would know it? Here they are, I think, sitting on their upholstered chairs, talking in mundane ways about mundane things. Committees. *Tenure*. Even their comments about the people they have lived with are matter-of-fact.

Clearly, they have not been In the Field as I will be In the Field, I decide. For me, fieldwork will be like Emily Dickinson's definition of poetry: I will "feel physically as if the top of my head were taken off." Whatever these people have failed to experience, *I* will be blown away!

3

Niu Guinea

May 1969, Port Moresby. At last we are in New Guinea. We feel that our trip has finally begun.

In fact, Port Moresby—or *Pot Mosbi*, or simply *Mosbi*, as it is called in Pidgin—is only a brief destination. We have come for the maps and reports that are housed here, in the government offices of the Territory's capital. If it were not for these records, we wouldn't have made this a stop. All air routes to New Guinea pass through Moresby, but you stay in the town only if you have to. It is a seedy, unsavory place, a magnet for people seeking adventure or work they seldom find. The young New Guineans, cut loose from their tribes, often become lowlifes. The expats, cut loose from their tribes, are often lowlifes to start with.

But the bad elements of Moresby do not faze me: I grew up on New York's Lower East Side. Far more pressing, literally, is the heat. Leaving the airport, I feel a weight descend upon my head: I am in a pot, and someone has just pressed down the lid. I cannot breathe.

This misery comes as a surprise. I have always loved summer. But I have never encountered such heat. At our hotel I lie flat on the bed and do not move. I watch our ceiling fan circle, chasing its tail. At dusk, I rise to join the expats on the veranda for gin and tonic and then return to my bed.

"We have to move," I say in the morning, still in bed. "We need a place with air."

I try to say this nicely, but I know where it will lead. Money is a tender issue. We cannot afford the town's better hotels, which cater to businessmen and wealthy tourists who want to "experience" New Guinea without discomfort. Seedy as it is, Port Moresby is expensive.

We glower at each other.

"You hate air-conditioning," Jeremy observes.

This is true. But I have never been this hot.

"There won't be air-conditioning in the bush," he says.

This too is true, and probably not a wise thing to say. I announce that I am going home.

We move to a classier hotel with icy air, a minibar, a buffet lunch! We roll our eyes at the tourists and snigger to ourselves. We are terrible snobs. But these tourists, it turns out, look down equally on us—scruffy hippies! One night is all that we can stand or afford, and we return to our lowly hotel.

The next day we set out for the government offices, eager for facts. All these months, and you could fit what we have learned about the Baining in a very small cowrie shell. We have read the wacky reports of the Catholic missionaries, we have absorbed the emotional impressions of Gregory Bateson, we have picked up bits of rumor and hearsay in Canberra, and we long for facts: we still know almost nothing about the people we will be living with or even where we are headed. Now at last we will find out the locations of Baining villages, learn about their size and population and accessibility, gain some sense of what we will find and how we will be received.

But these hopes wilt fast. The information is there; the records lie within reach. But apparently we haven't clearance to access them.

Clearance? Are the Australians afraid that we will infiltrate the rain forest? Preach communism in the bush? Unionize the plantations? Organize indigenous demonstrations against the Vietnam War? We have no idea, nor is anything explained.

But getting clearance, we are told, will not be quick. Indeed, it will take longer than we care to stay in Port Moresby. We decide to move on to Rabaul, the capital of New Britain. We will have access to the same information (once we are "cleared"), and we will surely make better progress: we will be closer to Baining land.

Moresby then appears to have been a waste. Even our contacts at the University of Papua New Guinea—young anthropologists and teachers—know nothing about the Baining. But they identify someone who does: a missionary who has worked in the Central Baining village of Gaulim, not far from Rabaul. We arrange to meet him before we leave.

This is my first encounter with a missionary—off the page, at least—and I do not look forward to it. I have a deep antipathy to missionizing. As I see it, the world is filled with various visions of gods, and I cannot understand how any culture can judge another culture's gods inferior when none can even be proved to exist. In an undeveloped, barely postcolonial country like New Guinea, where religious superiority is inevitably linked to the "proof" of power and wealth, missionizing seems to me not simply foolish and arrogant but unethical. I steel myself for this ordeal.

But as it happens, I like the man. He is intelligent, articulate, amiable, and respectful of the Baining, whom he clearly likes. Unlike the anthropologists we have met, he does not call them dirty, unattractive, or uncooperative. He does not complain about their language. His main concern, he tells us, is to protect them from the Tolai.

Historically, he explains, the Tolai have been the enemy of the Baining, who are thought to be the original inhabitants of the Gazelle Peninsula. At some unknown date in the past, these Tolai invaders drove the Baining from their coastal land, and they continued to raid their villages, enslaving and eating them. As we will later learn, it is even the Tolai who gave the Baining the name by which they are known: *Baining* is a Tolai word meaning "bush people." This is not a compliment. It is not what the Baining called themselves: no people calls itself "Hicks." The Northern Baining, the largest of the Baining groups and the one we plan to visit, call themselves "Chachat," which means "people."

Today, the missionary says, although the Tolai no longer eat the Baining—this has now become illegal fare—they remain the stronger, more populous, and far more savvy group. Imbued with their own entrepreneurial spirit—"They have their own monetary system," he explains—they have adapted swiftly to Western mores, as the Baining apparently have not. The missionary is concerned that in their role as catechists, they are trying to turn the Baining into "little Tolais."

It's true his proposed solution appalls me: he believes that the Baining should perform their rituals for tourists. But while I shudder at this notion, which strikes me as commercial and demeaning—a *sideshow*—I understand that his intentions are worthy: he wants the Baining to emphasize their Bainingness. He wants them to survive as Baining in a changed world. He is a decent man. And although we cannot know this at the time, he will be one of the few non-Baining we will meet who appreciates these people, who does not have that complex and often negative impression they seem to leave on outsiders, New Guineans and Europeans alike.

We are happy to leave Port Moresby, and though the journey to Rabaul isn't long, the distance, we discover, is immense. Rabaul is as beautiful and loved as Moresby is unsavory and loathed. Built in a caldera, its setting is magnificent: the town sits on majestic Simpson Harbor, overlooking Blanche Bay, dramatically surrounded by the volcanoes that will ultimately bury it. Unlike urban Moresby, Rabaul does not seem quite separate from the jungle, which encroaches everywhere lushly. And unlike Moresby, Rabaul is safe, a place where anyone can wander freely. It is a place we like at once and will come to love.

We move into the Australian National University house, which the school rents to academics for a pittance, which is exactly what we can afford. The house itself is a boxy thing, constructed in European fashion with vinyl siding—no *native* stuff, please, we're white!—and destined to be hot. The living room has just a small fan. But it is spacious, furnished (if sparsely), and superbly located on Mango Ave., a short and quiet tree-lined walk to the center of Rabaul, which serves the town's varied populations. For the Tolai, there is a large open-air market, the *bung*; for the whites—or *Europeans*, as whites are usually called—there are well-stocked Australian department stores, Steamships and BP's; for the Chinese, there are small trade stores, always dark, their shelves mysteriously half empty. The town has several restaurants, a movie theater (open weekends), and a newsagent, our link to the outside world.

Although the ANU house has several bedrooms, we have the place to ourselves, and we settle in at once. "We're here," we murmur at night as we curl up beneath the tangled mosquito net. "We're finally here."

Gail in her Marimekko shift, at the ANU house in Rabaul

But if we are excited to be in Rabaul, we are also desperate to leave, restless for fieldwork to begin. "Our last stop before the field," says Jeremy. We can sense that we are getting closer. But by now we feel that we have wasted weeks, and we still do not know where we are going. The Northern Baining live in both mountain and subcoastal villages, and a mountain village—more remote, more populous, and, above all, more traditional—is our ultimate destination. But first we plan to spend time in a village nearer to the coast. We know that in any village near the coast, contact will have influenced the culture. Contact in this region has been extensive. Unlike the Highlands on mainland New Guinea, which has only fairly recently been explored by white people, the Gazelle Peninsula has been inhabited by foreigners for decades.

Germans settled in the area toward the end of the nineteenth century, and missionaries were soon at work in the region. Major World War II battles, including the Battle of Rabaul, took place in the region, with local villagers assisting the Australians and enduring internment in Japanese camps. Cacao and copra—cocoa and coconut—plantations, now owned mostly by Australians, pepper the coast. Rabaul itself has a large Chinese community, the industrious descendants of laborers imported by the Germans early in the century, who now run businesses of their own. The town is also a travel destination for tourists who come to dive and snorkel at the nearby reefs.

No village with easy access to the coast will be untouched by these incursions, and for the anthropologist seeking an "uncorrupted" culture, this is far from ideal. But contact creates advantages as well. Villagers will have met whites; they will not be shocked to see us. Everyone will speak Pidgin, which will help us both to connect immediately and also to learn Baining. And near the coast, access and escape will be relatively easy, allowing us to correct the inevitable errors we will make in supplies and also to take breaks.

We figure that with six months in this first village, we will have time to make a knowledgeable choice for the second. What we need right now is to identify that first: our starting point.

We rent a jeep and immediately experience that sense of power and freedom the possession of wheels seems to bring. For the moment, our spirits lift. For the first time since leaving London, we feel that we are on our own as we cruise around Rabaul in the evening, catching the moonlit water through the palm trees and skirting groups of people walking, standing, sitting, or conversing in the road, which seems to be the meeting place of choice.

But we quickly discover that the power of our newfound mobility is illusory. We can drive only where there are roads, a limited terrain. And even when we reach people, they can tell us only what they know, which turns out to be limited as well.

We drive to Gaulim and speak to the missionary who has replaced our Moresby friend. "You might try Yalom," he says, and suggests that we talk to a linguist who has been working there. We visit the linguist, who says that Yalom may be involved in resettlement: the village may be moving to a location better for growing cacao. "Probably not a good choice unless you want to study the process of resettlement," he says. "What about Rangulit?" But Rangulit is soon dashed down by an agricultural worker who tells us that the village is small, missionized, and so busy growing cacao that people might have no time to teach us the language. "Also," she says, "there is no water." She mentions Luan. Someone else suggests Riet, which, so far as we can determine, is not a Northern Baining village at all.

We cannot easily visit these villages, which aren't on any roads: each would require an expedition. The maps and records, to which we now have access, in which we had such faith, do not tell us what we need to know. Indeed, they do not tell us very much at all. For all our consultations, we mostly sit around the house, waiting. We are so impatient.

"We may never get out of Rabaul," I write in my journal.

We shop for food. We talk to Tomas, the caretaker of the ANU house. We join the Ambonese club, where we meet some drunk plantation managers, whom we cannot shake off. We listen to Canned Heat sing "Goin' Up the Country" on someone's backyard radio, over and over, wondering what on earth this song can mean to listeners here in New Britain: the song of the week, it will stay with us for life. Our sole accomplishment during this time is to acquire a kitten, ostensibly to catch vermin in our house in the bush, should we ever get there, but mainly to love. We name her Loki and vie jealously for her affection.

At last we find succor from a German priest at the Catholic mission, Vunapope, which in Tolai means "place of the priests."

As Teutonically efficient as we are disorganized, he takes us in hand.

"I myself know nothing about the Baining," he tells us frankly. The man to see, he says, is Father Mayrhofer. The place to find him is Vunamarita. He instructs us to radio ahead to New Masawa, the plantation adjacent to the mission station, to say that we are coming. He explains how to radio ahead. He tells us where to find out about a boat to get there. Along the way he puts us down for the purchase of a book about the Baining. As it happens, this book, written by a priest and published by the mission, is in Italian, which neither of us reads. We order it happily, a small price to pay for a working plan.

At midnight on June 3 we catch a small freight boat to Vunamarita, the mission station near St. Paul, the site of the Baining massacre of 1904. By the time the boat leaves, we have been waiting four hours on the busy dock, staring into the dark, trying to make out words in the calls and murmurs around us, growing stiff, restless, thirsty, and increasingly anxious that this boat we can hardly see will suddenly just set off without us.

Four hours. This, we learn, is how you catch a freight boat in New Guinea: just be there—for as long as it takes.

Once on board Jeremy stays awake all night, watching the shadow of the coast. He is too excited to rest. I pass out on a bunk bed, my head on some burlap sacks. All night I feel things scampering across my body, mice or perhaps New Guinea roaches, which, although lighter, are much the same size. Squeamish as I've always been, I do not seem to care. I am so tired, I just sleep on.

We arrive around five thirty, almost dawn, one half the sky alight, the other dark, a stunning mix of light and shadow. Jeremy takes a picture of the moon above the coconut palms, a bat flying in the distance. A small group of people meets the boat, which brings mail, supplies, us. Father Mayrhofer is among them. He is slight, wiry, spry, almost bouncing in his sneakers as he leads us to his house, sits us down to an enormous breakfast, and takes off at once to say Mass.

Shy but friendly, Father Mayrhofer turns out to be a quirky man, as you would expect of someone who has lived in the Territory for more than thirty years and never once returned to his Austrian homeland. Although he joins us at the table, he himself doesn't eat. "In fact," he smiles, his wire-rimmed glasses glinting in the sunshine, "I never eat." Indeed, it is to this he attributes his excellent health: more than three decades in the bush, and not once has he needed a doctor. He has never taken antimalarials, but he has never had malaria. Even interned by the Japanese in the war, he did well: "You see, they couldn't starve me," he says, with a laugh that takes me by surprise, flying so high and long that I fear it will end badly, a crash landing.

I feel sure that he must eat something, but in the next days, although he feeds us generously and apparently with pleasure, we never do see him eat. He smokes nonstop.

On the subject of our fieldwork, Father Mayrhofer says at once that he does not recommend Luan.

"The village is too scattered," he says. "No one is ever around."

We sigh: Luan is our top contender. Another village down.

But wait: "Puktas, I think, would suit you well," he says. And if we want, a visit is easy to arrange: in a couple of hours, Maxie, the manager of New Mobisberg plantation, will be arriving with his tractor—to pick up mail and supplies—and he can give us a lift to his house, just a twenty-minute walk from the village. We can see for ourselves.

We wait for Maxie, sitting on the dock and watching the flying fish. It is good practice waiting, I think. I am not yet adept at this skill. This is hardly surprising, coming from a culture where we weave through checkout lines to save a minute and risk our lives at stoplights to save five. But so much of fieldwork involves waiting. We are learning this fast and will absorb it in the year ahead. Anthropology departments should require a course, I'll joke with Jeremy, Waiting 101, where students sit for hours and do nothing. Those who go berserk would be advised to reconsider their career choice.

But it is not too hard waiting for Maxie this morning: our spirits are high. At last we will meet the Baining. At last we are going to a village in which we might actually stay. Jeremy thinks through the little speech he has prepared in Pidgin to ask the villagers' permission, thrilled at the prospect of finally saying it aloud.

Maxie is a large, friendly fellow who is happy to give us a ride, and by late morning we are clinging to the back of his tractor as it bounces on the rutted path through New Masawa. When we arrive at his plantation, he invites us in for coffee, which we drink from small, dainty cups. Half Swedish, half New Ireland, with a cocoa complexion—*hapkas*, as they say in Pidgin—Maxie clearly sees himself as European. Sitting in his overfurnished living room, he seems a lonely figure, stranded at the edge of the bush.

Around noon, with great anticipation, we set off for Puktas. It is a short but steepish climb, the narrow path scattered with snail shells, broken and crushed. The heat, as we walk, is fierce. Hiking with us is a worker from Maxie's plantation, a replacement for the Baining Maxie asked to guide us in, who has somehow disappeared. In fact, when we arrive at a small hamlet—two huts on bare earth in a clearing—everyone seems to have disappeared. The place is deserted. We wonder whether the fellow who ran away dashed ahead to warn people that we were coming. We wonder whether even now they are watching us from behind the trees.

Our guide, although he is not from the village, seems best suited to scouting around, and he sets off in search of life. Jeremy and I sit down on the steps of a house and sweat. We are very thirsty. Thirty years from now people will carry water bottles everywhere, as if they might suddenly die of thirst in San Francisco or New York City. But we, in the jungle, dumbly, have not even brought a canteen.

In a while, when our guide has not returned, we fear that he too has abandoned us. We start to wonder just how long we should wait here, parched, bitten by sandflies, and just possibly being spied upon by people who do not want to meet us.

But suddenly our guide gives a shout and leads us to his find: a group of people clustered on a porch, a teacher and his pupils. As we clamber up the steps, a dozen children jostle about, eager to touch us. They rub our skin; they caress my hair, which is long and at the moment very wild.

We must look pretty forlorn because the teacher offers us water at once, handing us a cup and scowling when our guide throws the last drops away. "*Riva i stap longwe*," he says tersely, and even I understand: "The river is a long way off." So here, as in Rangulit, water is scarce. He sends some children to fetch a young coconut, which he splits with his long bush knife, to offer us the cool, sweet liquid inside. "*Kulau*," he says.

The teacher's name is Alois—or this at any rate is his Christian, not his given, name; as we will learn, all Baining who have been missionized have both. He himself is half Baining and half Tolai, and when he hears who we are and why we are here, he offers to teach us Baining if we stay.

"It will take you just *tu mun*," he says—"two months."

Apparently, we are dealing with an optimist. Indeed, he begins to tutor us at once, pointing and naming, word by unpronounceable word.

Alois sends the children off and leads us around the village, but no one is about. Everyone, he tells us, is working in the gardens. We meet only one old woman, hunched over her fire cooking taro, her mouth bright red with betel juice, her teeth black and sparse, and her speech rapid and guttural. She is amused at our efforts to repeat words after Alois and totally involved in her discourse, which she continues after we walk on.

By four thirty, when no one has yet returned from the gardens, we decide that we had better leave: night falls quickly in the tropics, and we have to make it back to the coast before dark.

"I will tell people you have come," says Alois. "I will tell them that you want to stay. Come back tomorrow, early."

We thank him, stutter some mangled form of the Baining greeting we have just learned (*Amrs!*), and take the day in reverse: down to Maxie's, where, again, we drink coffee in small, dainty cups; down to the coast, bouncing wildly on the back of Maxie's tractor; and down to the mission station, where Father Mayrhofer serves us a hefty meal of tinned foods that he doesn't touch.

In the evening, after I have showered—the good father having graciously removed three huge black spiders from the bathtub with brave bare hands and his special laugh—I contemplate New Guinea wildlife and reconsider the value of missionaries, Jeremy runs through his speech for the morning, and Father Mayrhofer smokes.

By seven the next morning we are on our way to Puktas, debating the odds that anyone will be there to meet us. It is a two-hour walk from the coast, we have been told, but halfway up we meet the tractor that takes us to Maxie's house. There we meet Mathias, a former catechist, and then Alois, who has heard the village dogs barking and left his class to guide us in.

By now it is eight thirty, which is late in the bush: the Baining are already at work. We wait in the hamlet where we sat the day before as people gradually come in from the gardens. Around fifteen men and ten women arrive, singly or in pairs. Both men and women wear *laplaps*, cloth wraparounds that are worn throughout New Guinea; some of the women wear blouses as well—*meri* blouses, as they are called, after Mary, meaning "woman" or "wife." Everyone carries a bush knife.

The villagers are short and solid, and very quiet. I notice their dark, liquid eyes. One by one, they shake hands—for our sake, a Western custom. For their own greeting, they exchange betel nut, or *buai*, a careful ceremony we will learn: cut the tip, set the white of the nut in the stem of the *daka* leaf, fold the leaf around the nut, and hand it over, nut side up. For us, whites who they assume will not chew *buai*, they have brought three *muli*, enormous pomelos with green skin.

We all stand around in silence until Alois says that we can speak, and Jeremy at last recites his piece.

"*Mi na meri bilong mi*," he begins—"I and my wife"—want to come and live here in Puktas and study "*ol pasin bilong Baining*"—"Baining customs." He says that we come from America, we are students, and we are here to learn. And after, when we return home, we will tell people in our own country how the Baining live.

When he has finished, no one says a word. What do they make of this? There is no way we can know. Their faces, it seems to me, are masked. They do not look hostile. They do not look welcoming. I see no response at all.

Finally, Mathias speaks. "*Em i orait*," he says. "*Em i orait*"—"It's all right."

Now other people speak up as well: they agree. Yes, they say, it's all right. But they do not have a good house for us, they say. For now, we can stay in the *haus kiap*—the house that is used by the district's Australian patrol officer, the *kiap*, when he comes to the village on patrol. But "*riva i stap longwe*," they say—"the house is far from water." We will not be able to *waswas*—to bathe—easily. Also, it seems—although this we gather only from uncertain exchanges—it is isolated. And we will not be able stay there long: the *kiap* will need this house when he comes through.

"But when you are here," they promise, "we will build you a house of your own."

"*Namel*," they say: "in the middle."

And that's it. It's all right. At last, our fieldwork can begin.

4

Pig Food

What do we take with us to Puktas? This is our question as we traipse to the trade stores in Rabaul, to BP's, Steamships, and the mysterious Chinese shops we cannot name, trying to decide what to buy.

In general we travel light. But in general we visit places where we can count on finding certain basics: beds, towels, plates. In Puktas we already know that there is almost nothing we will find. We will have shelter, our own house, if they will build it for us: walls, thatching, steps, an outhouse. We will have the food they grow, if they will give it to us: mainly taro. But anything else we will have to bring in.

So what do we really need? A table? Chairs? *That toasting fork?* What do we feel we cannot do without?

Even as we shop, we know that we are dealing with more than purchases. Questions of identity loom. Just what kind of people are we? Compulsive, fearful, culture bound? Tough? Soft? Spoiled? Am I someone who cannot do without a watch? Do I have to have a cup of coffee in the morning? Does a day feel incomplete—unbearable—without a bath or a book or a decent meal? And what would I call "a decent meal"?

Pig Food

What we bring, of course, is not entirely a matter of choice. In the Baining Mountains, we will not have a phone. We will not have an oven. We will have nothing that requires electricity—unless we haul in a generator, as the priest in the village of Raunsepna has apparently done, thereby generating a small amount of power and a great deal of displeasure. As the Baining will tell us later, indignant at all the carrying this man requires for his building projects (no fee): "We are not a car!" Which is something else we will not have, as there aren't any roads.

Overriding everything, perhaps, is the nature of fieldwork itself: a peculiar form of travel. As an anthropologist, you live in a village for more than a year; essentially, you are setting up a home. But your position in the village is ambiguous. You may be living in the village, but you aren't a villager. So what kind of home do you set up? Do you try to re-create as much as possible the home that you know? Or do you try to live like the people around you?

If you go too far in replicating a "European"-style home, you will be more comfortable, but you risk creating distance: you might well remain *masta* and *misis* to the villagers, who may then be far less willing to confide in you, which is the very point in your being there. But if you try to emulate the villagers—if you "go native" or "go bush," as they say—you risk losing your bearings. We may think of identity as *soul*, but down on the ground it is just habits and the possessions that support them.

We ourselves do not intend to go bush. Not that we will dine on china on a tablecloth. Actually, we do not plan to bring a table. But we see ourselves as sensible young people. Our aim, we decide, is to sustain a life that is moderately familiar. We purchase two cots and two beach chairs, so that we will not spend our entire lives on the ground. We purchase a large pressure lamp so that we can work and read at night. We buy a small kerosene stove and tinned food so that we can supplement our taro diet: we will have oatmeal and biscuits for breakfast and meatballs with rice at night.

We plan this carefully. We have been warned about the lure and the dangers of *going native*. We have heard that an anthropologist we know, a young doctoral student from the States, succumbed to this temptation and went mad.

When I think about this, I find it intriguing. I picture him running half naked through the jungle, waving a bush knife. Clearly, I have no real sense of what it means, to *go native*. Indeed, I have so little sense of what it means that I will not recognize it even while it is happening.

On the morning of June 10, we arrive at Vunamarita with our gear and our kitten. Once again we stop at the mission station, where Father Mayrhofer serves us a breakfast that he doesn't eat. Once again we catch the tractor that takes us up to New Mobisberg plantation, where Maxie gives us coffee in small, dainty cups. And once again we wait, this time for the carriers we've been promised who will tote our baggage to the village.

When they arrive, we discover that the Baining have sent the children of Puktas to escort us in. "Just kids!" I say. And it's true: these are youngsters—the oldest in their teens. Are we surprised that not one adult is there to greet us? We are. Do we mind? Actually, we do. We are not self-important people. We did not expect a parade. But we do think the arrival of two strangers to live in the village might warrant a greeting.

Still, the youngsters are strong, and our procession along the bush paths, if ragtag, is efficient. At the house, they deposit our baggage, fetch water, accept our pay—which they do not seem to expect—and disappear with extraordinary speed, leaving us in solitude.

We are intensely aware of this solitude as we look around. The *haus kiap*, it turns out, stands in a hamlet of its own. This includes the house itself, a sturdy two-room construction—with woven bamboo walls and thatched roof—raised on stilts, as required by Australian regulations; a smaller house, a *haus polis*, which is used by the *kiap*'s assistants; a *haus kuk*, a lean-to where you can set up a fire or small stove; and a *haus pekpek*, an outhouse. It seems a complete little setup, but it is definitely isolated, just as the villagers warned. All around our small clearing is dense bush. We have not given this isolation much thought, excited as we've been to have found a village home. But standing in this enclave, we realize that living here, we will see little of Baining life.

Traditional Baining hamlet

"It's only temporary," we say. We remind ourselves that the Baining have promised to build us a house of our own—a house that will be *namel*, "in the middle."

In fact, although we do not yet know it, Puktas does not have a center: the village consists of small hamlets, each with one or two houses—just like this one—scattered through the bush and connected, one to another, by footpaths. If we knew this, we might have asked what "in the middle" could mean in a village that has no middle.

By the time we have surveyed our small domain, it is well into the afternoon. "We'd better set up quickly," says Jeremy. "It gets dark so fast." We dash about, putting things in order.

For all our scurrying, there is not all that much to set up. The house has just the two rooms. The back is enclosed, a bit private: this is where we will sleep. The front is open below the thatching and seems almost like a porch: this is where we will visit and eat. We store most of our supplies in the back. Light equipment—a pot, a kettle, a small kerosene lamp—we line up against the walls. More fragile or perishable items—film, our camera, food—we leave exactly as we packed them, in two patrol boxes: strong metal trunks the *kiaps* take on patrols to protect their goods against jungle rot. Our clothes, stuffed into a large duffel bag, will remain in the duffel bag.

We prepare our cots, we lay down our eating mat, we open our beach chairs. We place our two large metal basins outside, to collect rain, and in the *haus kuk* we set up our kerosene stove. On one burner we heat up our meatballs, and on the other we cook the rice that we discover is already permeated with wogs.

As we eat, settled on the floor, we peer out our door, staring down the path to our hamlet, hoping that someone will come. But no one does.

———

Now it is dusk, and we need to hook up the pressure lamp before dark: it is a large, elaborate contraption that requires light to assemble. As we sit cross-legged on our porch, lamp parts strewn around us, I read aloud the instructions, which seem to be half in Japanese; Jeremy struggles with these parts. This is a serious lamp: we have been promised that it will light up the night.

And so it does: hanging in the doorway, it illuminates the porch magnificently. A second moon. Worn out from our day, we relax now in our beach chairs and bask in its glow—until suddenly we hear a great *whoosh*: Has it fallen? Has the bulb blown? Has it exploded?

Every insect on the Gazelle Peninsula has descended on our hut.

New Guinea has been called an entomologist's paradise. An entomologist's wonderland. Bug heaven. This is something I viewed with fear and trembling back home. Before leaving we talked with a friend, an anthropology student headed for the Sepik, about which insects terrified us most.

"Spiders," he said at once.

"Waterbugs," I said. "The praying mantis."

But our choices reflected the narrow limits of our experience. Around us in the hut tonight is an array of spectacular creatures unknown in Western apartments and gardens. In size, in shape, in color, these specimens are fascinating. They are gorgeous.

We flee.

For some time we stand outside the hut, staring up at the porch in awe. We are especially taken with a large horned beetle—a rhinoceros beetle, we later learn, an invader of coconut trees. This one seems oblivious to the fact that the coconut thatching on our roof is dead. With demented persistence it rams the thatching, falls, hits the floor with a hiss, and then rises to strike again.

What is this hiss? I have never heard an insect hiss. I have trouble with that horn. We have no idea what to do.

At some point as we stand there, our mouths hanging open, I realize that we have a weapon of our own: "Loki!" I cry. "Where is Loki?" Our kitten whom we have brought for precisely this purpose—to catch vermin. Well, here it is: the vermin! We send in our troop.

Our little kitten does exactly what she should: she heads straight for the falling beetle, drawn by the motion. But as the beetle lands, almost, it seems, as large as she is, it hisses.

She too flees.

By now we are getting tired. We feel like fools. At this moment I am grateful to be isolated, alone in our hamlet with no one to witness this humiliation. But we have to reclaim our house. We know that we have to take down the lamp, but first we have to deal with that beetle. Jeremy braves the house to fetch some Raid we brought—*Raid! In the jungle!* He approaches the bug. But the beetle, sprayed, is undeterred. At last, Jeremy fells the creature with a boot and removes the lamp.

We wait a half hour for the hut to clear and then return gingerly to our cots. Of course, the hut is not really clear. We know this. Antennae waggle in the shadows. I hear a chirp. But we're exhausted. It has been a very long day.

The first days in Puktas, we see almost no one at all. Our house seems to be en route to nowhere. A few couples do pass by, perhaps returning from the gardens: they walk slowly, carrying *bilum*—string bags—filled with produce and the bush knives that, we will find, no Baining goes without. But although they nod in greeting, they do not stop to talk.

Pig Food

Only one couple, Mran and Tuvuan, come to visit: "*Amrs!*" they say, as they sit down. "*Amrs!*" we reply. Apparently, they are neighbors—Mran points in the direction where they live—but we cannot see their house through the bush. And though they do not say much, and though I understand little of what they say, we are excited that they have come.

We wander out in search of people, but the village, we now see, consists of hamlets, we can barely find these hamlets, and when we do, there is no one there. We know that people are working in the gardens, and we head off on bush paths to find the gardens. But perhaps we are on the wrong paths—they fork in all directions. Or perhaps the gardens are far and we do not go far enough. We are wary of getting lost in the jungle. Who will find us? Who will look? No one seems to care.

We deal with practical things: rearranging our possessions, seeking a better setup for that lamp, getting water. Already we have run through the water the youngsters left, and our rain-catching system has not been a success. The rain arrived, as heavy as we could wish, and we looked with pride on our huge metal basins—so efficient! But all we captured was a tenth, perhaps a hundredth, of an inch of rain. Enough to brush a tooth.

"We'd better go to the river," says Jeremy, not unhappy to have something to do, and we set off with our jug. We will bathe and bring back what we need, or as much as Jeremy can carry, which will certainly not be what we need. But *need* can mean many things. Back home in such heat I would bathe twice a day. Back home I would wash my clothes daily. Back home we have faucets and water runs.

The way to the river is clear: basically, you just head down. The path itself is fairly steep. It is also rocky and full of roots, and as it traverses the hill, it zigzags between sun, where we sweat, and shade, where we slog through mud. I go slowly, sliding in my flip-flops. The river is lovely; getting cool and clean is a delight. But coming back, as I scramble over rocks, trip on roots, and grasp at shrubs, the mud mixes with my sweat to form an excremental paste. By the time we get home, I am dirtier than when I left.

Ha! we laugh. Ha-ha! Ha!

We have lunch: tuna, biscuits.

Another day. We wake up early, to the cries of the birds, the piercing call of the cockatoo, the *koki*, cutting through the bush and our dreams.

It is still cool at this hour, just past dawn. I put on my little orange Marimekko shift, which I belt with a string, or my little blue trade-store shift, which I belt with the same string. We have breakfast: biscuits with jam for me, oatmeal with honey for Jeremy, coffee for both. We take our pills—our iodine so we do not have to boil the water, our Chloroquine against malaria, our Enteroviform against stomach bugs, our multivitamin for our limited diet. And we wash them down with Tang: Tang with its vitamin C, Tang, ubiquitous among whites in the bush. All my life I will be able to call up the nasty taste of Tang.

I wash up with our few drops of water. I roll a cigarette with tobacco from my small round tin. And there is the day, stretching out before me. Jeremy goes out to find people and mostly comes back despondent. There is the day, stretching out before him. Or we go out together, with him leading and me sliding behind in my flip-flops, returning puzzled and lost, to find the day stretching out before us. We can read. We can write in our journals. We can study our guide to tropical diseases, perhaps learn why my sandfly bites have suddenly ballooned to the size of boils.

This is not how we imagined village life would be. But after all, it has been only a few days.

"It's only temporary," we say again. We say this often, hoping that it is true.

We cannot understand why no one comes. The few people we have seen do not seem hostile. Several, although they do not stay to visit, bring us gifts of food. Coconuts. A long stalk of small bananas. A pineapple and corn—introduced crops, we assume: this isn't even Baining food. The corn is so tough that after eating several cobs, we feel ill: we can feel the kernels popping inside us.

No one brings us taro. We find ourselves longing for taro.

In truth, we are frightened of taro. We plan on eating it, of course, but we bring certain issues to the table. Jeremy is fearful of foods; he is especially sensitive to textures. Once, after eating breadfruit, he takes to bed for a day. He dreams of being chased by breadfruits and wakes up clutching his belly. Now the very word makes him shudder. I myself like almost all foods, and I am certain that I will like taro. But back home, whenever we mentioned taro, people, if they knew the food at all, would say, "It's like potatoes": I am worried that a diet of taro will make me fat.

But as we sit alone in our hut, the absence of taro takes on meaning. It is true the lack of taro matters: we have counted on taro; we do not have enough tinned goods to manage without it. Already we can see our small stock of food quickly diminishing. But the absence of taro becomes symbolic. As it is, we are outsiders, living in isolation. We feel that isolation most fiercely in the evening, when we are eating our meatballs.

"Still no taro," I write in my journal.

The lack of taro and people eats away at us.

It does not occur to us that the Baining do not bring taro because they assume that we do not want it. We do not know that they haven't seen white people eat taro—the *kiaps*, the plantation managers, the missionaries do not eat taro, and the Baining cannot imagine that we will want to eat it either.

It does not occur to us that the Baining do not come to visit because they are an intensely private people. We have already forgotten that Bateson called them shy. And we do not yet know that these are people who would not intrude on one another, let alone on us.

Nor do we know that the Baining are so matter-of-fact, so utterly down to earth and pragmatic, that our arrival is just that: our arrival. *So you have come. So you are here. Amrs! No big deal.*

We do not yet understand that even if we were two-headed Martians setting up house, the Baining would simply note it mildly. What would interest them most would be our journey: Where did you come from? they would ask. How long did it take to get here? How far is it to Mars? Did you pass through Raunsepna, Alakasam, Galavit, and Wilaimbemki on the way?

By the by they might observe among themselves: these Martians seem to have two heads. And in their next ritual dance, their *singsing*—if they lived in the mountains and still had *singsings*—they would no doubt include a two-headed Martian among those extraordinary masks.

An exception to all of this is Mlung. Mlung is not shy. Mlung is willing to intrude. Mlung is curious; he is interested in us. Mlung soon takes over our lives.

Mlung is not in Puktas when we arrive, which is why he does not visit us at once. But he comes as soon as he is back. Here he is, bustling up to our house, ready to take charge.

Like most Baining men, he is short and stocky. But where others are muscular and firm, he seems to me soft, almost flabby. This softness, combined with rheumy eyes—the effect of some medical condition—makes him seem older than he probably is.

Pig Food

How old, I have no idea. At twenty-two I find that everyone looks old. He is not a young man, but neither is he a *lapun*, an old man. He is probably around forty.

Mlung greets us, he enters the house, and as we sit together on the porch, he tells us that he has been at Lassul Bay, at a meeting: he is councilor for Puktas to the local government.

Councilor: we know this is an Australian position, but we do not yet know what it really means. Jeremy has said that often village leaders who are associated with the Australian government are not the true leaders, the "big men" and shamans the villagers themselves look up to. Is councilor an important position among the Baining? We have no idea.

"I have heard why you are here," Mlung tells us and says at once that he would like us to live in his hamlet. It is near water, he says. We can *waswas*; we can bathe. He says this twice: it seems very important to him that we *waswas*. I wonder if he has noticed that I look dirty.

He promises to bring us a chicken. He will bring a coconut as well and show us how to scrape it to make *gris*, or sauce. I assume that he will help us eat this chicken as well. But when he arrives with the bird, bound upside down and still alive, to our dismay, he simply hands it over, leaving us to mangle the job so badly that an image will haunt us for years: fully plucked, the creature opens its eyes!

As for Mlung, when he comes the next day, all he wants is *ti*.

"*Misis inap wokim sampela ti?*" he asks. "Can the missus make some tea?"

Over time, I will make Mlung a great deal of tea.

From the start we have a complex relationship with Mlung. He is a complex man. He is also an irritating man. Clearly, he is generous: we cannot blame him for the fate of the chicken. But he has a fawning manner and perpetually pious expression that we find off-putting. Perhaps this comes from dealing as he does as councilor with government whites and missionaries. But we are not whites who want to be kowtowed to—I am most definitely not a *misis!*—and his conspicuous humility makes us squirm.

Moreover, for all his fawning, he tries to dominate our lives. As we struggle to establish our presence in the village, that presence, it seems, is always filtered through Mlung. He is everywhere. Life in Puktas becomes life with Mlung.

We begin to attend the small church on Sundays, and there is Mlung, to accompany us. We stay on after the sermon, when people gather in the clearing outside to mingle and chew *buai*, and there is Mlung, eager, I feel, to keep us to himself. He appears at our house every day. He monitors our activities. He always seems to know where we have been, whom we have seen or talked to— if we have actually found someone to see or talk to—and possibly, I suspect, even what we have said.

When Jeremy asks a youngster to give us lessons in Baining, assuming that a student who has attended a mission school will have some sense of the teaching process, Mlung lets us know that he finds this inappropriate: our teacher should be an older man. (And we think we know who.) When Jeremy decides that instead of shorts he will wear a *laplap*, the cloth wraparound that has replaced the traditional Baining dress for men (which is nothing), Mlung lets us know that he finds this inappropriate as well: Jeremy should not dress like *ol kanaka*, "the natives." Mlung is endlessly, obstructively solicitous about my welfare. Any expedition we mention—a plan to visit gardens, or a distant hamlet, or, God forbid, another village—he will claim that the distance is too far, or the path too steep, or the journey in some way beyond what I can do. What is most frustrating is that he is generally right.

———

Pig Food

The problem, of course, is that Jeremy needs Mlung, who is the only Baining in Puktas to take an active interest in his work, the only Baining in Puktas who seems to care why we are here and is willing, even eager, to talk. Jeremy may find Mlung annoying, but the anthropologist in him finds it hard to complain.

I, however, am not an anthropologist, and I find it quite easy to complain—especially when I learn that Jeremy has agreed that we will live in Mlung's hamlet, that this is where the Baining will build our new house.

"In Mlung's hamlet?" I cry. "How could you have done that?"

Jeremy shrugs. It is not a question worth answering. We both know why he has done it. Mlung is an assertive man.

"Mlung!" I say. "He treats us like children."

This is true: Mlung does treat us like children. Indeed, in anthropological parlance, he has adopted us. And in many ways, in Puktas, we are like children. I realize this. It is partly that we look so very young: only Baining adolescents are thin as we are thin; our young language tutor and his friends have asked if Jeremy and I are *really married*. But it is also that, like children, we cannot yet talk—not, at least, in Baining. Like children, we do not know the customs, we do not know how to behave, we aren't yet socialized. Like children, we cannot get around without getting lost. Indeed, I cannot even get around without falling down. And I am prone to stepping in the poop of the mangy village dogs. We do not have gardens, we do not grow taro, we do not know how to cook it, we have no livelihood. On our own here, we would not survive.

Obviously, this is the lot of the anthropologist in any new village, to be learning the ways of an unknown setting and culture like a child. But somehow I cannot see Levi-Strauss allowing himself to be treated as one.

We bicker constantly over Mlung. He is like family.

In fact, I do not whine without compunction. I know that Jeremy needs Mlung: I know that Mlung is the best—so far, the only—informant he has. We still have no other visitors, our excursions still lead mostly to empty houses, our tutor is just an adolescent, his knowledge limited by youth. And what does it mean to *dislike* someone from such a different culture—and before you even know anything about that culture? I think of the variability of customs even among cultures that are close: Americans find the French rude because they do not smile enough, while the French consider Americans imbeciles because we smile too much.

Am I responding to mannerisms that I'm misreading? Am I stuck entirely in the personal? But wouldn't it be demeaning to ignore the personal, to treat all Baining as though they were the same, simply Baining, as if they as a people—unlike us—were not made up of individuals?

I feel confused, I feel guilty, I feel ashamed, but I cannot help myself: Mlung in loco parentis drives me wild.

These feelings erupt one day in a curious culinary showdown.

Although by now we have tasted taro—on a visit to Mran and Tuvuan's house—we still live mainly out of tins. Desperate for fresh food, for something green, I have supplemented our tin-and-rice dinner with *angamingl*.

Angamingl are long, green bean-like pods that grow on a tree near our hut. I know their name because in a language lesson with our young teacher, we used these pods to learn declensions, the forms getting increasingly more intricate—*anamigrim ama yurisingle, "the two pods their seeds"*—until all three of us burst out laughing. I know they are edible because the youngster told us that they are.

Pig Food

As it happens, I am cooking these pods one day when Mlung arrives for a visit. He greets us. He peers into the pot, which is uncovered. He shakes his head.

"What are you doing?" he asks, though what I am doing is pretty obvious.

"*Angamingl!*" I say, as proud to know the name of these pods as I am to be cooking them. I tell him that I am boiling them for dinner.

He looks at me in horror. "That isn't food," he says. "You can't eat that."

I tell him that that is exactly what we intend to do. "*Bai mitupela kaikai dispela samting*," I say in my rudimentary Pidgin. We will be eating them.

"But it isn't food," he says again, staring intently at the pot, as if he would like to overturn it. "You'll die!"

"But we've eaten them before," I reply, my smirk implicit: and we aren't dead yet, are we?

Unable to watch—he cannot bear it—he walks off, while I proceed to cook my *angamingl* with stubborn pleasure.

In fact, they aren't very good.

A few days later, at a village meeting, Mlung, as councilor, is reporting on local matters, when suddenly we hear: "*Angamingl.*" Although we cannot understand the Baining, we cannot fail to recognize the topic, and we stare at the ground, struggling not to laugh as Mlung works up steam.

After the meeting, he comes over to translate for us what he has said.

"You aren't dogs! You aren't pigs!" he says. "You are men, and you should eat the same as us!"

This is such a grand and heartfelt statement that I am mortified; I feel foolish for my petty rebellion.

Yet this incident turns out to be just the shake-up that we need. Suddenly—disgusted perhaps by our eating *angamingl*—the people of Puktas acknowledge that we are here. We, who had somehow been invisible, are now the center of the meeting: people murmur and shake their heads and gently stare. A man named Kuluga steps up at once to take us on a botanical tour, to teach us which plants we can and cannot eat. Back in our hut, people bring us taro, a great deal of taro, far more taro than two people can consume. They seem determined that we should never be so ignorant or so hungry that we will ever eat pig food again.

5

Taro and Gin

Taro—*andumgi*—forms the bond with the Baining that we have needed. Luckily, we love it. And once the Baining see that we do, they acknowledge their pride in this food that is so central not only to their diet but to their very identity.

"*Taro, em i bun bilong mipela*," says Mlung. "Taro is our bones."

He takes pleasure in bringing us many types of taro, which so differ in size, in texture, and in taste that they remind me, in their variety, of cheese. Mlung says that the Baining especially prize *kamanauvum*, a large and handsome tuber whose white flesh is veined with purple streaks. My own favorite so far is the smaller *mawilki*, which is off-white, dry, and very dense.

At first the Baining give us only cooked taro. I'm sure they find it strange enough to see a white woman eating taro; they cannot imagine a white woman actually cooking it, and certainly not cooking it as they do. Baking taro Baining style is a dirty business. First you char the tubers on a high fire, and when they have thoroughly blackened, you scrape off this char. Then, as the fire has burned down, you set the taros on the embers, and you turn and scrape, turn and scrape, turn and scrape until the crust has turned white and you have turned black.

Mbar in the gardens, cooking taro and *pitpit*, scraping a taro

It is a long and messy process, but I am a cook. I love to cook. In Cambridge I made my way through Irma Rombauer's *Joy of Cooking*, in London I made my way through Julia Child's *Mastering the Art of French Cooking*, and here in Puktas, I intend to bake my own taro. I learn by watching Tuvuan, who, though shy, lets me observe and is happy to give me some tubers. She also gives me a scraper—*aivaki*—a small metal tool that, according to Mran, has replaced the shells that the Baining once used.

My early taros are fairly poor, smudgy and unevenly cooked. But soon they acquire the steamy fragrance and crisp crust we love, a cross between potato and the bread that we deeply miss. We eat our taro with butter, which we purchase at the New Masawa trade store in tins and consume long after it has gone rancid, with no apparent harm.

As I cook, Mlung hovers over me, torn between pride and disapproval. Just as Jeremy should not be wearing a *laplap*, I, a white woman—a *misis*—should not be cooking taro. "*Ating i no tan,*" he says repeatedly of my taro. "Perhaps it isn't done." But although he criticizes, I can see that his heart isn't in it. Behind his eyes, it is easy to perceive the smile.

I remember Bateson's shock at the Baining obsession with taro, his disbelief—his dismay—that this tuber could hold such interest. But I find that I share their fascination: taro becomes *bun bilong mi*. My journal fills up with taro. "Five small taros from Sil," I write, "the best we've ever had." "A new kind of taro today, but I'm not sure what it was called." "Baked an enormous *kamanauvum*, but it didn't come out right—very depressing." "I wonder if I'm getting fat."

But if taro provides a bridge to the Baining, we do not seem to find much on the other side.

It is true we feel welcome now. After church on Sunday, when everyone gathers in the clearing outside, the women invite me to sit with them. They take me around. They offer me *buai*, betel nut, and laugh when I find it too bitter. They give me *brus*, their strong native tobacco, which I find that I love: I wrap the leaf in newsprint and inhale it down to my toes.

The men gather around Jeremy. Now he has acquired a shotgun, and they ask him to shoot them *blakbokis*, or flying fox, the bats that circle our hut at dusk. He begins to go hunting with Kanga, an extraordinarily dignified young man, who says little, moves fast, and can somehow see the birds in the thick canopy of the rain forest.

We visit people often: as we learn our way to the different hamlets, we more frequently find the villagers at home, and they seem pleased when we join them on the earthen floor, careful to choose a spot free of scarlet betel spit. And people come to visit us. Sometimes they bring us taro, or bananas, and we in turn offer something, mainly trade-store tobacco, a valued gift.

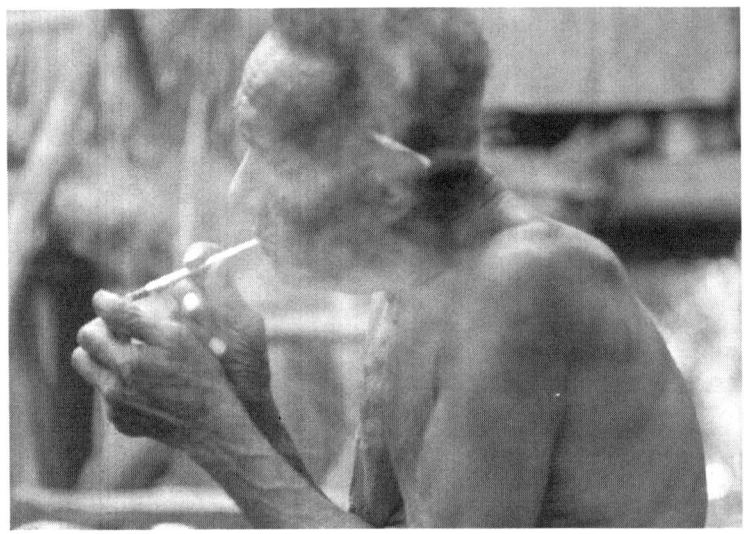

Ngoanangait at his house in Puktas

But a visit, we discover, mostly means that someone sits himself down on our porch and says nothing. They have come, presumably, to be friendly. This is a social undertaking. But conversation is not the Baining way. Dialogue is not big in this culture. They respond if we ask a question, although they do not necessarily answer the question, and they do not speak or ask on their own. They are a taciturn people who dislike those who talk too much: they call them *maus wara*—or *agerapki mutki*—"full of spit." The Baining are comfortable with silence.

I am not so easy with silence myself, and I find these visits awkward. Yet I do not say very much either, whether people visit us or we visit them. I am hesitant to ask personal questions of such reticent people, and I find it difficult to speak about my own life as well. I have shown some photos of my family and tried to describe them: who they are, what my parents do for a living, where we have lived. But I have to lay so much groundwork, and even then I feel that little comes through.

How could I describe the tensions with my mother, so commonplace back home, so out of place here? How could I possibly describe my troubled sister, whom no one understands even back home? What would it mean to say that I want to be a writer or that I have studied Greek literature? And I'm afraid that to talk too much about how we live—with all our possessions, our *stuff*, our *things*—would seem boastful. To talk personally at all is to leave out so much that what I do say seems distorted, even untrue.

Nor do I believe that the Baining want me to talk about my personal life any more than they want to talk about their own. In the end, on these visits, I feel as though I have to block out who I am—and I sense that Jeremy feels very much the same: there is no room here for who we really are.

In any case, we are here to find out about Baining life. What we would both like is to talk about things that are happening around us, to use events and activities as entry points to converse, or, for Jeremy, to pose his cultural questions.

The problem is, almost nothing happens in Puktas. It isn't simply the absence of everything that fills up a day back home. I am aware that I grew up in New York City, that I have lived in Cambridge, and that I have come from London to the bush: I understand what this means, the level of bustle and enterprise that I am used to.

But don't most societies have activities? Don't they usually have some kind of political life, with leadership and rivalries, status and possibly power grabs? Don't they usually have some kind of social life, with kinship and friendship, obligations and arguments? Don't they usually have some form of religious life, with beliefs, superstitions, and rituals, perhaps shamans and magic? Don't they usually have some kind of ceremonies, to celebrate birth, or marriage, or coming of age? Don't they usually have some form of artistic life: weaving, pottery, sculpture? Don't they usually have some form of wealth they need to strive and bargain for: yams, or pigs, or shells?

We cannot find any of these things in Puktas. It seems that people work in the gardens, and in the evening they go home and cook taro. They visit, which seems to involve hanging out and chewing *buai*. Every day is much the same except Sunday, when there is church and sometimes a meeting, which usually touches on mission or local government issues—Australian affairs—and is generally dull. No one in Puktas seems to care much about these affairs.

So far as we can tell, the Baining here have no political life at all. People in the hamlets all consider themselves Puktaskina, people of Puktas. But as a group, they seem to lack a formal or a semiformal or even an informal organization that gives authority or power to anyone. It has been clear to us from early on that they have no "big men," as many New Guinea societies do. But we are now realizing that they have no leaders at all. No group of elders to make decisions. The only formal political role we can identify is that of councilor, Mlung's position. But this is an Australian creation, and although Mlung is respected, the role itself does not seem to mean a great deal.

Nor do the Baining of Puktas seem to have religious beliefs and activities, outside those of the church. They take church seriously: after all, this is the home of the St. Paul Mission, the scene of the ancient massacre; indeed, the Baining are still required to tend the Graves of the Martyrs, in everlasting penance.

But they do not worship Baining gods or a Baining god—we have heard no mention of their own gods at all. We are aware that they no longer practice the rituals they once had, they no longer perform the dances—the *singsings*—with extraordinary masks. But they seem now to have almost no rituals at all. We have been told that they do not have initiation rites. They do not have complex marriage rites: according to Baining custom, the wedding couple shares a taro. They do not have shamans. Nor are they an especially superstitious people. They do not seem as superstitious as Americans. They are certainly not as superstitious as my mother.

The Baining of Puktas do not appear to have a complex kinship system, one of those elaborate webs of relationships and terms that exist in so many of the societies anthropologists have studied. It seems clear that they have stable marriages. They care for their children. But each family unit seems to be distinct, a nuclear family much like ours in the West, without extensive obligatory ties. They have only a few kinship terms: Jeremy has counted six. They do not worship or even seem to remember their dead ancestors. They do not seem to consider bloodlines or even blood ties particularly important.

One day Jeremy tries to take his first genealogy, an initiation rite for the newbie anthropologist. There he is, sitting on a mat in the front room of our house, across from his young informant, a large blank piece of paper between them.

"*Orait*"—"All right," Jeremy begins. "*Nau husat mama bilong yu?*"—"Who is your mother?"

His pencil is poised. Anticipation is in the air. He is about to become an authentic anthropologist.

"I don't know," the young man replies.

He doesn't know. How can you not know who your mother is? We have no idea what this can mean.

As it turns out, this episode reveals an intriguing Baining practice, a system of cross-adoptions: when two women give birth at around the same time, they might trade babies, each family raising the adoptive child as their own. Also, we learn, children might simply choose to go and live in another household that they prefer, and he or she will be adopted.

These adoptions are by no means secret: the names of the couples are known. But sometimes, as in the case of Jeremy's informant, children—even if they know they have been adopted—will not be told the name of their birth parents, or over time these names might be forgotten.

Here then is a truly Baining custom. It is a custom that challenges our Western notions of mother-child bonding. It is also a custom that puts into question whether the Baining, before the church arrived, had an incest taboo: in this system, after all, how could you know for certain who your blood relatives were? It seems likely, especially if you marry close to home, as the Baining apparently do—indeed, we learn, as close as possible!—that you could marry a near relative, even a sibling.

It is Mlung who explains this custom of adoption, but he speaks of it cautiously, as a topic he would rather avoid. The church, it seems, does not approve. The church, however, has not been able to stop it: the practice is too deeply embedded in Baining life.

We are relieved to hear that the power of the church has limits. We have to wonder, though, as we reflect on this opposition, just how much *has* been stopped by this church, which has foisted its beliefs, and its catechists, and its holy days, and its schools, and its burden of guilt on the Baining.

Have the church and the government between them stopped just about everything? We know that the Baining in this coastal region used to have *singsings*. Did they also have gods and shamans? Initiation rites? Leaders with power? This intriguing custom of adoption seems to us to open a window into a different world, a Baining world that we are coming to believe—in Puktas, at least—is sadly gone.

This view of a cultural void, with contact as the villain, seems confirmed when we discover that alcohol is a problem in Puktas. The villagers drink. Water might be in short supply, but beer and gin seem to flow, a river of alcohol that has snaked its way through the plantations—from New Masawa to New Mobisberg—and, as we see it, filled the hollows where a culture once flourished.

One day, fairly early on, while we are hunting out the elusive Baining, looking for someone to talk to, we follow the sound of voices to a house. People! A dozen Baining gathered on the wide steps of a porch—and they are talking! We feel that we have struck gold.

We greet them—"*Amrs!*"—only to realize, too late to turn away, that they are plastered.

"*Amrs! Amrs!*" they call, as they make room for us on the steps, and offer Jeremy a bottle. With me they are unsure: Puktas women, it turns out, do not drink, and though the men in this gathering offer, they do not expect me to accept. I can refuse without fear of wounding feelings. As I watch Jeremy squint and suppress a grimace, I am grateful to be spared the pleasure of warm gin on a torrid afternoon.

But neither of us is spared the experience of inebriated Bainings.

The Baining, we discover, typically so reserved, so polite, so laconic, are transformed by liquor: gin makes them raucous and maudlin. Verbose! Old Tulu, normally so dignified, nearly falls on me, leaning over, nose to nose, to lament how the black man, *ol kanaka*, and the Baining in particular, have only *rabis nating*, "just rubbish."

"*Mipela gat sem*," he says—they have shame—that Jeremy and I are living as they do: sleeping in a hut, sitting on the ground and eating taro, scrounging for water to *waswas*.

"Ay, poor us! Ay, poor you!" the group moans, "us" and "you" gradually blurring in the mist of heat and booze.

In any case, the men's laughter belies these lamentations. Clearly, they are glad that we are here and that we are living as they do. Indeed, they decide at this point to give us each a local Baining name—a *ples nem*. I become Lukun, which I believe is some kind of river weed. Jeremy becomes Mbalu, although they later change this to Kuluga when, at a more sober moment, they realize that Mbalu is Lukun's brother—the incest taboo at work!

We feel depressed by this outing and vow to avoid drunken gatherings. But this proves to be impossible. We need too much to be included, and drinking is too extensive. Attending church one Sunday, we hear the catechist, confronting a small turnout, declare that twenty-four hours of drinking is quite enough. "*Wanpela de inap!*" he says. No one needs two or three days and nights. People should start drinking on Thursday, he proclaims, so they can sleep it off by Sunday and come to church. He has given up trying to stop the drinking: all he can hope to do is change the party time.

Six weeks in, we are feeling increasingly frustrated. We knew even before we came that in Puktas we would be dealing with the consequences of contact. We came here only for a basic introduction, a place to acclimate ourselves to the bush, to master Pidgin, and to learn as much as we could of the Baining language before heading inland. Jeremy did not expect to find answers to probing anthropological questions.

All the same, we did not expect to find as little Baining life as we are finding. Between our isolation in the *haus kiap*, the need to avoid parties, Baining reticence, and the fact that *nothing happens*, Jeremy is making little headway with fieldwork. He goes off each morning, visiting, mapmaking. But he feels that he is marking time.

I too feel that I am marking time, although for me the issue isn't fieldwork but life—or, as I think of it more melodramatically, Life. Sometimes I go visiting with Jeremy; sometimes I just stay home, in my little clearing, with Time.

I have never had so much time. I never knew there was so much time in a day. How can there be so much time? Some days, it feels enclosing: a box or a bubble that I can't escape from. Some days, it seems the opposite: a medium, moist and humid, that I dissolve in. Mostly, it is simply a void that I feel desperate to fill.

I draw out every act, to use up time. I eat my breakfast biscuits slowly. I clean our dishes slowly. I wash up slowly. I roll my cigarette slowly. I write in my journal slowly. I cook taro twice a day: this takes up hours.

I read: some Penguins that I have picked up in Rabaul and *Time*, which comes with the mail and makes home seem very far away. I write letters and look forward avidly to this mail, which arrives haphazardly—delivered to the mission station at Vunamarita, handed over by Father Mayrhofer to a Baining from Puktas who happens to be returning from the coast, and carried, eventually, to our hut. These letters too make home seem far away.

"How fascinating it all sounds," write family and friends. They have no idea. For them, of course, eating taro or bathing in a river or watching the Baining clear bush all sounds so different, so new. How can they see these things as routine? And for them, we describe every incident of any interest in detail: When a malarial team comes through to spray, we turn it into a story. When Maxie throws a party, we turn it into a story. When a villager asks Jeremy to shoot a wild pig that he has trapped but can't kill—because the Baining have no weapons—we turn it into a story. How can they grasp that this was the only interesting incident in the week—and that it lasted all of two hours? How do you convey the weight of all those other hours, when nothing at all is happening, the minute-by-empty-minute day?

By mid-July, we feel that we are still waiting for fieldwork to begin. We cannot claim that there is no progress at all. We still have language lessons, although our student no longer comes to teach us: fired, we assume, for the *Angamingl* Affair. "The children mustn't lie to you," says Mlung, who has taken over the lessons himself. We have begun collecting stories, which seems promising: people do know stories, it seems.

But when we go to someone's house to tape a story, it is very artificial. Language lessons are artificial. Visiting is itself artificial. We still have little sense of daily Baining life. How can we even know that it is as empty as we think? Maybe there is more that we are missing? With the Baining so laconic, so unwilling to talk, we need to observe, and for that we need to be living in a hamlet. Yet here we are, still waiting for a house *namel*.

From the start, we told the Puktaskina that we would be staying in Puktas six months and then moving on to the mountains. We did not, of course, say that we planned to stay twice as long in the mountain village. We did not in any way suggest that we viewed Puktas as a stepping-stone to the mountains. This would be incredibly rude, especially since there seems to be some rivalry between the coastal and the mountain Baining. Indeed, as we have come to know the villagers, and as they have embraced us, we feel guilty even thinking in these terms. Still, we did tell them that our six-month deadline is fixed: we have to leave before the rainy season—*bipo taim bilong ren*—when it will become impossible to hike into the mountains.

What the Baining have made of this schedule, I can't say. It seems to have left no impression. Although they said from the very first day that they would build us a house, although they have long since decided that it will be in Mlung's hamlet, and although they mention it often—reminding us that we will soon be able to *waswas* more easily—we have yet to see any signs of construction.

Beyond frustration, we have begun to fear that by the time the house is finally built, we will live in it for just a month before leaving: all that work for just a month—we will feel rude. But we also feel that it would be rude to pressure them—after all, they have other things to do besides building us a house, they have lives of their own, they have land to clear and gardens to tend to, and they have already refused to take payment for this work. And so we only hint at it from time to time, so feebly that I doubt they even hear us, and nothing progresses.

Our desire to be nice, to be polite, to avoid rudeness of any kind is more than a preoccupation during our lives with the Baining: it is an obsession, a pathological need. I understand this desire. We want to show that we are not your stereotypical arrogant colonialists, that we have nothing to do with people like the manager of New Masawa plantation, who has gotten into trouble for chaining and striking his "*bois*." And who, after all, can argue with being nice?

But we go to extremes. To begin with—and we know and acknowledge this—we are both insecure, afflicted with a craving to be liked and approved of. And in this, as in everything, we compete. We strive to outdo each other in suppressing our own needs and wants.

Has a visitor been sitting in our front room for two hours saying absolutely nothing? He has. Will either of us say, I want to eat now, or sleep, or go for a walk, or just be alone—and will you please, please, please, go home? We will not. Will either of us simply read or eat or write, proceed with life as if the visitor weren't there? Never! No, we will simply sit there playing silent host to our silent guest, who does not really wish to be asked any questions. To do anything else, we feel, would be unacceptably rude.

In the tacit competition we wage to be egoless, I seldom win. I am simply not as nice as Jeremy. Not that I take action. But often I will say, in English so our visitor doesn't understand, "I'm getting hungry," or "I would really like to read now," or "My God, I don't think I can take this for one more minute!" And Jeremy will shrug, or say, "Well, eat then," or "So go read," swiftly proving in three short words that he is the better person. How smug he looks! How ugly I feel! This will lead to some nasty scenes later, in our own bitter privacy. However nice we may be to the Baining, we seem to have no qualms about being rude to each other.

In fact, we argue constantly. Jeremy feels that I am always finding fault with everything. I feel that he is always finding fault with me. Jeremy feels that my antipathy to theory is obstructive. I feel that although he has dragged me on this field trip, he doesn't really want me to participate in his work. We find that we can quarrel about anything: family and friends, food, housekeeping, Loki, photographs, even the phonemes in the stories we have started to tape: "*Nga!*"—"No, *ngwa!*" "*Nga!*"—"No, *ngwa!*"

We have a particularly vicious spat about a bat—a *blakbokis*—that Jeremy has shot; young Tomamia has made off with it, and I feel enraged.

Taro and Gin

Jeremy with young Tomamia, who took our bat

"Did you want to eat that bat?" Jeremy says, knowing full well that I did not: we have already eaten bat and found it wanting a certain *je ne sais quoi*. But I am angry that Jeremy is always willing to shoot these bats for people who come around asking at dusk, our dinnertime. He jokes that anthropologists often hire a villager to hunt, but he himself has become the village shoot-boy. I'm not amused. Mr. Nice. He wins again.

Too much closeness, we're both aware, is a strain. Too much dependence, too much need. To have no social mates but one another. To have just one person who shares your language, your culture, your simplest frames of reference. And for this person to be so imperfect! For this person to be so insensitive, so unempathic, so arrogant, so totally *unsimpatico*. Every morning we wake up and there it is: you again!

Will things be better in Mlung's hamlet?

In truth, I am anxious about this move. I realize that our isolation has been absurd: it defeats the very point of being here. And I have found so much solitude a bit numbing. But I have also enjoyed our privacy. The ability to observe means also being observed. I dread the sense of being watched.

Most of all, I am concerned about our niceness, our *politesse*, our apparent need to be doormats. If we have had trouble holding our own in isolation, what will life be like smack in the middle of a hamlet? And Mlung's hamlet, no less. If he has monitored our lives from a distance, what will it be like when we are living straight across from his house?

There he will be every morning: "Does Lukun need help with the fire?" "Does Lukun need water?" "*Dispela taro, ating i no tan.*" "*Lukun inap wokim sampela ti?*" He will sit himself down, and we, with our Emily Post–in-the-bush rules of etiquette, will never ask him to leave: he will be there until nightfall, the Man Who Came for Tea.

But Jeremy is hopeful. His work is so utterly stalled. He is here, after all, to observe, and he has found almost nothing to observe. His thesis topic is the ritual expression of opposition between the sexes. But the Baining of Puktas have neither ritual nor opposition between the sexes. Here, there does not seem to be the great distinction between gender roles that occurs in so many societies—including our own—and if couples are not demonstrative, they seem to get along extremely well. Indeed, the main opposition between the sexes in Puktas takes place in our hut.

If he can learn anything at all in this village, he feels, it will be in Mlung's hamlet, and he is eager for a new beginning.

We argue about this, too, right until the day that we move.

6

Moving Day

On August 7 we move at last to Mlung's hamlet. Our house has finally been built because the *kiap* needs his: he will be coming to Puktas, he sends word, in early August. The *kiap*'s visits are rare, but when he comes, the villagers take heed: under pressure, the Baining work fast so we can just squeak in before the deadline. But in the rush, we are warned, the house is not quite finished. The *haus kuk* is not complete. Actually, it hasn't yet been started. But August 7 is the date, and though the *kiap* delays his trip for several weeks, we move on August 7 all the same.

We have planned for this move to be easy. Our cargo, light to start with, has diminished. We are aiming for a simpler life. As the Baining feel shamed by how little they have, we feel shamed by our goods. Wealth! The stuff of imperialism! Our goal has been to strip it down.

We have given away our clumsy cots and now sleep on mats on the floor; these roll up neatly for transport. We do not have much tinned food to carry, living as we now do on taro and the occasional pigeon or hornbill that Jeremy shoots when hunting with Kanga. And though we haven't quite abandoned our stove or pressure lamp, we use them so seldom that we have little kerosene to haul.

It's true this cutting back has had a downside. I do not miss our meatballs, but I suspect that we are short on protein these days, and I wonder what this will mean for our health. I do not miss our cots, but I do have some issues with the mats, which Loki loves to use as a mouse run: mornings, we wake to see whiskers approaching; small rodents enter our dreams. And while I do not miss that lamp, with the multitude of bugs that it lured, I truly miss the light. I am a night person. I have always been a night person. I watched the *Late Show* with my father when I was ten. Now, with our small kerosene lamp too dim to read by—just barely light enough for a game of Scrabble—we go to bed early and wake at dawn. A more natural cycle, I tell myself—repeatedly—but it feels entirely unnatural to me.

Still, we take pride in this basic living. We are pleased at how few people we will need to help us move.

"The big move," I write in my journal. "Much dreaded," I also note. And moving day itself is not encouraging.

Loki seems to share my misgivings and puts up such a fight that we are forced to put her in a box. We put the box in a sack to carry. As we trek through the bush paths, she cries pathetically the entire way.

When we arrive at Mlung's hamlet, Mlung, curiously, isn't there, and the house is even less finished than we thought. The missing *haus kuk* is the least of it: we quickly set up a cooking area under the hut. But the outhouse isn't ready. There are no front steps: we can't get in!

While the men see to these details, Mlung finally turns up, and for Mlung he seems suspiciously gay. It turns out that he has been drinking, perhaps celebrating our arrival in advance. Not to be outdone, our movers whip out a bottle of their own. As our little band settles on the ground by our new house, I already foresee a long line of boozy sessions in the weeks ahead. And we have barely moved in.

Conversation turns quickly to the party that Jeremy and I have agreed to sponsor, a housewarming and also a thank-you, since the Puktaskina will not accept pay. Somehow—perhaps it is the alcoholic haze—someone suggests that we buy a cow at New Masawa for this feast instead of the customary pig.

"*Bulmakau!*" the word goes around. "*Bulmakau!*"

A cow? The villagers have never cooked a cow, and as they toss the idea around, it is clear that no one knows how. They will *mumu* it, of course, like a pig, burying it in a pit with hot stones. But what size pit? For how long? How many stones? And who will carve this cow?

"*Maski,*" they say. "No matter." A *bulmakau* it is.

To us, this sounds ominous. We see complications. We see delays. We suspect that this shindig will turn out to be a farewell party. Indeed, we only hope that it takes place before we leave.

The first days in Mlung's hamlet, it seems that life may be even more intrusive than I feared. People come and go. Children and chickens run wild. The house of our neighbors Takiap and Hapaluk, a young couple who also live in the hamlet, seems to be a gathering place at night. After weeks of solitude, all this activity comes as a jolt.

"A wretchedly uncomfortable night, a noisy morning!" I whine in my journal the day after we have arrived. "I really don't see how I can stay here without an ounce of privacy!"

But as it turns out, life is better in the hamlet, even for me. Taro and wood are forthcoming, we never have to ask, and our exchange of gifts is simpler. Although the proximity of water, so long promised, proves useless since the river path here is even steeper—something no sure-footed Baining would have noticed—

we now have the children to help fetch water: Jeremy sets up a bucket shower in our hut. The children also guard against bugs: if they see us run suddenly from our house, they know at once that some exceptional creature has arrived, and they rush over laughing, pluck the monster up, and crisp it on the fire to eat.

Life feels fuller here. *We* feel fuller here, the place is so much richer in food. Hawilki accidentally kills Takiap's pig, and a packet of *vlumga* arrives. Nawe shoots a cassowary, and a packet of *murupki* arrives. We are treated more often to the *mumued* taro we love, *ahindumgi*, which has been sauced with coconut milk, wrapped in a banana leaf, and buried with hot stones. Takiap and Hapaluk introduce us to *agahaip*, a wild green they cook in coconut milk: it is one of the most delicious foods we have eaten in our lives.

In this setting, Jeremy can observe what there is to observe in daily life, and he no longer has to hunt down people to talk to. There is usually someone visiting the hamlet, or Mlung arranges for us to visit others.

And in this setting, Mlung shines. Perhaps he can relax now that he "has us in his clutches," as I write in my journal. He needn't worry where we are or who we're seeing: he has us in his view. As he becomes less hectoring, I come to appreciate how helpful he truly is. As we focus increasingly on collecting stories, he arranges for various people to tell their tales. When we struggle to transcribe the tapes, he proves to be a patient translator, even jovial at times. He sits with us for hours, a mediating presence in our phonemic disputes. A moderate drinker, he protects us from drunken orgies, even hiding some bottles of gin at the cow roast that finally takes place in our hamlet, with *ahindumgi*, music from someone's radio, and a very large crowd—even Maxie comes: it is a big success.

Heating stones for a mumu

Loki too is happier here. To our surprise, she soon goes into heat, and for several nights she goes off with the *wailpusi*—the "wild pussy," as he is aptly called in Pidgin—a bush tom who immediately responds to her call. Doting parents, we worry about her absence, but she returns, looking quite chuffed.

In Mlung's hamlet, while it's true I miss my solitude, I like feeling part of Baining life. By now I have acquired a bush knife, and though I cannot cut big logs, I gather branches for my fire. I have grown adept at using fire. I bank the embers in the evening to keep them going overnight, and I start the fire in the morning without a match. Twice a day, like the other women in the hamlet, I cook my taro. My fingers have grown sufficiently calloused that I can move the hot taros in the embers barehanded. I can even move the embers.

Dalinda, Mlung's wife, says that she feels shame to see us living as they do. "*Mi gat sem*," she says. But when Hapaluk, who is younger and more open, says frankly that she is pleased to see it, Dalinda admits that she agrees.

One day Takiap watches me cook. I am sitting on a log in our *haus kuk*, which has finally been finished, shooing off the chickens. I am blackened from the char of the taro.

"*Nau em i Baining pinis*," he laughs, pointing at my sooty limbs. "Now she is truly a Baining."

Whatever this might imply about the Baining self-image, he looks immensely pleased—as, I confess, am I.

But if life feels better in Mlung's hamlet, for fieldwork the move makes little difference. Jeremy can observe what there is to observe, but that doesn't prove to be much. Nothing new emerges. No rituals, no fascinating customs that we had missed. Life seems very mundane. The Baining of Puktas go to the gardens each day, they get food, they return in the evening to cook dinner. It strikes us that this could be suburbia. They might be going to the supermarket and returning home after work. There are a few arguments, some illness, a child's death in another hamlet, which is briefly mourned, but everything seems to move on an even keel, cycling through days that feel unmarked and empty.

To us, the Baining look sad, and we believe that they *are* sad as they go about their daily lives, which seem to demand and offer so little. Men and women certainly work hard in their gardens, but there is little challenge in growing taro. Land itself is abundant and free; it is there for the taking: claim it, clear it, and it is yours. Taro thrives in the fertile soil; there are no floods, no killing frosts, rains, or drought, and as yet no disease or insect infestations to wipe out crops. Cooking taro may be a time-consuming

Moving Day

business, but the Baining—like me—have ample time with so little going on in a routine day.

Life here is so insular. Outsiders so seldom come to the village that I can easily recall the few who have. The malarial team that came to spray, a procedure the Puktaskina seemed to consider useless. Some Baining who came down from the mountains, en route to another village, and stayed in the *haus polis*; the Puktaskina seemed to ignore them. Once, finally, the *kiap* came on patrol, dealing briefly with the villagers, chatting with us over tea; he was gone the next day. And once—thankfully only once—a white plantation man appeared, to visit *us*: he seemed to think we were in desperate need of racist company. Even Father Mayrhofer is a rare figure in Puktas—indeed, although we have heard of a ceremonial appearance, we haven't seen him here at all.

To us, the Puktaskina look bored, as bored as we feel when they come to visit and sit in our front room and say nothing. To us, they look as though they suspect there should be something more to life, but they don't know what it is. Now that they no longer perform their *singsings*, not only do they have no rituals, but they have no crafts, no music, no art.

The older people can dredge up stories from memory, tales of the folk hero Hrini that are exactly the same as those gathered by Father Rascher at the turn of the century, and tales so strange—filled with siblings, snakes, holes in the ground, and, always, people going somewhere, journeying from village to village, from mountain to mountain—they give us a sense of how extraordinarily different the Baining worldview must be, or must have been.

But these stories do not seem to be part of the Bainings' daily lives. People do not tell them to one another for entertainment. We do not hear them telling them to the children. They tell them to us because we ask. They enjoy the telling once we do ask, immersing themselves in the tale: "*Na i go, i go, i go, i go,*" the narrator will say as he takes his protagonist on some long journey. And Mlung, at the repetition, will joke: "*Ah, i olsem masin nau!*"—"Ah, now he's just like a machine!" But neither the storytellers nor the audience have anything to say about these tales. No interpretation, no comment. The stories seem to have no context. We believe that the context has been destroyed.

In Mlung's hamlet, we see our previous view confirmed: the Baining of Puktas are living in the remnants of a decimated culture.

We have promised the Puktaskina six months, and we will honor that promise. We try to make the best of it. We continue to collect stories; we make a trip to the village of Ranganga, to collect more stories. This focus helps us learn the language as well; although linguistic progress is slow, although the language, as we were warned, is hard, we manage. Like people everywhere, the Baining love to hear us try. If we mangle words, no one minds.

But Jeremy sees his work stagnating: he uses up hours hunting, his notes are copious but scattered, and his journal is all about food.

I feel that I am stagnating: I use up hours cooking taro, I write nothing but my journal, and my journal is all about food.

Jeremy feels increasingly depressed: Is this really all there is here? he keeps wondering. Or is he failing as an anthropologist?

I feel increasingly depressed: Is this really all there is in life? Is everything else invention to mask this flatness that is real? And how can I say that what we in the West have invented is better, with all our personal discord and discontent, our wars and dissension?

Moving Day

We pore over our book of tropical diseases, its pages already yellow and worn, its binding broken from use, imagining, fearing, hoping for the worst: ulcers, fevers, parasites—this is our major source of entertainment.

We feel desperate to move on.

At the end of the summer, Jeremy visits the village of Raunsepna, in the mountains, to observe a traditional *singsing*. It is a difficult journey—his first experience hiking in the real Baining mountains—and he nearly collapses en route. But he returns exhilarated, fired up with tales of the spear dance, and the fire dance, and those extraordinary masks. I haven't seen him so energized since we arrived in New Guinea: it is as if he has suddenly been reminded of why he is here.

While Jeremy is in Raunsepna, I spend the week in Rabaul, and when he returns I meet him with my own vivid saga: of solitude and quiet, of reading and reflection, of real showers and a real bed and meals with bread. I haven't felt so energized since we arrived in New Guinea: it is as if I have suddenly been reminded of who I am.

After this we both find it hard to return to Puktas, though our reasons are diametrically opposed. Now Jeremy longs to be in the mountains; I long to be in Rabaul.

Back in Puktas, we are edgier than ever. "I'm going to Rabaul," I say every other day. Sometimes I say I'm going home. One day, after an argument, I even start to walk away. Mlung, ever watchful, rushes over and asks me where I am going. "Nowhere," I say, barely holding back my tears. And it is true: I am going nowhere at all. These threats are as empty as our daily lives. Every morning, there I am. There we are. You again!

At last it is November: we can leave. We know that we have to conceal our joy, and then we realize that in fact we don't feel very joyous. Although both we and the Baining are too reserved and too shy to express affection, although I cannot say that I know these people as I think of knowing friends, we have woven our way into Puktas life. No one wants us to leave, and they especially do not want us to go to the mountains. They do not think highly of their mountain cousins. For days before we leave, the Puktaskina visit, and the same terse dialogue repeats.

You are going *antap*? people say. To the mountains?

Yes, we say, we are going *antap*.

It is cold in the mountains, people tell us. You will get sick.

Yes, it will be cold, we say. We will have to dress warmly.

In the mountains, they warn us, they do not have *taro tru*.

Nogat? we ask, wondering if this is true or just a hostile myth about the mountains.

Nogat, they say. Something, it seems, has wiped out real taro—perhaps a *binatang*, an insect—and they have only Singapore taro, *singapo. Agalun.* Pig food. You will be hungry. You will get thin.

We will eat *agalun*, we say.

They shake their heads. You will get sick in the mountains, they say again. *Bikpela sik*. Very sick.

We promise that we will take care.

The night before we leave, people come to the hamlet for a farewell feast, and in the morning the entire village lines up to say farewell. Everyone shakes our hands in solemn Baining-Western fashion. They hold out their babies' hands. "*Amrs*," they say, one by one. "*Amrs*."

They weep. We weep. Dalinda goes off alone, behind a hut; we hear her wailing. Mlung himself cannot speak. He accompanies us to the coast, where we wait for the boat. We reach the dock by seven thirty, but the boat does not arrive until two, and it doesn't leave until three thirty. All these hours, just sitting in the sun, the three of us staring at the water. I long for this to be over. I think about our house standing empty in Mlung's hamlet. Will someone else move in? Or will it stay vacant, a constant reminder of our desertion?

"We will visit before we leave New Guinea," we promise Mlung when at last the boat is ready to leave. "We will visit before we go home," we say, honestly believing that we will.

Leaving feels unbearable. Yet how glad we are once we have left. We feel guilty about this; it seems a kind of betrayal. But we are glad nonetheless. We have needed for so long to move on, and we are excited about going to the mountains. By now I seem to have abandoned my reservations: I no longer talk about staying in Rabaul. By now I have seen the photos from Raunsepna, and the *singsing* does look amazing: the fire dance, the spear dance, those extraordinary masks. By now I too feel the pull of this new realm. Life there, we know, will be altogether different. At last we will be with the *real* Baining. At last our field trip can begin.

7

Jungle Boots

At the end of November, we prepare to set off for Wilaimbemki. We have chosen this village with care. According to patrol reports, this is the largest of the Baining mountain villages. Judging by our maps, it is sufficiently remote to have remained traditional.

Just how traditional Baining culture is in the mountains, we do not really know. We know that these villages still perform their *singsings*: Jeremy has witnessed this in Raunsepna firsthand. We know that they do not grow cash crops: neither cacao nor coconuts will thrive at the higher altitude. We know that although the coast of the Gazelle Peninsula has been invaded by outsiders for decades, the interior has been largely ignored, protected by its inhospitable terrain. Outsiders need to have a good reason to tangle with the dense bush of the Baining Mountains, and few do. Even missionaries are sparse on the ground: with just one resident priest in the mountains, Father Hesse in Raunsepna, we know that Wilaimbemki has been spared an active white mission presence.

But we have been able to learn little more, even right here in the region. The terrain that has protected the Mountain Baining from contact has made information difficult to come by. And

Jungle Boots

if outsiders do not visit the Baining to observe, neither do the Baining emerge to report. As we have learned in Puktas, they are an insular people. They keep to themselves. Rabaul, like any town, might attract young men, eager for jobs or adventure, but you will not find many Baining among them. The Baining will work on a plantation to earn the cash that by this time is necessary—to pay taxes now that taxes are required (one dollar per person per year), to buy knives now that metal knives are available, to buy clothes now that clothes are expected to be worn. But the Baining return to their villages.

Looking back, I now understand an incident that took place in May—our very first days in Rabaul—when we went to a health clinic for some shots we had somehow neglected to get. A missionary there, when he heard we were off to visit the Baining, told us that five Baining boys had just run away from his school. He couldn't understand it. "They were so far along in their studies," he said. "I brought them here to take them further. And now they have run away." He was mystified—so mystified, apparently, that he told us this story twice.

But having lived for six months with the Baining, at this point I could explain: the Baining were not being "uncooperative," as he assumed; the youngsters were simply going home. The Baining may not like to stay in houses, but they like to go home. They may like to move around—to their gardens, to other villages—but they want to move among Baining on Baining land. Home is not a house: it is a link to a particular area on Baining land. And if you want to find out anything at all about the Baining, you will have to meet them on their land.

As we set out, we feel renewed from our break. We have taken a trip to the town of Lae on the mainland, where we've met up with a London friend doing fieldwork in the Sepik. In yet another

ANU house, ensconced in a quiet suburb, we have had the cheering, invigorating pleasure of just talking to someone from our own world who isn't us. We have also had a brief stay in Rabaul, where we have—very lightly—resupplied.

We are traveling lean, even leaner than when we moved to Mlung's hamlet, and we are looking forward to a stripped-down life in the bush. We do not bother to bring the equipment that we have long since abandoned. We have given even the kerosene stove to the Puktaskina. We do not bring in much food, only some rice, a few tins, powdered milk, mainly breakfast items: we will live on taro, even *singapo*, if that is all they have.

"Less to carry, less to replace," we tell ourselves, as if practicality was the issue, as if something more were not going on in this drive for basic living.

"We have learned that you shouldn't try too much to do without," I write to my family, though it seems obvious that we have learned no such thing. "Living as fully 'native' as possible is really extreme and a bit foolish as you can't *be* native any way you look at it," I write, as if we weren't trying to do just that. I do not seem to think that I am lying as I write this, either to them or to myself.

Most of what we do bring is intended for the Baining, gifts that we plan to trade for food, information, and help: salt, cigarette paper, batteries, pens, thread, but mainly trade-store tobacco, the thick, sticky stuff that the Baining prefer to their own far superior *brus*, and the tinned mackerel that New Guineans so unaccountably love, though we feel it is most aptly described by the Pidgin name for canned fish, *tinpis*.

We are high on expectations and resolutions. Jeremy hopes that now, in a traditional village that still practices rituals, he will at last get some grasp of this culture that has seemed so diluted:

he sees himself digging in, observing, *finding out*, spending more time focusing on his notes and fewer hours hunting in the bush.

Together we have vowed that we will be firmer, more adult, more assertive in setting up our own lives, meeting our own needs, insisting on some privacy—at the very least, a time for meals.

Personally, I have vowed to be more gracious, more industrious, more independent, and less whiny. I will stop threatening to leave. This last promise is easily made: I suspect that if I actually make it to the mountains, an expedition I am viewing with some terror, I will not be going anywhere for quite a while.

We take the trip to Wilaimbemki in stages. First we have to reach Pondo, a coastal plantation on the western side of the peninsula, and then Poiniara, a subcoastal Baining village nearby: this village will be the starting point for our inland journey.

Reaching Pondo turns out to be more trouble than we expect: the "company boat"—the plantation freight boat that we plan to take—is out of commission, and our efforts to charter a speedboat fail. Fretting in a Chinese restaurant in Rabaul, we meet the *kiap*, who happens to be going to Pondo the very next day.

"Why not come with us?" he asks.

Why not? No overnight journey for the government officials. No bedding down with roaches on bags of copra. No, this is a day trip, with deck chairs, a bathroom, and lamb chops for lunch. On board, lazing in the sun, we laugh at how the bureaucrat arranging our passage warned us that the boat would be "uncomfortably crowded."

"Ha!" we say. "Obviously, he has never traveled by freight boat."

But then we realize: the "crowd" he referred to so sourly was probably us.

The boat lands at Pondo, where the *kiap* meets briefly with the councilor from Wilaimbemki, Karigyungi, who is waiting on the dock. We tag along, taking this chance to meet the councilor ourselves and ask permission to stay in his village. This is something we have not yet arranged: we know that we are taking a risk, just turning up with our baggage. What if he says no?

But Pondo is such a distance from Rabaul, we couldn't see making this boat trip twice. And we feel pretty certain that he will agree—as he does. Indeed, Karigyungi is just as casual as we expect a Baining to be. "*I orait*," he says, smiling so easily, you might think that young Americans asked to live in his village weekly instead of never before. He promises that when he returns to the village the next day, he will send down carriers to help us in.

In the meantime, we stay at Pondo with John, the manager of the plantation, a quiet, friendly Australian, just a few years older than us, who does not seem much like a plantation manager at all. He certainly doesn't resemble the stereotype personified by the manager at New Masawa, the rough-edged bigot notorious for abusing his "*bois*."

John seems to treat the New Guinea workers decently, or at least to speak about them decently—I can't say that I ever see him doing much plantation managing. He seems mainly to read and play records: his collection of rock and blues is superb. As we sit in his living room listening to Bob Dylan, the Rolling Stones, and Muddy Waters, feeling not unhappily displaced, I wonder what on earth this man is doing at Pondo. I suspect that he may wonder this himself, every day.

In the morning we visit Poiniara; John drives us over in his jeep. It turns out that the village isn't far, nor is it very much of a village. Apparently, it is a village in progress. The Baining of Wilaimbemki are building it as a place to grow cash crops.

"Then we will move the village here," says Solmet, a dynamic and handsome young man from Wilaimbemki, who speaks rapidly in Pidgin and Baining with bits of English tossed in and at once becomes our host. In his sunglasses, Solmet looks cool. And in fact, Solmet *is* cool. He is the only cool Baining I have ever met. Listening to him, I feel certain that he could sell you a bridge, even if you knew there wasn't a single bridge in the region.

Having described the Bainings' plans, he now lays out ours.

"Later," he tells us, "this afternoon, people will come down from Wilaimbemki." They will rest for a day, he says, and then on *Mande*—Monday—we will all go *antap*. "*Bai yutupela stap hia long Sande nait*," he says: we should sleep in Poiniara Sunday night, so we can get an early start.

"*I orait*," we say, amazed at how smoothly this has gone.

On Sunday, when we arrive with our gear, Solmet swiftly takes charge. He sets us up in an empty hut, he arranges for food, and in the evening he calls a meeting, to explain to other villagers why we are here.

"They will live in Wilaimbemki—they have come to learn *ol pasin bilong Baining*," he begins, and goes on to elucidate our goals quite as well as we could have done it ourselves. Indeed, when he takes out his sister's tape recorder to play us a *singsing*, I wonder who is the anthropologist here—and just how "authentic" these "real" Baining will be.

Monday morning I wake up very early, ready to confront this hike. I have been nervous about it for weeks, but I suspect that I haven't been nervous enough, and I am eager to have it over with at last.

But the day does not start well. As soon as we awake, we discover that our cat is not in the hut. By breakfast she hasn't returned. Loki, who after her dalliance with the *wailpusi* is pregnant, seems to have run away.

In truth, I cannot blame her: we have given her a rough time. There she was, a little town kitten assuming she would hang out in Rabaul her whole life, living on fresh milk and mackerel. Then suddenly, we come along and drag her off to the bush to face hissing beetles and feed on woggy rice. She has already been moved several times, once in a sack, and God knows where we are taking her now.

People run around, calling her name: they search through the village and on the edges of the forest. But Loki doesn't appear. The Baining think she has been killed by wild dogs. Wild dogs! This is even worse than I have imagined. I fear that she has gone off to have her kittens. I know absolutely nothing about feline pregnancy; I know neither how long it lasts nor how far along she is. But if she has run off to the bush to have her babies, I do not believe that either she or they will survive.

"I really don't want to leave," I say. But Jeremy is getting tense: we have to start. Hiking in these mountains is well known to be arduous: the heat, the mud, the density of the bush. The climb is not that steep, but you are always going up or down: the ground is never level for more than a yard. "Exhaustion sneaks up on you," Father Mayrhofer warned. Jeremy recalls his own struggle on his solo trip to Raunsepna, and he knows that for me the day ahead will be long and hard. Even in the easier terrain of Puktas, after all, I was always falling down. My one long excursion, to Ranganga, was not what you would call a success: confronting a log stretched high across a river, I freaked, and neither of us has forgotten the incident, which we refer to simply as "The Log."

Remarkably, in all these months, my hiking skills have not improved. Measuring in time, not miles—as distance in bush

Jungle Boots

like this has to be measured—the Baining say the hike will take three hours; the *kiap* has said four. But Jeremy and I both know that for me, it will take at least six, that we have to reach the village before dark if not before the afternoon rains, and that there will be many log bridges to cross.

"*U tit*," the Baining murmur, the words echoing through our scattered group—"Let's go"—the byword of a people always on the move. They promise that they will bring Loki to Wilaimbemki if she returns to Poiniara, but I do not expect to see her again.

I set out with a heavy heart. But it turns out that this is nothing compared to my heavy boots. These boots are Jeremy's solution to my perpetual hiking trials. He is convinced that my major problem is neither acrophobia nor innate clumsiness but footwear. If I will only wear the right shoes, he thinks, I will be sure-footed and fleet.

It is true that in Puktas I trudged around in flip-flops, as they are all too aptly called. But we both know that in this terrain, there is no ideal footwear, only ideal feet—and the Baining have them. With their thickly callused soles, they can move easily over the most gnarled jungle floor; with each big toe splayed outward like a brake, they have firm control as they move up and down the undulating ground. As an agricultural worker tells us, he likes to point to a Baining's feet and say, "I want shoes like that!"

But if there is no way to acquire the feet, I can at least acquire better shoes, Jeremy has argued, and a few weeks back, he ordered rubber jungle boots, rumored to be excellent, through a Chinese trade store in Rabaul. When they arrived, gleaming nausea green in their box, he was ecstatic, certain that we had the problem solved.

I had my doubts. For a start, they were stiff and clunky. They were also at least a half size too large. They rode up most of my calf. They would be hot—rubber doesn't breathe. And besides—I had to say it—they were hideous.

"Hideous!" Jeremy cried, latching on to what he believed was my main, and frivolous, concern. "This isn't a fashion show. We're hiking in the bush."

Setting out this morning, I sighed and hauled them on. But we haven't gone long before I can hardly move in these boots. Heavy to start with and now encased in viscous mud, they have become dead weights. It's true the gluey paste on my soles gives me traction, but it also sets me off balance. I fear that while crossing some log, I will simply stick in place and then tumble sideways down a ravine.

Slow at the best of times, I am now even slower. I am sure that the Baining have never seen anyone move so slowly. To them, I must seem like a different kind of animal, another species. At length, the mud on the boots grows so thick that I cannot lift my feet at all, and I come to a halt, stuck in the mud. For a while, no one even notices my absence, I am already so far behind.

At this point, as I sit down to clean my boots, the mud now further moistened with a mix of sweat and tears, I am saved by the *komitiman*, as they call him, though I have no idea what this means. (What committee?) He is a compact, wiry man who moves with an almost military bearing and elegance and who apparently recognizes my plight, foreign as it must be to a Baining. Once we get moving again, he stays near me, always just slightly ahead, gallantly offering a strong hand at every difficult passage, which for me, he seems to realize, is just about every passage. He leads me firmly over each log bridge until at last, around dusk, we reach the village. Briefly, I fall in love.

Jungle Boots

The first days in Wilaimbemki are delightful: they are the happiest I have spent in the bush. Perhaps I am simply thrilled to have arrived. But everything starts out smoothly. Even Loki is returned, hauled up in a sack from Poiniara, still pregnant and apparently unharmed by her adventures.

As in Puktas, no one makes much of our arrival. Only the children are curious. The grownups take us in stride: So you have come. So you are here. No big deal. "*Atlu!*" they say, which we learn is the mountain version of *Amrs*.

But if they are blasé, they are friendly and generous. The first night, they set us up in the *haus kiap*, and they bring us plenty of cooked food and firewood: as the Puktaskina have warned us, the taro is *singapo*, and it is indeed chilly in the mountains at night. Here, we note, the *haus kiap* has no separate *haus kuk*; here, they set up their cooking fires indoors.

In the morning, we take in first impressions. Unlike Puktas, Wilaimbemki has a village center: as we sit in the *haus kiap*, we are facing it, a large clearing with houses all around, some on stilts, some in traditional Baining style, on the ground. This clearing is absolutely clear, just red-brown earth scraped so bare that there is not a spot of green. Later we will see that it is the women who keep this plaza clean: a woman clears the space around her house in much the way she removes the lice from her children's hair, slowly and obsessively, looking almost at leisure as she bends, leaning over from the waist, and chops with her knife at every sprout.

The women here, apart from young girls, do not wear *laplaps*, as they do near the coast; dressed traditionally, they are naked except for a cane belt resting on the hips that carries a small skirt of grass in front and also a tuffet behind, where it serves as a cushion to sit on and—as Jeremy notes—resembles a cassowary's

Wilaimbemki

tail. The men in the village, as in Puktas, wear *laplaps*, but the older men who live in the bush still go naked—as we soon learn when old Suga appears.

This is definitely more *real*, we decide.

Traditional dress, a central village where we can visit, a friendly welcome—all seems to be going well, and in the mix of names and faces, one man stands out at once: Teingan. He is short, a bit roly-poly, probably around Mlung's age, and extremely high energy—he speaks even faster than Solmet. Like Solmet, he is someone whose intelligence is quickly apparent, and he seems immediately interested in what we are doing. Apparently, Teingan was Wilaimbemki's first councilor, a position he tells us that he—like other Baining—did not want and took only under pressure. As councilor he made a trip to Lae. So he has been outside these mountains. He has been in a plane. He is clearly not your average man, and we hope that he might play a role comparable to Mlung's—and perhaps play it even better.

Jungle Boots

Teingan

The very first day, with an efficiency unheard of in Puktas, the Baining of Wilaimbemki discuss getting wood to build us a house. But then my hero, the *komitiman* (I still do not know what this means!), suggests that we stay in Solmet's house: "Solmet will be away," he points out. "He will be teaching in Komgi."

Ah, yes, everyone agrees. Solmet will be teaching in Komgi.

At first we don't know what to say. Solmet's departure comes as a blow: we had assumed he would be here in Wilaimbemki, an outstanding informant, a friend. And how can we simply take his house: what if he wants to return?

But once Solmet consents—"*i orait*," he says, happily, it seems—we agree, and the men set to work. Dismantling some unused house, they get enough wood to make repairs: they secure the roof for the rainy season; they partition off two rooms and a space for a bucket shower; they build an outhouse.

I'm so thrilled with our little house and the speed with which it has been finished that I ignore what happens next, when I point out to Jeremy that the outhouse has no door.

"It doesn't need a door," he says.

Is he joking? I stare at him in disbelief.

It's true the men have worked hard, and I can understand not wanting to ask for anything more, which is surely Jeremy's issue. But this outhouse sits on a raised mound of land overlooking the village. Does he really expect me to squat there in full view?

Apparently, he does.

"No one can see in," he says as we stand there looking straight in.

Luckily, before we can work ourselves up, we find a large piece of burlap to hang up as a door. It will suffice. But this incident does not auger well for our fresh new plan of seeing to our needs.

No matter. I'm so charmed by our new abode that I'm not looking for signs of trouble.

"You wouldn't believe the house," I write to my parents that evening and again in my journal. "It's about 20 steps from the river—a lovely view, it has screened windows, shelves and an iron cupboard and a table! With our books lined up and a fire going in our stone hearth, it's amazingly cozy."

I rave on: it even has a door.

Am I delusional? So deprived that a cupboard makes me ecstatic? So determined to be upbeat that I'm blind? The house, however adequate, is just a hut—and not even quite as large or as neatly made as our house in Puktas. It has an old iron cupboard, some shelves, and a view of a small swimming hole out the back window, which is simply a square opening cut out of the bamboo wall, though it does have a screen. Our fireplace, set up in the front room, consists of some earth with a few small rocks as a border. A stone hearth indeed! But at this point, I seem to see our hut in Wilaimbemki as a lovely house in Provence.

Our house in Wilaimbemki

8

"Our Fathers Never Told Us"

These early days in Wilaimbemki are deceptive; everything seems to come together with such ease.

Here, we are finally close to water: we can *waswas* daily. We can also easily *waswas* our plates and our clothes. Every morning I slide into the swimming hole just behind our hut, a small shallow pool surrounded by grasses and trees that has been dammed with stones and is used, I discover, only by the children and, now, me.

Here, we are close to other houses: our house is truly *namel*. Our hosts bring us *bilum*, net bags, filled with *singapo*. They bring wood. We hand out various goods in exchange, which seem to go over well.

Most important, work begins at once. Teingan, when he hears that we are collecting stories, sits down with us and belts out three tales at rapid speed. People tell us that soon they will perform a night dance, a fire dance. Very soon. In just a few weeks. At last Jeremy can see his fieldwork taking shape.

Yet even by the end of the week, the picture has shifted. As we walk through the village, we suddenly find that it is nearly empty.

"*Ol i go long singsing*," we are told—apparently, people have gone to a *singsing* in another village.

We wait, hopefully, for their return.

But fairly soon we realize that the village is almost empty most of the time. It is empty not only in the daytime, when we know that people will be working in the gardens, but also in the evening, when we expect they would have returned. They do not return. So here we are, finally, in a centralized village, surrounded by many houses that we can easily reach. Yet we find ourselves once again searching for people to talk to.

We cannot understand what this means. Where has everyone gone? We are aware that some people have returned to Poiniara to work on the new village they are building: clearing bush to make space for houses and gardens and the cacao shrubs that they will plant. Unfortunately, this group includes Teingan and his wife, Kandimgi, who depart almost at once.

Still, this is only a handful. There should be many more people here. We chose this village for its size. According to the census, out of some three thousand Northern Baining living in the mountains, around four hundred should be living right here in Wilaimbemki. This is a sizable number of people to have disappeared.

We soon come to realize that the village is in some sense a sham. Traditionally, the Baining do not live in centralized villages. They live in an *area*, in hamlets or single houses that are either scattered through the bush, as in Puktas, or built right in their gardens. But in the dense Baining Mountains, this setup did not accommodate the new world. How could the government, charged with administration, administer—and how could the church, charged with saving souls, save them—when no one could even find these people?

The Australian government needed a village for census taking, *kiap* patrols, and tax collection. The missionaries needed a village for churchgoing and schools. So the Baining obliged. They built a village. But the Baining did not need a village, the Baining do not live in villages, and they did not intend to live in this one. They have continued to live mainly in their hamlets and houses in their gardens out in the bush.

Wilaimbemki is not quite a movie set: people do use it, as we learn, not only to be counted and taxed. The clearing is a meeting place and a place to have *singsings*. The village is a place where children attend school with the local catechist, and a few adults will always be here to look after them. And it is a home place of sorts. People like to return here—there are always people arriving from the bush or from Poiniara.

But they do not stay: they turn up, and in a day or two, they may be off again. We remember that Bateson called the Baining nomadic, but this is not the case. The Baining do not move as a group, nor do they move seasonally or in any distinctive pattern: individuals simply come and go. Early on Jeremy can see how hard it will be to establish any long-term relationships, to find informants whose presence he can rely on: he speaks to someone, and the next day they are gone. Sometimes the village is crowded; sometimes as we stroll among the houses, we have almost the whole of Wilaimbemki to ourselves. All we can count on is a small horde of children gathered around our hut—or even under our hut—staring in, and our closest neighbors, Kyimkyim and Madeilas.

Kyimkyim and Madeilas do not leave the village overnight. Every day they go to the gardens, but every evening they return. We do not think about this much in the beginning, but in time we suspect that they remain in the village just for us. It seems they have unofficially adopted us. Kyimkyim, with his long face and sad Baining eyes, is always leaning over our way to look in on us—we can see him hovering just past the pawpaw tree. He pretends to be just walking by, as he checks to make sure that we have food and firewood, and maybe just to see that we are still alive.

Why he and his wife have taken on this burden isn't clear. Unlike Mlung, they seem to have no curiosity about our lives, our culture, or our country, nor have they an interest in using us to enhance their status. In Wilaimbemki we cannot perceive any sense of status to raise. Although Mlung had some awareness of it, being closer to Western people and Western ways, status is not a Baining concept: this is a society remarkably free of class or rank. Perhaps the reason for their care is simply proximity: they are stuck with us. Or perhaps it is because they are nurturing: after all, they have nine children of their own, by birth or adoption—what are two fledglings more?

Kyimkyim with thatching for roof work

Madeilas with her baby in a taro garden

Kyimkyim then should be an ideal informant: he is always around. But although our mutual warmth is tacit, although we greet one another daily—"*Atlu!*"—we say very little more. Madeilas, like most of the women in Wilaimbemki, does not speak Pidgin—or won't: we can't believe that the women do not know it, as they claim. Kyimkyim, for his part, if we speak, will make a small endearing sound—to acknowledge that something has been said—but he does not seem to enjoy talking at all.

In this, he is like most of his fellow Wilaimbemkina. Indeed, we have discovered that the Baining of Wilaimbemki are so laconic, they make the Puktaskina seem chatty, verbose. It is true, there are exceptions: Teingan and Solmet seem to thrive on words. Old Suga, if we meet him coming into the village from his bush house, will talk nonstop, but we cannot figure out what he is saying. At first I think he must be mad, though I come to see him as merely eccentric.

But the others, we find, not only do not talk very much, but are especially loathe to answer questions. In Puktas, although people did not initiate questions, or necessarily answer them, they would at least say something if you asked. They made some effort to relate. Here, in response to a question, people cast their eyes downward, they fidget with their bush knives, they look thoroughly miserable, as if implements of torture were being applied. They give a one-shoulder shrug, which indicates a negative, meaning anything from "I don't know" to "I would rather not say."

We struggle with this. "Are they hostile?" we ask one another. "Do they view us as intruders, invaders who should not be in their village at all?"

Yet we can't believe that this is true. No one treats us with hostility. If they appear to take us for granted, we know that this is normal for the Baining, and they seem to have welcomed us warmly. They have given us Wilaimbemki *ples* names to replace the ones from Puktas, laying claim to our presence: Jeremy is Iara, his *wannem*—or "namesake"—a thoughtful, gentle young man. I am Kusaiki, my *wannem* is Solmet's wife. It is a lovely-sounding name; I believe it is another river weed. People smile when we come to visit. They make room for us on the floor of their hut, away from the bright-red splashes of betel spit, and offer us food. They seem happy to visit as well. So long as we do not ask questions. Preferably, if we do not talk at all.

In time, we come to see that this reticence isn't personal. Indeed, the way they treat us appears to be much the way they treat each other. Dialogue, we learn again—this time more forcefully—is simply not the Baining way. They do not like questions, they do not want them, and by God no one can make them answer unless they choose.

One day, Jeremy is sitting with Teingan's wife, Kandimgi—who has returned, briefly, from Poiniara—when Mranmotki enters the house.

"Have you come from *antap*?" asks Kandimgi, tilting her head to indicate the direction, "up there."

A simple question, but Mranmotki does not reply. She makes a gesture that is hard to discern: it might be a shake of the head, which for the Baining means yes, or it might be that single-shoulder shrug.

"Have you come from up there?" Kandimgi asks again, and Mranmotki murmurs, "Mmm." Apparently, the answer—which seems to have been wrenched from the very core of her being—is yes.

Now Kandimgi, perhaps encouraged by an actual reply, pursues another question. "Was Ngava up there?" she asks.

To this, Mranmotki does not reply at all.

"Was Ngava up there?" Kandimgi says again.

But again Mranmotki neither replies nor gestures, and the question is dropped.

To us, of course—to most Americans—ignoring someone's question seems rude. To us, such behavior would seem to show contempt, for the question or the questioner. But among the Baining, this is apparently not the case. Kandimgi shows no anger at Mranmotki's silence. Nor does Mranmotki show anger at being asked; she simply chooses not to answer, and this is perfectly acceptable. Actually, among the Baining, to be insistent or annoyed when someone fails to answer a question would be rude.

We cannot understand the nature of this behavior; we do not grasp its underlying source: Does this stem from an intense sense of privacy? A need for autonomy? We have no idea.

For me, the Baining reticence is overriding. I am shy and reserved to begin with, and I know that I myself would not welcome probing questions about my personal life. I can't imagine telling someone I don't know about my sex life. I too would refuse to answer. I soon decide that when I visit, I will ask nothing beyond, "Are you well?"—a question that seems to be acceptable.

But for Jeremy, the situation is devastating. He too is shy. He too is reserved. He too respects privacy. But what can he do but ask questions? It is the anthropologist's job not only to observe but to ask about what he has observed: without someone to explain, to interpret, to provide a context, how can you know what it is you are observing? And to begin with, here, as in Puktas, there is so very little to observe.

Although it causes discomfort on both sides, although Jeremy, laughing dryly, tells me that he often feels like a policeman trying to extract a confession, he proceeds with his questions, trying to unearth whatever may lie behind this apparent blankness. But whether he asks about religion and rituals, myths and superstitions, the battles among different Baining villages that are said to have taken place in the old days—or even something as small and trivial as the name of a common plant—the range of responses remains the same. Sometimes people ignore the question; they give that shrug. Most often, if they say anything at all, they will reply: "I don't know. Our fathers never told us."

"*Our fathers never told us.*" He hears this again and again. In Puktas people might say this too. But here it is a mantra.

"I am just a young man," says a man who is not so young at all. "*Mi pikinini nating*"—"I am just a child," says a man of forty. "Our fathers never told us." We realize that the Baining, curiously, see themselves as ignorant little children. The elders, they say, knew these things and did not pass them on.

Are there any *lapun*, any elders, we can ask?

Kyimkyim invites us to visit his father, Baiki, one of the oldest men of Wilaimbemki, and one day, when the weather seems good, we set out for the bush hut where he lives. Kyimkyim leads the way with one of his sons. He has warned us that the trip will be long, but the hiking, it turns out, is not a challenge: no swollen rivers, no ravines, *no log bridges*. I move better in any case these days: I have taken to going barefoot. I have cast away not only my jungle boots, but also my flip-flops, which offered neither support nor protection—not even from dog poop—and on wet ground would turn into slides. With newly toughened soles, I trundle gamely, if still slowly, along.

Jeremy is very eager for this visit: at last, a *lapun* with whom he can speak. As I watch him walking up ahead with Kyimkyim, I feel that he seems focused, even hopeful, upbeat.

We arrive at Baiki's house around midday. It is a traditional Baining house, built flat on the ground. A thick log embers in the middle of the single room, drying the tobacco that hangs from the rafters and smoking up the air. Pigs root and snuffle just outside.

We greet Baiki, who is sitting by the log, wearing nothing but a shirt and a cloth around his neck. Kyimkyim explains the cloth: his father has a cold. From the moment we arrive until we leave, the old man carries on a running monologue. We cannot call him laconic: we cannot say he doesn't talk. But without teeth, his speech is hard to understand, and I get very little of what he says. Gradually, we come to wonder whether there is much to get. Gradually, we realize from his son's responses that Baiki is probably senile, and whatever knowledge he has from his own father is locked forever inside his head.

By the time Kyimkyim suggests that we go—with a warning about the afternoon rains—we aren't sorry that the visit is ending. A bit dazed, we thank old Baiki and leave.

Undeterred, Jeremy decides to visit another *lapun*, Sireigi, who lives out near the village of Alakasam but considers himself attached to Wilaimbemki. A large man with a full white beard and an impressive paunch, Sireigi reminds us of Santa Claus. He is truly a *lapun*: his own father, he tells us, saw the very first white men. He himself is old enough to remember Bateson's visit in 1928.

But Sireigi walks tall and straight, and he has his wits about him. He even seems happy to talk. He shows us the kind of shell the Baining used for scraping taro before they had metal scrapers. Garden magic? he says, when Jeremy asks. He knows of no techniques to ensure that taro will grow. If there is such magic, the Baining fathers never told them. Origin myths? He is sure that the fathers knew, but no one has passed this knowledge on. Why didn't they? Ah, he shrugs, that he doesn't know.

In time we grasp just how deeply embedded the Baining sense of their own ignorance is. They see themselves not simply as a people who know nothing but as a people who now know nothing but who at one time knew more.

We begin to feel that here in the mountains, we have encountered the very essence of Bainingness—just as we had hoped. But that essence appears to be the very opposite of what we had hoped for. Convinced that contact had destroyed authentic Baining culture in Puktas, we came in search of a richer, fuller way of life. But what we have found is that life in Wilaimbemki is, if anything, even more spare. It is Puktas in the extreme.

In Wilaimbemki, as in Puktas, nothing much happens in an ordinary day. The Wilaimbemkina clear gardens, they work in the gardens—here, they even sleep over in the gardens. They gather wood and they cook. As in Puktas, they do not seem to have much social or cultural life. Jeremy has uncovered no elaborate kinship systems, with special relationships and obligations. We have seen no sign of traditional political organization or leaders, only meetings with the councilor, which tend to be bureaucratic affairs. And though the teachings of the Catholic Church seem weaker here, we have found no evidence at all of Baining religion and very little of what we think of as spiritual. We have struggled to understand the concept of *aios*, which the missionaries have translated as ghost. When someone dies, the Baining do refer to him as *aios*, but if this means "spirit," it also seems to mean "corpse." A down-to-earth people indeed.

But if life is in many ways the same as in Puktas, here it seems even flatter. People talk even less. They seem more self-contained. They seem more passive. They wander off into the bush, alone, more often, and if you ask where they are going, they will simply say, "*Mi go long bus*"—"I'm going to the bush."

With some exceptions, like Teingan, Solmet, and Iara, who are rarely around, the villagers seldom reach out to talk to us, to teach us the language, to explain, and the women do not reach out at all. In Puktas, Tuvuan, though shy, helped me learn to cook taro; a group of women taught me how to chew *buai*; Dalinda showed us how to weave a simple basket. Here, the women, although not unfriendly, mostly ignore us.

Over time the Puktaskina came to enjoy us: they took pleasure in the way we tried to live as they did; they laughed at our foibles. We sense little of that engagement here. And if there is less engagement with us, there also seems to be less with each other. Apart from mothers and infants—where affection is open and abundant—the Baining hardly seem to interact. One day we visit a house and find a group of men simply dozing on the floor.

"Our Fathers Never Told Us"

This, we are coming to feel, is the *real* Baining, undiluted by proximity to Rabaul, plantations, a mission station, visitors—or alcohol. The Wilaimbemkina do not drink: we cannot blame gin for eroding the culture; we cannot say that it has filled the hollows where a culture once flourished. All we can see are the hollows, unfilled.

In Wilaimbemki, though, they have their *singsings*, both the day dance and the night dance, and it is here, in these rituals, that we hope to find the meaningful core of Baining existence. They do not perform the day ritual, with its spear dance, often—only every few years—but they have promised to organize one for us after the rains. The night dance, however, the fire dance, they put on relatively often. Indeed, they mentioned plans for this dance as soon as we arrived, and so we see this early on.

Fire dancer

Fire-dance masks

The night of the dance, as we gather with people at dusk in the village clearing, we are excited, especially Jeremy, the anthropologist who so far has been deprived—starved—of all he had expected to find. He has seen this dance once, at Raunsepna, when he saw the day dance as well: a night dance may be performed separately—as they are performing it now, on its own—but it always follows a day dance. In Raunsepna, though, he knew no one to ask about the masks or the moves: this is his first chance to ask questions and find out what this ritual is about.

When dark falls, the dance begins. The fire, piled with wood, is huge. A chorus of men chants vigorously in high-pitched falsetto through the night, beating their bamboo drums in riveting, addictive rhythms so complex that we cannot work them out. One by one the young men in their extravagant masks salute the chorus: some of these masks are white and ghostly, a bird's head on a long, thin neck, a head with large round eyes and the open beak of a hornbill; some are oblate and colorful, huge and unwieldy. The men dance straight through the fire, the sparks flying brilliantly against the dark sky.

It is a spectacular event. Yet, for all the spectacle, for all the eeriness of the masks and the wild drama of the fire, this seems to be a very informal, even casual, affair. The dancers, the chorus, the spectators, all seem to be enjoying themselves immensely. They are having a good time.

When the dancers approach the chorus, to present themselves, onlookers yell out directions: "A little to the side!" "A little forward!" When a singer's voice, exhausted, cracks, everyone laughs. When a dancer slips on the wet plaza—it has now begun to rain—people laugh as well. The chorus is often out of sync, and the singers take many breaks, to smoke and chat. Young boys without masks join in and dance around, practicing for their own fire dances in the years ahead. And people do not feel obliged to stay: as the night wears on, the audience drifts away, heading to their houses, leaving it to the young men who are dancing, and the chorus, to carry on.

Clearly, this is entertainment, and that in itself is extraordinary, given how little entertainment the Baining seem to have. But is there more to this ritual? Has it meaning? This is Jeremy's central question: after all, the anthropologist looks for meaning. It is my question as well: after all, we have both been raised to look for meaning—and in our Western world we seem to find it everywhere. Cultural meaning. Religious meaning. Personal meaning. Emotional meaning. Symbolic meaning. We long for meaning: Jeremy needs it for his work; I need it for my life.

But in the days that follow, when Jeremy asks about the meaning of this dance, the Baining reply with their one-shoulder shrug.

"This is not truly our dance," they say.

Indeed, Jeremy has read, in missionary writings, that this fire dance has come from the Central Baining, where it is sometimes performed with snakes, and apparently the Northern Baining—the Baining of Wilaimbemki—say this themselves: "This is not our *singsing* the way the day dance is our own," they say. They have borrowed it—though they themselves do not dance with snakes. The one thing they loathe—and fear—is snakes.

As we see it, then, the Wilaimbemkina have adopted the dance, but they seem to have left its import behind. The young men love it: the fire dance is a young man's dance. But it doesn't seem that this ritual has more significance for the Wilaimbemkina than a Saturday-night hop.

"Ah, but the day dance," they tell us, repeatedly, "the day dance, *ahirei*, that is something."

In fact, the Baining call all their dances *pilai*, or "play"—the day dance too is in some sense entertainment. But it is different: the day dance matters. And the day dance, they make clear, is truly theirs.

We wait eagerly for the day dance. We now have a mantra of our own: *After the rains.*

9

A Time of Rain

The rainy season hits us hard. It isn't that the rains are monsoons. There aren't floods. It doesn't even rain all the time. Indeed, there is little drama to this weather. It is all just a slow wearing down. The grayness. The damp. The cold. "It can't really be that cold," I say—and it isn't. But my body has so adapted to the heat that this cooler weather feels like winter.

I cook to get warm, which is a comfort, but cooking here is not rewarding. Unlike *taro tru*, with its subtle varieties, *singapo* comes in one type and a single flavor: bland. We long for the taste, the texture, the crust of the taro we know. Though *agalun* cooks fast compared to *taro tru*, I cook just once a day and reheat: it simply isn't worth it to bake twice—and this also helps us to save wood. Most days now I cannot go for wood, and I miss my solitary treks to the bush, which have become the high point of my day. I feel so cooped up—but I cannot get around in the mud. I can hardly get to the outhouse, which I seem to need hourly in the rain. I am tempted to devise some kind of chamber pot.

Even the good things go bad. Loki's kittens are born to great excitement. We have never seen a cat give birth. When the time comes, she scurries past the box we have prepared and settles into our cupboard. We watch the tiny blind kittens pawing as they struggle to nurse. There are six: four gray, like Loki herself, and two ginger, whom she licks most of all, as if to make them gray.

But one by one they fall ill. They tremble and cry and cannot feed. "Is it distemper?" I ask Jeremy, as if either of us would know. Other than rabies, this is the only animal disease we can name. I nurse the sick kittens with powdered milk mixed in a bamboo dropper, but the ginger two die all the same, and a pair of the gray ones are weak. Only Buster and Blackjack, named for their aggressive hardiness, truly thrive.

At night a neighbor's cat comes prowling: she too has had a litter, and she is after Loki's milk and bowl of rice. She is big and tough, a bush cat. Loki is pampered and slender, still kittenish. Nightly, we evict the enemy; nightly, she returns. For a while, between the hissing, the mewing, the feeding, and the mating season of giant roaches—who fall down on us in pairs from the beams—no one sleeps.

In time, Loki starts hunting in earnest: after dark she heads into the bush and brings home tiny bats and mice. Nearby, just outside the house, she snares frogs who come up from the river. She eats only the legs—a gourmand! Frog corpses litter the floor; she leaves them for us to dispose of.

Fieldwork isn't helped by the rains. Already stagnant, it stagnates still more. Jeremy sees less of the people he would like to see. Along with Teingan and Kandimgi, Jeremy's friendly *wannem* Iara works often at Poiniara, and they cannot come up to Wilaimbemki so easily now. When people visit, we all sit and listen to the rain.

Mostly, people visit for goods. Everyone wants goods. *I gat tabak?* they will ask. *I gat sol? I gat tinpis?* Tobacco, salt, mackerel, even thread. They love it that we have goods. They drive us crazy.

A Time of Rain

It is not that we don't want to dispense these goods: we do. We brought them for the villagers, to exchange for food, for wood, for information. But people come at all hours, and our barter system is badly out of whack. Someone offers a single coconut for a packet of tobacco, a rate we cannot afford. Children bring kindling when what we need is wood. No one offers information.

On the whole it seems the Baining would rather pay than barter. They have even suggested that Jeremy and I open a trade store, right here in Wilaimbemki. As they see it, we can afford to bring in a lot, while they can afford to buy just a little at a time. They think a trade store is a great idea.

Politely, we decline. I can just see the two of us, shopkeepers in the bush, doling out tobacco and *tinpis*. It is not a career move we have in mind.

We wonder if things can get any worse.

Despite my vows, I have already threatened to leave, many times. We fight more than ever these days, once with burning embers. We are so tired of each other, so weary, so bored. We never make love: we are too exposed, with people wandering in, asking for goods, with our horde of children besieging us, watching us, gathering under the house even in the rain. And no desire. We never cuddle: the mats and the kittens make it hard even to get close. We hardly touch one another at all: for the most part, the Baining themselves do not touch—not, at least, in public—and physical contact has come to feel awkward, even wrong.

Anger and guilt bleed together in the rains. Every night, every morning, there it is: you again!

At last, I decide to rent a flat in Rabaul. We talk it over for days. I mull it over in my journal. Is this a good move, or is it cowardly? Is it a sign of independence or defeat? Is it pragmatic or capricious? I write with great drama.

On a day that is dry enough, we hike to the coast. Just the two of us: Jeremy can find the way. For the first time in weeks, we feel hopeful. We look forward to the plantation: a bed, music, company other than each other. We look forward to Rabaul, and separation. We look forward, at last, to making a change.

But the story line quickly unravels. John, who had been so friendly, is not very happy to see us. No boat has come through for so long that he is running low on supplies. He hasn't much food. He and George, the manager of Odnop—Pondo's sister plantation (and "Pondo," we note, spelled in reverse)—commiserate daily, over beer. They seem to be well stocked with beer.

One day, over beer, he and George decide that they are hungry enough to eat a horse, and they shoot one: they chase it in a jeep; the kitchen workers hack it up. It is an ugly business, and no one wants to eat this horse. John won't even join us at the table.

Another day, over beer, they decide that they too will go to Rabaul. They are sick of waiting for this boat that doesn't come. No doubt they are also sick of life on these remote plantations. They radio B. B., another manager, to take us in his speedboat. He is reluctant: the water will be rough in the rains.

Over beer, he agrees.

"But we have to leave early," he says.

"Can they do this, these managers?" I say to Jeremy. "Can they just abandon the plantations?" This isn't something we can ask.

The trip to Rabaul is indeed rough. We leave late, of course, the men still bleary from drink, and the water knocks us around. And in Rabaul things grow rougher. John and George get sacked—we never see them again. And though we run around searching, though we talk to a real estate agent and the agent for the ANU house, we find that there aren't any flats to be had, not at once, not at a price we can afford.

A Time of Rain

B. B. takes us back to Pondo, where we remain, somewhat battered, and marooned by the rains.

At Pondo we hardly talk. Jeremy does not want to discuss the fact that we are back where we started. I do not want to discuss what I have done. Actually, I'm not sure what I have done. Were there really no flats I could rent, or did I give up looking too soon, because my heart just wasn't in it? Was I afraid to live alone? Did I feel that I had to see this field trip through, to show that I could take it too? I brood on all of this alone. Days, we watch the sky for signs of clearing; nights, I keep dreaming that our two weak kittens have died.

At last the weather turns, and we decide to take a chance on Wilaimbemki, though we plan to break up the trek. In Poiniara, Teingan tells us we can stay overnight in the house that he has built en route, about halfway to the village. It feels like an adventure: we pack a food kit to camp out.

The path, we find, is passable—just. The storm the day before wreaked havoc. Branches and fronds lie everywhere; even trees are down. The paths are thick, wet mud.

"You can get through," some villagers coming down from Wilaimbemki shout in greeting. "But the river is high," they say.

I can picture that last river before the village. Crossing will be rough.

"*Atlu!*" we shout back, and thank them for the warning.

We plow on through the wet forest, pausing often to rest, to shake ourselves out, to remove the small, dark leeches that attach themselves to us in streams. We're relieved to make it to Teingan's hut.

But the night, we find, is eerie. It isn't that we have anything to fear: no wild animals, no poisonous insects or snakes, no thugs.

But we hadn't foreseen the total solitude: just a hut, with no one around. We hadn't anticipated the silence. We hadn't realized just how dark it would be. We build a fire; Jeremy gathers leaves for a bed. But the fire dies down, the leaves have bugs, and we lie awake through most of the night, bitten and cold. The next day, we barely make it across the swollen river, to get home.

Home.

Back in the village, I am ashamed to face my journal. What can I say? I am back. The two weak kittens have died, exactly as I dreamed.

Iara, who has returned now from Poiniara, tells us how happy everyone is to see us. "They are very happy," he says. "It is their wish that you would stay in Wilaimbemki forever."

We wonder if things can get any worse.

In March things come to a head. The crisis begins when Jeremy develops a toothache. A toothache in the bush.

So far we have been lucky with our health. For all that we have imagined, poring over our guide to tropical diseases, nothing serious has occurred. An insect stung Jeremy in the eye—but it healed. Those sandfly bites on my legs swelled to enormous boils—but they deflated over time. Digestive ailments have been frequent but brief, often brought on by an excess of *ahindumgi* or *agahaip*.

From the first, though, we have been worried about teeth. Before coming to the field, we were warned about the insidious dangers of dental infections and decay. This is why, back in England, I consulted with a dentist about having my wisdom teeth removed beforehand, to avoid an abscess while in the bush. This is why, when Jeremy had a toothache in Rabaul—on our break—he had gone straight to the dentist, and why he didn't even complain when the man pulled a tooth for what we suspected was just a cavity.

"He probably doesn't know how to do a filling," we had mocked. But now we realize that he knew even less. It seems he pulled the wrong tooth.

At first Jeremy tries to deny the pain he is feeling, but soon he is clutching his jaw. At last, the ache grows so intense he decides that he cannot wait at Pondo for one of the boats that do not come. He will walk to Rabaul.

"Walk? You're going to walk across the peninsula?"

"I can do it in six days," he says. "I've worked it out."

Six days? I see six weeks—or worse: I see him collapsing from exhaustion, floating down a river, falling into a ravine.

But there is nothing to do: he has to go. I wave good-bye as if I may never see him again.

Alone in the village, I feel at a loss. Without Jeremy it is clearer than ever that I have no reason at all to be here. I try to live my daily life. I cook my two *singapo* taros. I visit Madeilas and Karigyungi. I read. Long before Jeremy could possibly return, I am staring hopefully across the village clearing, as if he might suddenly appear.

The Wilaimbemkina are kind; they bring me food. Kyimkyim sends his son Langi with a special culinary treat: larvae, precious to the Baining, and the larvae's mother, *aharang ar nan*, a huge bug!

"*Tambu*," I manage to whisper, as I stare at these delicacies in his hand, shaking my head and thanking him profusely. *Tambu*, taboo in my religion, whatever that is.

But in Jeremy's absence, people take advantage: they are constantly at my door, asking for goods. The children especially drive me wild: they bring their sticks and twigs, laughing—it is all a game; they want pens, tobacco, fish. I have trouble saying no, and I am running out of stock.

In the meantime, a Baining neighbor coming up from the coast brings our mail from Pondo—ordinarily a cherished moment. But the post is upsetting and out of sync: my mother discusses my uncle's death as if it is something I know about—but I have no idea what has happened. Somewhere a letter has been lost. We are a close if hostile family, and this death is distressing. I grew up with this man. I start to worry about my father. He smokes, he has diabetes, he drinks coffee all day and hardly sleeps: will he die before I return? I lie awake nights. Will Jeremy die before *he* returns?

In just a week he is back, and we are so glad to see each other. We hug for the first time in months. We had forgotten there was love. But we are both exhausted, worn out from our separate ordeals, and too depressed to fight our demons: familiar demons who now gain strength.

For me, it is the emptiness, what I see as a world without meaning. It casts a shadow on everything I know. The Baining, I think, have it right. All our *things*, all our objects and technologies, all our *beliefs*, our thought and art seem mere artifice, created to mask this emptiness, which is all that is real.

For Jeremy, the haunting question is whether the emptiness we perceive here *is* real. In Puktas, although he had doubts, he assumed that contact had destroyed the culture. Here the doubts have grown. Is he really finding nothing or merely finding out nothing? Is there nothing to find, or is he simply failing to find what is there?

A letter comes from Bateson, to whom Jeremy has written for advice. "History is repeating," Jeremy told him. "We are encountering what you encountered. Should we too leave?"

Bateson replies that if the problems Jeremy is having with the Baining are specifically what is interesting about the Baining, he should stick it out. But don't look for the social organization and culture that you expect a society to have, he writes. The Baining don't have them. Just look at what they have. At how *little* they have, is what he says. View them as truly *primitive*, he concludes.

In one way I feel grateful for this confirmation that the problem doesn't lie with us. But Bateson's letter also disturbs me. I feel a deep sense of unease. I perceive a touch of malice in his tone, his response, I suspect, to the fact that the Baining so confounded him. I feel that he too wants it confirmed, after all these years, that the problem did not lie with him. But really, I am not so sure that the problem does not rest with the three of us. After all, the Baining live their lives.

"Maybe we're mistaken," I write in my journal, "and the aloofness of these people is extremely sophisticated."

We reflect on the Baining mantra, "We don't know. Our fathers never told us." What does it mean?

It is possible that this is in some sense true. Perhaps there was once a Baining culture that was fuller, more complex—more articulated—than the one that now exists, and that culture has disappeared. This is what we believed in Puktas, where we assumed that the Europeans, the government, the missionaries, the Tolai, and contact with outside life in general had reduced the Baining culture to a shell that was quickly filling up with Gilbey's gin.

In truth, it is hard to believe that here in Wilaimbemki, isolated as the Baining are in this bush they have so entirely to themselves. It is hard to see how the amount of contact they have had could have wiped out an entire culture.

Still, they have certainly had contact. The young men go for periods of work on plantations, the *kiap* comes on his annual patrol, the missionary baptizes the young and sends catechists, often from other New Guinea cultures, to "educate" the children. Who can say what level of contact is necessary to so alter, or even shatter, a society's core beliefs that the elders do not pass them on?

It is also possible that it isn't true that knowledge that once existed has been lost, but the Baining believe that this is what happened. Just as we in the West have a myth about the Garden of Eden where everything was innocent and happy, just as we have a general and perpetual belief in a past, always past, Golden Age—whether in government, morals, or education—when everything was better, so the Baining might have their own myth of an era when their people had knowledge and more success than they now have.

And, of course, it is also possible that they are putting us on. We aren't cynical, but, after all, we are not entirely naive. It may be true, as we believe, that the Wilaimbemkina aren't hostile. But there can be other reasons for secrecy. Fear. Superstition. A sense of inferiority. Perhaps they think that if they told us about their culture, we, like the church, would disapprove. Perhaps this is why they were so offhand about one of the only ceremonies we have seen, where they try to contact someone in the afterlife who has just died to find out the reason for his death. Perhaps they took it more seriously than they let on. Perhaps they see us as critical intruders and do not wish to disclose the beliefs, the rituals, the myths, the traditional knowledge that they actually have.

Are the Baining taking us for a ride? In a way it feels better to consider that they are withholding information about their culture than to consider they have so little culture to impart. In another way, it feels much worse. Seeds of anger, sown by our demons, sprout.

———

Everything grows fast in the rain forest, and these seeds are already bearing leaves when we are visited by Father Hesse, the German missionary from Raunsepna, the fellow who is always building in the village, demanding carriers. To our surprise, he openly expresses his own frustration with the Baining. Over tea, he complains that people tell him nothing.

"They do not tell me when a child is born," he says. "They do not tell me when someone dies. They do not tell me when a marriage will take place." He discovers these events by chance, if he learns about them at all.

"Yes," we reply. "We know. They tell us nothing either."

Together the three of us lament the Bainings' "evasiveness." Although we do not use the word, the epithet "uncooperative" is in the air.

At first, it feels good to commiserate. We cannot say that we like the missionary: though he must be around our age, he does not seem youthful at all; to us he seems chilly and odd. But isolated as we are with the Baining and each other, Jeremy and I have no perspective on the problems we are having, and as with Bateson, we appreciate having it confirmed that these problems do not lie entirely with us. We need this badly. As I write in my journal that evening, referring to the priest, to Bateson, and to ourselves, "The Baining certainly do fill one with a sense of failure."

But soon we begin to brood. Do the Baining evade us as they evade the missionary? Or the *kiap*? Do they see us as the same? How can this be? We are nothing like the missionary. Nothing like the *kiap*. We are not here to proselytize, to criticize, to encourage or enforce or even suggest any changes. We are not building up the village with churches and schools, compelling people to haul and carry, for free. We do not tell them that the Lord is their shepherd, when they have never even seen a sheep.

We do not make people line up to be counted; we do not demand taxes. We do not tell them that they must *waswas*.

We are anthropologists, neutral, here only to observe and accept. Don't we live as the Baining live? Isn't our house their own house? Don't we cook and eat their food? We are not colonialists, we are not imperialists, we are not missionaries trying to impose our beliefs and customs and will on these people. To be seen this way grates terribly. We feel deeply, miserably hurt.

The frustration we have been feeling for weeks now turns to fury, fueled by this unsavory image: colonialists! And dumb colonialists at that. How could we not have seen? All the goods we brought to trade—for food, for information, for goodwill—we have been handing out as people come for them. We haven't demanded any trade. And they come at any hour. A tin of fish at nine at night? Of course. Tobacco at seven in the morning? Why not? Batteries in the middle of lunch? No problem. The Wilaimbemkina treat our hut like a storehouse. Not only have we abandoned our resolutions to preserve some privacy, to establish our own lives—but we have gotten almost nothing in return.

I mutter about greed. I feel that they have played us for fools. "Maybe we should just stop handing out goods," I say. But no, says Jeremy, hand them all out, empty the store, let this miserable business end!

I take to isolation: I do not visit. I move my little hearth from the front room to the back, where no one can watch me cook. Alone I can wallow in self-pity. There is no one to bring me out. No one cares if I hide. No one even cares if we speak the language: there is no effort here to help us learn it—they would prefer if we do not talk at all.

A Time of Rain

We think of speaking out at a meeting: we will announce that if people do not want us here—if they won't speak to us—we can go to another village. Other villages have asked us to come and stay and collect stories: Malasait, Rangulit, Ranganga. And then there is always Puktas.

"If things keep up," I write in my journal, "a return to Puktas wouldn't be such a bad idea."

A return to Puktas? Not a bad idea? *Really?* Can memory be so fickle? So porous? We were wretched in Puktas. By the end, all we wanted was to leave. How have things gone so very wrong?

All of this is festering when suddenly one evening a delegation of young men arrives at our hut. They sit down, filling up our front room, and even grow boisterous as they say that they have been sent by their fathers to tell us to turn away the children who come asking for goods. The children, they say, have been keeping the goods for themselves, not turning them over to their families. The parents are angry at the children for bothering us all the time and for finishing up the goods that we have worked so hard to get.

This strikes us as extraordinary. It takes us so entirely by surprise. We have said nothing, but apparently the Baining must have noticed our dismay and our anger. I didn't think they were aware. What was it, I wonder, that they perceived? Now I am embarrassed as I picture myself muttering around the house, making faces to Jeremy, ranting in English. Did I think I was invisible?

In any case, they have found this most politic way of dealing with what has been happening. It was by no means only the children who came for goods. But why not blame it on the children? After all, no one really blames the children—who can blame children?—and we can all move on.

We regain our bearings. We reflect on how easy it is to come unmoored in the bush. "Imagine judging the Baining greedy—greedy!" we laugh. It seems surreal. But things seem righted now.

And then a second extraordinary incident occurs: Teingan returns from Poiniara, and at the meeting where we intended to speak out, he does it for us—although we haven't asked. He urges people to talk to us. They should not treat us like *kiaps*, he says. We are two people who live in their village, and we ought to be included.

What, we wonder, has brought this on? Even Teingan is not clairvoyant. But we realize that Iara, Jeremy's *wannem* in whom he has confided, who has been spending time in Poiniara, must have spoken to Teingan, and Teingan, never shy, has taken it upon himself to speak to everyone else. Will Teingan's pressure make a difference? The possibility gives Jeremy such hope.

That very day he sits down with Teingan and old Ngoneingmot, who has come into the village from his bush house. He asks about Baining beliefs—about the origins of men, the significance of masks. He knows that Teingan will be open. It is impossible to imagine Teingan anything but open. He is not a secretive or deceptive man.

But both men profess ignorance.

"Many times I have wanted to know these things, and I get angry that my father never told them to me," says Teingan. "He knew these things, but he didn't bother to teach them to me, and now all the old men who knew these things have died." Why did his father not transmit this information? Teingan doesn't know. Ngoneingmot doesn't know. "The ancestors were *longlong*," he says. "They were 'crazy.'"

We decide that we will go to the coast: we are desperately in need of a break.

10

Masks

Can this field trip be saved? It is April now, and both of us have serious doubts. March has left us chastened. We have returned from our break facing facts: Jeremy, just how little his work has progressed; I, just how badly I have behaved. We acknowledge that the vows we first brought with us to Wilaimbemki have all dissolved: we have not been firmer, more adult, or more assertive; we have not seen to our needs or protected our private lives.

Having failed in these resolutions twice, we shrewdly abandon them. We decide that if we cannot assert ourselves with the Baining, we can at least establish independence from one another: although we seem unable to go our separate ways, we can live our separate lives. Jeremy will devote himself to fieldwork. I will remove myself entirely from fieldwork. This vow draws a line in the mud so we each know where we stand. We know this is our very last chance.

"This can work," we tell each other quietly, hopeful but subdued.

For me, this new approach is not so very new. I have long since stopped asking questions where questions are so unwelcome. When I visit our neighbors, I have taken to sitting in silence like a Baining. I still take photos—I have hopes for these photos—but I now work very little on story collecting. Language learning has slid. What I cannot now say in Baining I will never be able to say: in self-indulgent moments, I find this poignant.

Nonetheless, there is a point to this vow. Now that we have formalized the decision, Jeremy can feel free to work, and I can look to a life of my own.

I can't say there is much to this life. I do not develop any interest in the wonderful birds of the region, other than the few that we eat. I do my best to ignore the entomological wonders. I gain no knowledge at all of the extraordinary flora around us, oblivious of a latent passion for gardening that I do not foresee and cannot at this point even imagine. Mainly, I learn to fill time. Having practiced since Puktas, I now master this skill, which I will use and abuse for the rest of my life.

I cook our *singapo*. I clean our meager belongings. I smoke. I swim, watched intently by the children, who will swim later, on their own, but who never join me in the water. I tend to my sores, which I realize aren't healing so well anymore—the lack of protein, I assume—and I study our book of tropical diseases, in search of more concerns.

I look after the kittens and Loki, who is conspicuously pregnant again: another "wild pussy." When her new kittens are born, I look after them too, forcing her to nurse them when she insists on feeding the older ones instead. She chases after Buster and Blackjack—now almost as large as their mother—corralling them into her box, where the little ones mew pathetically, ignored.

"What on earth is she doing?" asks Jeremy, as he watches this curious scene.

"I think she's gone mad," I say sadly. "She's gone mad in the bush." I feel sympathetic: I understand.

As the rains subside, I can return to gathering wood. Every day I cross the little river behind the house, stepping carefully on the stones across the swimming hole, and I follow the path into the bush. The ants bite fiercely here, and I cannot go far—I'm afraid of getting lost—but I love these excursions. I love to be alone in the bush, to sit in a bamboo grove and listen to the reeds creak, to hack the wood, swinging my long knife with fury, delighting in every *thwack*. I cannot identify the trees, but I learn the different woods by how they burn: which ones are dense and provide long-lasting embers, which are lightweight and flare out fast. The one kind of wood I know by name is *awilainga*, the tree for which Wilaimbemki is named. It is everywhere.

From the first, when gathering wood, I have carried it in a bundle on my shoulder. But the women of Wilaimbemki don't approve. It is not the Baining way. And they are right, of course; it's inefficient. The women bear their bundles on their backs, where they are bound with a carrying strap—*amalunga*—that is suspended from the forehead, freeing up their hands. We see

Woman returning from gardens with firewood

Gail carrying wood the *right* way, with her *amalunga*

Masks 131

Woman returning from gardens with *bilum* of taro and baby

Woman tying up her *amalunga*

them returning from the gardens, bent double under enormous loads: a bundle of wood, a *bilum* of *singapo* resting on the wood, and sometimes, perched on the very top, a baby. The husband, carrying his little tobacco and *buai* purse, ambles behind, smoking and swinging his knife.

I have avoided this strap partly out of fear: how, I have wondered, will I walk? But one day while I am out getting wood, I meet some young girls in the bush who give me an *amalunga* of my own and show me how to use it. Adding some of their own wood to mine, they bind up a bundle so heavy my neck snaps back at once.

"Ha!" they laugh as my life flashes before my eyes. "Ha-ha!"

From now on, although my own bundles are minuscule, and poorly bound, everyone is pleased that I am doing it *right*.

One day, the *kiap*, on patrol, drops by for a visit; he is standing at the house with Jeremy when I arrive home, carrying my wood.

I see him staring at the *amalunga* strapped across my forehead, at my bush knife, my bare feet. He is polite, a Boy Scout type; he doesn't comment. Nonetheless, I see his eyes, wondering just how far around the bend I have gone.

Still, there are so many hours in a day, and these basic chores are not enough to fill them. Hours remain. I decide that I will read. Of course, I have been reading all along. There are the books that I have purchased at the newsagent in Rabaul, a quirky selection of Penguins and schlock: *A Room with a View, Lord Jim, Moby-Dick*, and a rancid little book of horror tales in which people are satisfyingly boiled and flayed—people even more unhappy than I! There are the books that my mother has occasionally sent, also a quirky selection—a James Bond thriller, *Portnoy's Complaint!*—which have made their way slowly to Vunamarita or Pondo, where they would wait until some kindly Baining from our village, coming home, would bring them to our hut.

But all of this has been haphazard: now I read in earnest. I have found a bookstore in Australia that has everything and sends it anywhere, offering literary succor to the outback. I study their catalog: I want it all. I make my way through Randall Jarrell, luxuriating in the intelligent wit. I follow his leads to Hasek's *Good Soldier Schweik* and Turgenev's *Sportsman's Notebook*, drinking in the humor and compassion I so desperately need. One by one I take in the novels of Thomas Hardy, whose steely worldview may be what I need most of all.

Reading becomes my dream sleep. I read as if quenching a deep thirst. I read as I once read as a child, huddled in a huge red armchair in our living room, my island in a sea of family chaos: I read to be *not here*.

What the Baining make of all this reading, I have no idea. They do not ask. Only the children, as ever, are curious: they never seem to tire of watching me. They gather around the hut to observe me in my utter stillness. They are quiet, but they do not let me be. As I sit on my beach chair, on my porch, I am their local theater, playing a silent film. They are my audience, reminding me—painfully—that in fact I *am here*.

At one point I get so annoyed that I let loose with a tirade: "What are you doing here?" I yell. "Why are you crouching outside my hut? Why don't you go home? *Go home!*"

Fortunately, my Baining, poor at best, grows so garbled in my rage that whatever I say apparently has no meaning. Affable as ever, the children smile and do not budge.

I return to Wessex, as far from Wilaimbemki as I can go.

While I am wandering abroad, immersed in other people's woes, Jeremy struggles on the ground, immersed in his own. It turns out that removing myself from fieldwork does not prove so hard. His is the tougher task.

By now, he has scrapped his original thesis: the ritual expression of opposition between the sexes seems no more pertinent in Wilaimbemki than it was in Puktas. There are no secret male societies, no exclusive male dwellings, no particular social tensions between men and women that we have discerned. It is true the girls start helping with work earlier than the boys, who still seem chore free in late adolescence. But as in Puktas, there is no emphasis on gender distinctions or division of labor, and the marriage arrangements seem to work: we learn of several fights, but couples mostly get along. We are not aware of much extramarital sexuality. Actually, we are not aware of much sexuality at all.

Jeremy hopes that some new topic will emerge from the day dance, or preparations for the day dance, this elaborate *singsing* that seems to spring up out of nothing and has such import for the Baining. What that import is, he still doesn't know. But although the Baining are quick to call anything they have *rabis*—or even more strongly, *rabis nating*—this, *ahirei*, they never call "rubbish." They would never demean this *singsing*; it is a ritual that carries weight.

We have already decided to visit Alakasam, where we have heard that they are planning to perform a day dance soon. But in Alakasam, as in Raunsepna, Jeremy will be an outsider; he will have missed the preparations for the dance, which, he has been told, are extensive. It takes many weeks to prepare for a day dance: the Baining say that they consider this the hardest work there is. And it is this preparatory work he feels he needs to observe if he is to understand what is going on.

When will Wilaimbemki have its day dance? The rains have ended, but as yet we see no sign that any plan is under way. Jeremy probes, trying to grasp what lies ahead.

As the Baining have told us, there is no particular occasion that determines the date of a *singsing*, apart from the general "rule" that it will not be during the time of rain.

"Does it mark the end of the rains then?" asks Jeremy.

"*Kwasik*," the Wilaimbemkina say. "No." They just would rather not get wet.

"Has it something to do with crops?" he asks, wondering if it is part of an agricultural rite, perhaps a harvest. Although taro seems to ripen continuously, *pitpit*, a long, spongy vegetable the Baining eat, is seasonal, though it is hard to see this minor food as sufficiently important to warrant a ritual.

"*Nogat*," they say. "*Kwasik*."

"Is it part of an initiation ceremony?" he asks. "An occasion when boys become men?"

"*Nogat! Kwasik!*" they say. At some point it is simply decided that the time is right.

"But what makes it *right*?" Jeremy asks, desperate for some connection to meaning. The Baining will give that shrug. Perhaps it has been a very long time since the last *singsing*. Or perhaps a neighboring village has performed a dance, and they feel a need to put one on too: competition is clearly involved. Nowadays the church may arrange for a *singsing* to celebrate a Christian holiday. And in this case, in Wilaimbemki, *we* are the reason: they have promised that they will organize one for us. *Meaning* is a concept lost in translation. In the Bainings' eyes, it seems that the connection is implicit: they perform this *singsing* because they are Baining.

One thing Jeremy does learn is that the date of the *singsing* will be determined by a single man, who will also direct the preparations: this is the one area in which the Baining do have a leader. A leader! Jeremy's anthropological antennae vibrate. Is this evidence then, at last, that there is a political leader?

"*Nogat*," the Wilaimbemkina say. "He is a leader only in the *singsing*."

"Is he possibly a religious leader?" asks Jeremy. "Is he a shaman?"

"*Nogat!*" they say. "*Kwasik!* He has no spiritual or magical powers. He is simply the man who knows how to do this—often his father had this role before him—and he is in charge."

In Wilaimbemki this ritual leader is Ngoneingmot, and in June he says that it is time. Ngoneingmot moves from his bush house to the village, where he will remain until after the *singsing*. He will oversee all aspects of the preparations, which now—finally—begin.

Preparations for the *singsing* test our new vows. Although we have agreed that I will not participate in fieldwork, for this Jeremy feels he needs to ask. This is the most interesting thing the Baining do. After all these months where nothing has happened, he can understand if I want to observe.

In fact, these preparations facilitate our separation: this is men's work, one of the few occasions in Baining life when strict distinctions between men and women matter. The men build a hut in the bush where they will work on the masks, and though the location of the hut isn't secret from the women—indeed, the women bring the thatching to build it—after this, they must avoid it: contact with the ritual preparations will harm them. It is said that they will waste away.

"But there are exceptions," Jeremy tells me. "A few women do take part." These women are appointed by the leader and continue in this role from ritual to ritual until they are "retired." A woman who helps in this way is considered an honorary man and may be called *anopkusakta*, or *angwatki*, the latter a term created by adding a feminine suffix to the word for *man*: she is a "female man." It is the same word they use for a woman who cannot bear children.

"Do you want to be an honorary man?" Jeremy asks.

For a moment I hesitate. It would be easy enough, I know. I am already outside the society, I am in some sense neither woman nor man, and the Baining would probably not object. But I decline.

"No," I say, "I really don't." I understand that Jeremy is being generous, but I have vowed to withdraw from fieldwork, and I honor the vow.

Every day now men go off to the bush to work on the masks. They cannot all go all the time: the preparations take a long time—for the dance in Wilaimbemki they will take two months—and the men need to help see to their gardens. They go in shifts: around fifteen men make their way to the work site daily.

The women, for their part, begin to practice the singing that is their contribution to the ritual. The women's chorus will sing all day on the day of the dance: they have to practice songs from previous rituals sung so long ago that they are now half forgotten, and they have new songs to learn. Although these songs—which, not surprisingly, are often about journeys—are called women's songs, and although it is women who will sing them, it is men who compose them and teach them to the women, and some men also join in the practice.

Nightly, people meet in a house to sing, and they sing for longer and longer stretches of time, until the dance is close at hand, when they are singing through the night. These meetings are called "rehearsals," but they are part of the ritual itself. People sleep less and less.

With all this activity, the village is transformed. Daily life is infused with energy. When the men go off to the bush in the morning, they walk briskly, their gait strong and firm. They no longer seem sad and depressed. They hold their heads high. We have never seen such pride in the Baining. A people who feel they know nothing believe that this is something they do know: something important that their fathers *did* pass on.

Jeremy too goes off to the bush site every day, and he too walks with new vigor. Here at last is something to observe, a great deal to observe.

In a culture with so few artifacts, with so few tools, here he finds a complex process. The men build frames for the masks. They beat bark to make barkcloth to cover the frames. They draw geometric patterns on the barkcloth and make paint to fill them in. They craft splendid cassowary-feather rosettes for the cradles of the spears they will carry in the spear dance, and they paste bird feathers on the spears themselves, which are not literally spears but long poles. These feathers are saved from dance to dance: since the Baining do not hunt, feathers are hard to come by, and precious.

In a culture that creates no other art, here suddenly art flourishes. Each mask is skillfully wrought, put together with great care and covered with brightly colored geometric designs. The fanciful shapes, with their heads, eyes, ears, beaks, and tails, seem almost familiar—but these are imaginary figures, dream creatures.

And suddenly, everyone is an artist. On the barkcloth of the masks, the leader marks off portions, and each man designs his portion as he pleases, stopping his pattern only when he meets his neighbor's border. Here, as everywhere, the Baining need to be individual. Yet this is very much a unified effort. The large mask designed by many men will be carried by those men: it becomes one mask.

In a culture with so little ritual, here there is a great deal of ritual, specific and detailed, that pulls the group together. All follow rules in preparing the masks: they drop brush from the forest in one pile when they arrive, they drop something from the work site in another pile when they leave, they strew knotted vines over their work—knots are everywhere—and they cleanse themselves before leaving, to protect their wives when they go home.

Only here, Jeremy feels, do the people of Wilaimbemki become *We*.

The day of the dance arrives. It is an enormous *singsing*, the largest anyone can recall, Solmet tells us. There are dozens of masks and fifty-eight spears. They will be brought out throughout the day in their order, while the women continue to dance in a circle and the chorus, singing since dawn, continues to sing.

For me, the spear dance is the big event. I cannot imagine it beforehand. "We should photograph the piercing," says Jeremy,

Woman and child on day-dance day

and I stand by with a camera as the men kneel down to have their backs pierced with a cassowary bone and rope inserted to hold on the long pole, which rises dramatically behind. The pole is supported by more than the twine: it rests on the cradle with the magnificent rosettes that sits between the men's legs. Nonetheless, the spear is a great weight pulling on the rope. Sometimes the skin breaks while a man is dancing; sometimes, we have been told, the wound will later get infected.

"*I gat bikpela sua,*" Solmet says. There can be a deep sore, which in the jungle, where bacteria thrive, can be serious, even fatal.

Families cluster around individual spear dancers, helping to prepare them. They blacken the dancers with wet ground-up charcoal; they hang the new grass skirts that have been made for the occasion on the dancers' spears. Kyimkyim and Madeilas, proud parents, hover around Langi, who looks dashing in his *bilas*, his finery. Even Solmet joins in: cool Solmet has never danced with a spear. "Today," he tells us. "Today is the day."

The men dance out to the chorus; they dance in a circle around the circle of women dancers. There are so many spear dancers that they have to divide into batches. Some dancers last long; others drop out fairly quickly; none reveals the pain he must surely feel.

Between the spear-dancing acts, other masks come forward. Men carry in the large python mask. In an acrobatic feat, men run with a small mask that sits atop a tall pole that is balanced on their head. They are cheered on by the audience, who seem eager to cheer. The feeling of the day is festive, joyous, the culmination of two months of work, the culmination of a heritage, the proof that the Baining are Baining.

Langi dressed up for the spear dance

Solmet with spear-dance regalia

Masks

Spear dancer

Spear dancer and child

Masks

Aguruguruk mask dancers arriving at dusk

Aguruguruk dancers

The *singsing* lasts just the day, with a fire dance at night. Then everything returns to what it was. Spectators can take whatever masks they want: the masks aren't sacred, and the Baining either do not know or do not care how much money these artifacts could fetch if they were sold.

"We will send these home," we say, as we make a selection of masks. "We will give them to a museum, a place where everyone can see them."

The rest, their usefulness ended, will be left in the bush to decay. All that work. The jungle takes it in.

Within a week, we prepare to leave. I feel almost rude in our haste, but I have waited so long for this moment.

"I can hardly believe that we're leaving," I say, over and over.

We pack up the things we will be taking. We distribute the goods that remain. Tobacco, salt, rice. Towels, plates, bowls. The shotgun will be highly valued. But whatever we leave will be used. Although I am sad to leave behind so many books, even these, I know, will surely find a use. I see the pages wrapping hundreds of cigarettes: line by line, they will be happily smoked.

We do our best for the cats. People take the kittens, who we feel pretty sure will survive. But we cannot leave Loki behind. We do not believe that she will make it in the bush without us. Who will give her rice and powdered milk? We arrange for her to go to a plantation—the new manager at Odnop, a kind man, agrees to take her in. But we doubt that she will thrive even there. As we stroke her now for the very last times, our grown-up kitten, we feel sadness and a terrible guilt.

As in Puktas, the whole village lines up to say farewell. Teingan and Kandimgi, Karigyungi, gentle Iara, and of course Kyimkyim and Madeilas, our parents in absentia, who will now, at last, be free to leave the village. *Atlu! Atlu!* We shake hands. Everyone shakes our hands. As in Puktas, it is emotional, but this time the feelings are more complex. As in Puktas, we have woven our way into Wilaimbemki life, but here it has been a looser weave, with frayed ends and dropped stitches. We feel no sorrow at leaving. We are so tired, and we long to go home.

At Pondo we wait for a boat. The plantation house is quiet now. John is gone, and the conventional young couple who have replaced him do not listen to Bob Dylan or the Rolling Stones. I am sure they have never heard of Muddy Waters. They are gracious and generous: they even insist that we sleep in their bedroom. They are also bigoted, and very naive. I cannot imagine they will last. At dinner, we talk about cooking with coconuts, and the woman looks at me blankly. "But where will I find a coconut?" she asks. What can I say? This is a copra plantation. We are surrounded by coconuts. She is lucky, I think, that one doesn't fall on her head.

We stay outdoors as much as we can. We watch for that boat. I take comfort: this is the very last time that we will wait for a New Guinea freight boat. Yet I've gotten so good at waiting now. I think back to my first trip to Puktas, waiting that night on the dock, when hours were difficult to bear. Mere hours. Now whole days make little difference.

I am staring so intently at the water, thinking back, that I miss what Jeremy has said. I catch only the last few words, something about "not going on." But I have no idea what he is referring to. On the boat? With this marriage? *With life?*

"Not going on?" I ask.

"With anthropology," he says. He does not intend to write his thesis.

I stare at him, trying to take this in. I cannot believe that he means it. Surely, this is merely aftershock. Letdown. Posttrauma.

Anticlimax. He has never even mentioned it before. All these months in the field and not a word. This cannot be for real.

"You don't mean that," I say.

"Yes, I do," he says. He has thought it all through. He will never do fieldwork again. Ever. Not even without the Baining. Not even without me. Of course, he will write the report required by his grant. But he has already decided that he isn't suited to fieldwork. And if he doesn't do fieldwork, he doesn't want to be in anthropology: he has no desire to be an armchair anthropologist.

"I see," I say, trying to see. Why on earth, then, have we stayed all this time? I wonder. But I do not ask this. I am hardly the one to call on logic: what exactly was *my* reason for staying all this time? I find myself shaking my head and almost smiling. This is surely the final absurdity in this sorry tale, I think.

But in this, I am wrong: It isn't final. It isn't final at all.

PART 2

Lost in America

11

The Story of a Lifetime
Part 1

"Would you tell me, please, which way I ought to go from here?"
"That depends a good deal on where you want to get to," said the Cat.
"I don't much care where—" said Alice.
"Then it doesn't matter which way you go," said the Cat.
"—so long as I get *somewhere*," Alice added as an explanation.
"Oh, you're sure to do that," said the Cat, "if you only walk long enough."

—Lewis Carroll, *Alice's Adventures in Wonderland*

You got to be careful if you don't know where you're going, because you might not get there.

—Yogi Berra

It is an evening in 1972, Jeremy and I are living in San Francisco, and we have gone to the movies. Going to the movies is a rarity these days, a precious and expensive moment now that we have a child, and I ought to be enjoying every minute. But we have barely sat down—we are hardly past the opening credits—

when I find that I am crying. I do not make a fuss: I weep quietly, sitting very still as the tears course down my cheeks. But Jeremy knows that I'm crying all the same: we are so close, so terribly connected, that lying in bed side by side we sometimes cannot tell which of our stomachs is rumbling.

"What's wrong?" he whispers. "Are you sick?" No, no, I shake my head.

"Is it the movie?" he asks. No, no, I shake my head again.

"Do you want to leave?" he says.

I gesture *shhh*. But the tears keep on flowing, blurring our vision. We do not see this film. More guilt! I have wasted the babysitter's fee.

"I'm sorry," I say when we leave, as we're heading for the car. "I'm really sorry."

"But what was it?" Jeremy asks.

"I just can't do it," I say. "I just can't write about New Guinea."

"New Guinea?" he looks at me, puzzled. "Well, you don't have to write about New Guinea, do you?" he says.

And he is right: I don't. I really don't. My God. It's as if the sun were suddenly shining on the Golden Gate Bridge, where I have been perched for months in foggy misery, now lighting up the world and bathing me in warm solace. It's all right! No need to jump! I can walk off this bridge!

At the moment, bridges are very much on my mind. I have enrolled in a master's program in creative writing at San Francisco State University; I have been writing stories about New Guinea, hoping to connect them as a thesis; and I am currently working on one about the log "bridge" that I wouldn't cross on our journey from Puktas to Ranganga.

This story isn't going very well. It is better than the account I tried to write when we first returned from fieldwork, a muddled word trek that dead-ended in the bush. It is better than the poems I turned to next, which seemed to focus à la Conrad on "the horror" and "the maw of the jungle," although I couldn't actually recall any horror or, for that matter, define a *maw*. And it is better than the other stories I have written so far for this course. But I realize that people in my workshop do not particularly like it, that it leaves my writing adviser seriously unmoved, and that it probably isn't very good, although I do not understand why.

I have called this story "The Log," which is how Jeremy and I have always referred to the episode, and it is basically a simple tale:

We are hiking to Ranganga with six Baining from Puktas, our guides, escorts, and friends. Because I am such a poor hiker, we have moved slowly and stopped frequently for breaks, and by the time we reach the river near the village, it is already swollen from the afternoon rains in the mountains. For the Baining, this is no big deal: there on our left is a log, laid out bank to bank many feet above the water, and the group heads at once for this log.

"Are they kidding?" I say to Jeremy, pointing to this slimy, mossy death plank.

He passes on the word that I am frightened.

"*Bilong wanem?*"—"Why?" smiles Mran. "*Em i olsem bris.*"

It's just like a bridge? It is nothing like a bridge! A bridge is flat, it has handrails, or rope, or something to hold onto. This is not a bridge as I know a bridge, and there is no way I am walking across it. We wade through this river or we go home.

"They could carry you," Jeremy says, and this is true. I am small: I weigh well under one hundred pounds, far less than the sacks of rice that the Baining carry all the time. But although I know that I'm light and that the Baining never fall, I also know that there is no such thing as never, and this is absolutely not how I want to die. I stand my ground.

The Baining do not understand. They cannot conceive of this fear. Crossing logs over rivers and ravines is just something they do all the time, something they did as children. It is just how you get around in the bush. We all stand around for a while, uncertain, studying the water, eyeing the log, until finally Mran agrees to ford the river. The men align themselves in a V formation so that I, in the center, will not be swept away by the current, which is fairly strong. Holding hands, we calmly cross to the other side.

That is the entire story. Is there psychological tension? Not really. I don't suggest—I don't even hint—that I will try to cross the log, and I don't. Is there danger? Not really. Although fording the river is against the Bainings' better judgment, and they do not see the need, the river isn't roiling and they don't believe that anyone will die. Are there characters? Not really. We are all stick figures, playing our roles. In itself, the tale is pretty dull, and though I see this, I cannot figure out why: because it wasn't at all dull when it happened. It was tense and fraught in ways that simply aren't coming through.

But presumably this is a story: I am writing fiction. I can do anything I want. I can froth up this river, I can make the crossing perilous, I can make this white woman a careless colonialist *misis* willing to risk other people's lives for her own pride and fear. I can make the husband an arrogant bastard who compels his wife to cross that log. I can drown someone—anyone I want! I have that power!

But I can't do any of those things. I try, but I can't. The embellishments do not feel true. The story would not be true. I am stuck in the tedium of truth. And in truth this little story is autobiography, not fiction, and it is merely an anecdote. It is one of the many anecdotes that Jeremy and I tell about Life in the Bush that people love to hear. But an anecdote, I now see, is not a story: in itself it has no depth, no context, no meaning, or at any rate no meaning I have found. In fact, as I struggle to write about New Guinea and the Baining, I find that the experience itself has no meaning. And for that matter, I find myself brooding, what is the meaning of anything? The Baining had it right.

Jeremy and I do not talk about culture shock; we have never really talked about culture shock. But we have both had trouble coming home. It was not so bad at the start. The drive across the country moving west—in my father's old Buick, a gift—offered respite: a week in limbo, a vacation. We were still, after all, just visiting, foreigners taking in the sights. The motels, the diners, the highways—it was fun. And who could imagine Las Vegas after Wilaimbemki! But Las Vegas isn't supposed to feel real. Here in San Francisco, setting up lives, we have struggled to hold on.

Jeremy has fared better than I. In one sense it has been easier for him. He has lived in this city before, at one time it was home, and he likes it here: the setting, the hills, the fog. But in another sense—although I do not acknowledge this and at this point in my life do not even see it—coming back, for him, has been harder. Dropping his thesis, leaving his field, he has had to abandon a life. He has had to give up on a dream he held on to for many years. He has had to counter the arguments of his graduate school adviser, who thinks that the grant report he is writing, already in outline, is excellent and only one short step from his thesis, which he wants him to write. He has had to ward off the entreaties and expectations of his father and his mother, academic stars who saw a young star in the making and desperately want him to return to anthropology.

But Jeremy has stood fast, rejecting not only anthropology but all of academia. He has developed a distaste for the overreaching ambitions that permeate universities. Indeed, he now rejects all ambition. He doesn't explain, he would rather not discuss it, but I assume that the Bainings' prosaic view of existence, their pragmatism, their immersion in daily life have brought him down to earth. I assume that their impenetrability has cut all theories down to size. I assume that, like me, he is struggling with *meaning*. What he wants, he says, is something real, something down to earth, work that will support everyday life: a job.

A talented programmer, as it happens—in these earliest days of computers—he has been snapped up at once by a University of California researcher with vast ambition, iffy methods, and a vague link to New Guinea. It has turned out to be a good job, supporting not just the two of us, but also Jeremy's new worldview: his slick and sleazy boss proves to him daily that ambition—intellectually, ethically, socially, and personally—is indeed a nasty thing.

On the whole I have had a rockier time. I wanted to live in New York, I have always seen myself as a New Yorker, and I had always assumed I would return to *The City*, as I still think of it. But Jeremy has never much liked New York, filled as it is with noise, grit, and my family. While he has never said that he longs for San Francisco—longing is not his style—he did suggest it would be a good place to live.

And why not San Francisco, after all? I thought. It was true I hadn't liked California on my visits. But I had been there only twice, very briefly—the second time en route to New Guinea—and both times we had stayed with Jeremy's mother in Menlo Park, the essence of suburbia, which, on principle, I loathed. San Francisco was admittedly a city, if a small one, I reasoned, and

"Maybe," I said to Jeremy, "maybe after New Guinea, New York would be too much." I did not believe this for a second: I could not imagine New York ever being "too much." But I owed him San Francisco, didn't I? I had ruined his fieldwork, after all.

San Francisco has been a guilt trip from the start.

On arriving, we move at first to Polk Street, an area I like that we can barely afford. We just manage a seedy little place that we have no money to furnish. It has a living room mainly bare except for five large Baining masks that we have not yet placed in a museum, a tiny kitchen just inside the front door, and a bedroom we stuff wall to wall with a huge bed, an embarrassing bed, a California king that Jeremy coveted, no doubt to make up for all those months sleeping on a mat, not to mention a year without sex.

I like Polk Street for the shops, which remind me of New York City and which I need since I do not drive. I never learned to drive in Manhattan—no one I knew learned to drive in Manhattan; I had no reason to learn in London, where we didn't have a car; nor did I learn in New Guinea, where we had neither a car nor roads. But here in California I am a very odd bird. In the supermarket people gather around and laugh when I ask to have my food delivered. "*Delivered?*" they say. "*Where is your car?*" I suspect I am the only person in California who cannot drive. I have to carry my passport just to write checks, as if I were living in a foreign country.

In fact, San Francisco feels like a foreign country, and I find, even after months—a year—that this feeling does not change. In New York, in Cambridge, in London, I wandered everywhere. In San Francisco, I never learn my way around. In New York, in Cambridge, in London, libraries were my haven. In San Francisco, I never even get a library card.

For me, San Francisco isn't home; it is just another new place. And it isn't a place that I like. To me, with its trams and painted ladies, it feels like a toy city. To me, it seems terminally cute. I long for the size, the power, the energy of New York, the very grit that Jeremy hates.

I am always cold. It hasn't helped that my mother-in-law praises San Francisco as "permanently air-conditioned." I hate air-conditioning. It hasn't helped that she keeps rounding up ex–New Yorkers like herself to tout the virtues of San Francisco and badmouth Manhattan with the vehemence of ex-smokers denigrating tobacco. Actually, it hasn't helped that she is here.

I have no friends in San Francisco. When we arrive, I don't know anyone at all. We link up with an old friend of Jeremy's, indeed his closest childhood friend. "He was so smart," Jeremy says. "He was so funny." But he isn't smart and funny now. He has somehow turned sneering and mean. It was his family, says Jeremy. Or it was Harvard. Or that accident. Or maybe it was drugs. We spend hours soaking in his bitterness, we aren't sure why—mainly, it seems, because he is *there*.

We fight about San Francisco. We fight about Jeremy's mother. We fight about his friend. We fight about housework, which Jeremy finds pointless after living for so long in squalor. What's a little dust compared to mud? Dirty floors when you're used to dirt floors? A spattered stove when you've been cooking with blackened embers? Soiled sheets when you've been sharing a mat with vermin and rodents? Be glad you have a bed!

I long to go home, to New York, and I say this repeatedly: "I want to go home." "I'm going home!" My God—I sound exactly like I sounded in New Guinea. And here too I never leave. Will I never be happy anywhere? Will I whine everywhere? Will I always be threatening to leave and never leave? How do we stand it? And why does Jeremy stay?

We do not discuss it, but we wonder, each on his own, just what is holding us together. Tenacity? Fear? *Love?* Or is it only this intense experience we share? Who else will remember our surrogate fathers, Mlung and Kyimkyim? Who else will remember Solmet and Teingan, Jeremy's *wannem* gentle Iara and his hunting companion Kanga? Who else will remember the taste of mumu'ed taro—*ahindumgi* and *agahaip?* Who else will laugh when they play "Goin' Up the Country" on the radio, or say "*Hagap!*"—"Enough!"—when a conversation has gone on too long? Who else will remember the heat and the mud, and our poor cat Loki, the fighting, and all the waiting: to choose a village, to get a house, to find people, to be alone, to see a *singsing,* to come home? To understand?

Who else will see the deep abyss under that log bridge?

I try hard to find my way. I see how Jeremy has been grounded by a job, and in our first months I too try to get a job. But my classics degree impresses no employers; the publishing factories for unskilled, highly educated young women like me are located some three thousand miles away, and the fact is, I do not want a job. "I don't want to *just get a job,*" I tell Jeremy. "I want to write."

I too see the phoniness of ambition, but how can I abandon it? What would it mean to write without ambition? And I need to write. I wanted to write before we went to New Guinea: how can I give it up before I've even tried? And now I have my material: our fieldwork with the Baining. Surely, for a writer, this is the story of a lifetime.

Every day for several months, I sit alone in my tiny kitchen, which is also my office, trying to tell this tale. I do not have an outline. I do not have a plan. I do not read through my letters from the field, and I barely consult my journals. As I see it, I will just tell what happened. But as I write, I find that I am not at all sure what happened. Mostly nothing happened. How do I convey this nothing? How do I show it was precisely this nothing that mattered?

I type and I type, and I trash every page. I cannot get it right. Every word I write feels false. The very act of writing feels false. Increasingly, everything around me feels false: the striving, the conversation, the social life, the theorizing, the art, the bustle and busyness, the big deal we make about everything here in America, our so-called civilization—all phony. All invented to mask the reality the Baining knew: you're born, you live out your time, and you die. *No big deal!*

The Baining didn't cover this up. They saw it as it was; they lived it: the essential boredom of existence. They didn't create things to distract themselves from this truth, to make everything seem more interesting than it is. They didn't create meanings to make everything seem more significant than it is. They didn't lie. But how can I write so many words about these people who used so few words of their own? How can I make this trip significant when nothing at all is significant?

Daily I watch myself dissolve. I barely make it to the market. I leave the house, I go back, I leave again. I become one of those people who cannot cross the street, who hesitate at the curb, who go up, who go down, who cannot move forward, who cannot decide which way forward is. I am a bag lady without bags! I am a homeless person with a home!

I know that I have to pull myself together, fast.

Do I seek help? I do not. About this, I do not talk to anyone at all. I cannot imagine confiding in family, or the friends I've kept up with back east, or my single friend here, our bitter friend's girlfriend, whom I like. I am sure they wouldn't understand. I have found that people want to hear our anecdotes, our stories about life in the jungle, the exotic journey that we took. "It's all so *fascinating!*" they say. When I even hint at the deeper problems, or the struggle to come home, their eyes glaze over. They do not take it in.

I cannot imagine seeking professional help: a psychologist, a therapist, a shrink. I am sure they wouldn't understand. I am sure they would want to talk about my childhood, not the Baining, and I would spend months, maybe years—my whole life!—discussing my crazy sister, who is very much beside the point.

It does not even occur to me that I might talk to an anthropologist who has been in the field, though *this*, I will realize much later—years later—is precisely what I need: an anthropologist who has himself had trouble coming home. But at this point, I do not know any anthropologists, there is only us, and Jeremy would rather not discuss this at all. He believes that he has left New Guinea behind and that I should leave it too. He has already said what he thinks: "I think you need a job."

I feel that I am entirely alone with this, and alone I decide that what I need is a child. As Jeremy needed a job to ground himself, I need a child. As a job seemed real to him, a child seems real to me, and it is the only thing that does seem real. There is nothing phony about a child. Children do not mask the emptiness of life; they fill it. Even the Baining had children!

"I think we should have a child," I say to Jeremy. And although we agree on almost nothing, Jeremy agrees with me on this. We pause in our fighting to make love. We make love purposefully, exhaustingly, a bit desperately on our enormous, outsize bed, and it turns out there is even passion. It doesn't take long before I'm pregnant, and we're thrilled.

But a child! This changes everything. With a child, I cannot be this panicked. With a child, we can't be fighting all the time, arguing about San Francisco, and family, and work, and a jungle of unresolved issues. Something, I feel, needs to be done.

"Maybe we should see a marriage counselor," I say. I say this cautiously. I already know what Jeremy will think. As I expect, he rolls his eyes. All the same we get the name of a therapist from our bitter friend's girlfriend and start at once on weekly sessions.

But this woman hasn't a clue. For her, the past is our childhood; the present is the stuff of daily life. New Guinea is not on her map, and we are not inclined to take her there. In these sessions, we do not talk about the Baining. We do not discuss those long, strained months in the field. We do not bring up ambition. We do not go near Nothingness. We talk very briefly about our families. But mostly we seem to focus on housework. Mainly, we seem to dwell on a large and heavy pot that I insist Jeremy should help me wash. All discussions lead to this pot.

"The *Big Pot*!" we laugh after every session. Jeremy expected no better. But at least this draws us together and helps me see what I should do.

I decide that I'll go to school. School is something I know. In school, even with a child, I won't be *just a wife*, a role that still fills me with dread and now looms even larger with the addition to wife of *mother*. I decide that I will get a master's in creative writing: another useful degree!

"I can teach," I say to Jeremy, to prove that I'm as practical as ever.

I dig out the queer little novel I wrote in London, about a young man who also finds that he's dissolving, and I apply to San Francisco State. At last, I'll have a Project of My Own.

―――

The Story of a Lifetime: Part 1

By now, the crisis has passed: I can cross that street. Pretty soon I am even driving down the street, although I do not take readily to driving: it fills me with dread. On my first solo outing I'm a wreck. "You'd think you were Amelia Earhart setting off across the Atlantic," laughs my babysitter, a young Californian who has probably been driving since she was five.

The babysitter—yes! The baby has arrived.

To prepare for the baby we have moved to a larger place, a beautiful apartment in the Haight we can afford because the Haight itself is derelict these days. This is San Francisco in 1971: the Flower Children have gone. The Haight is now a depressing neighborhood of boarded-up shops, junkies, and debris.

To prepare for the birth we have conscientiously attended classes in Lamaze: this is San Francisco in 1971—natural childbirth is *in*. "Breathe!" the instructor tells me. "Breathe!" To Jeremy, whose role is to simulate the pain of childbirth, she says, "Pinch her while she's breathing! Pinch her hard!" He is happy to oblige.

And to prepare for a semester off, after the baby is born, I have worked hard in my writing program.

In this program, I can write about anything I want. This is San Francisco in 1971: any form, any topic will do. But I find that I cannot let New Guinea be. I cannot let go of the Baining. They are everywhere. A problem I cannot solve. A story I have to tell. When our son is born, we name him Gregory: even Bateson is never far from our minds.

But if the Baining are everywhere, in writing I still cannot find them. I cannot pin this story down. I feel it is a powerful story. I know it is the story of a lifetime. But weeping in the movies, I finally acknowledge what by now I know as well: I do not really know what this story is, and I will have to lay it down.

12

The Story of a Lifetime
Part 2

"Tut, tut, child!" said the Duchess. "Everything's got a moral, if only you can find it."

—Lewis Carroll, *Alice's Adventures in Wonderland*

It is three o'clock on a weekday in 1981. Gregory comes home from school: I hear him closing the door, coming through the kitchen.

"It's okay, Mom," he calls out. "Don't get out of bed!"

As it happens, I am not in bed. As it happens, I am sitting at my typewriter in the bedroom, which I use as a study, and I squirm with embarrassment as I realize that every day for several weeks I have been napping when my son arrives from school. The lure of the bed, for me, is like the pull of the bottle for the drinker: an escape, a place to go that isn't *here*, a place that is soothingly nowhere, a pillow of oblivion.

I have not been this low since the year we returned from New Guinea.

The Story of a Lifetime: Part 2

Jeremy and I are living in Massachusetts now, in Brookline, not all that far from where we met. Eight years back we came east, as I wanted, avoiding New York, as he wanted, and in some sense we are now living where neither of us really wants to be. But both of us knew Cambridge, it was an area that neither of us loathed, and this is just about as fair as it gets in our tumultuous relationship. We have chosen Brookline for the schools, reputedly top-notch; for its proximity to Jeremy's job—still *just a job*—at Harvard's School of Public Health; and for the shops at Coolidge Corner, which—as on Polk Street—remind me of New York City. On a very small scale, I like to say. Very small. I still bemoan the loss of New York, I still routinely threaten to go *home*, I still whine and do not leave.

A great deal has happened in the past eight years, in the last five much of it good. In fact, it seems to me that things came together before they fell apart. And I find myself wondering just how I have come to be here, at thirty-five, napping in the heart of my days. I have spent hours tracing the route, and I can always see how nicely A goes to B, how C would logically follow, but then I suddenly find myself at Z, the end of a road I never meant to take.

In this sketch, as I trace it, first I finish my master's degree in creative writing at San Francisco State, which is fine. I use the degree to get a job teaching writing in college, just as I intended. Also fine. I publish a poem in a small arts magazine. This is great. I publish some reviews in this same magazine. Excellent!

And then suddenly this little magazine, in the way of little magazines, is in crisis. Suddenly, it has a near-death experience. Suddenly, I am editor. Is this great? Well, yes: a magazine, a platform, my own perch in the literary world, and as it happens I love it. I love the constant busyness of the deadlines, I love dealing with the contributors, the illustrators, the printers, the advertisers, the debts, yes even the debts, the designer pleading on the phone, his wife yelling in the background, his baby crying, and me swearing that we will pay every penny we owe, we will!

And I love the magazine that appears, an actual product. I have never produced an actual product in the real world before. I have never felt so involved, so alive, so smart. I keep so busy that I never think about the meaninglessness of life. I never dwell on the futility of ambition. I am so far from the Baining. So yes, a very good step.

But this little magazine, in the way of little magazines, doesn't pay—I do not take a penny—and it consumes my life. It absorbs every minute of my day, inhabits every fold of my brain, takes up residence at home.

"Actually, we are not independently wealthy," Jeremy mutters from time to time.

"Please, Mom, don't answer the phone," Gregory whimpers after dinner.

"So how are you?" asks a friend who calls, and I tell him about the magazine's advertising (going badly), and the circulation (pretty good), and the material we are getting (first rate). He is silent. "But how are *you*?" he asks again, sounding puzzled. Now it is I who am silent, and I cannot decide which is worse: that I thought I had answered the question, or that I have nothing else to say.

I give up the magazine. A good move! But I have to keep busy; it's crucial that I stay busy to keep Nothingness at bay. I start to teach college full-time, I return to school for a library degree, I'm an instructor and a student, and I have no time to think about what all this activity means or if it has any meaning at all. Excellent! But I do not like teaching full-time. I hate the department meetings and the faculty meetings and the politics, I have no time to write, and the Catholic college where I teach pays so little—the nuns, after all, give most of *their* salary back!—that it hardly seems worth it.

I quit. "No one quits a full-time teaching job in 1981," says a friend. I quit. I am finished with the liberal arts. "In fact," I tell Jeremy, "I am finished with the arts." I now have my degree in library and *information science*, and I am headed for high-tech. Smart move! High-tech is the future. I pull together my résumé and take it to Honeywell, where they are looking for a technical librarian. The interviewer examines my résumé with its degrees in ancient Greek and creative writing, she scrutinizes my list of published book reviews and poems, she peruses the samples of my arts magazine that I hand her with a flourish of pride. She is bemused.

"And why do you want this job?" she asks.

Good question! I have no idea. In fact, I do not want this job at all.

So I have nothing. I spend a year of Sundays studying help-wanted ads, seeking not just a job but an identity, a purpose, a life, and playing Gregory's electronic football, which I totally master.

I sleep.

But I am not sleeping this afternoon when Gregory comes home from school. I am pulling my life together. I am drawing on my inner resources.

I have decided to freelance as a writer. I will not write literary criticism, which pays little, or poetry, which pays less: I will write articles, journalism, which I know will pay more. For a start, I have arranged to write a monthly column on magazines for a library publication. I have begun to seek out other assignments. And I have decided that at last I will write about our field trip to New Guinea. It is time to deal with that experience. It is time to make use of that material, which is surely a writer's dream. And it is also time to write a book. I have published essays and reviews, but I have yet to do a book. I think about this constantly: *No Book*, and I am thirty-five years old.

This time I am more organized: I have not forgotten my earlier efforts. It's true I still do not have an outline; I cannot say that I have much of a plan. But I have already rummaged through the basement and dug up our maps of New Britain, our letters from the field, and my journals still redolent of jungle rot. I will finally write about the Baining, about our lives among the Baining: the story of a lifetime.

Jeremy and I seldom talk about New Guinea. We do not discuss the Baining. But the experience enfolds us. It is the foundation of our tremulous marriage, the caldera in which that marriage has been built; it is the smoky medium in which we move; it hovers over us like the one large mask we kept that hangs above our fireplace, pinning us with its eyes, or what we take to be eyes, though one Baining claimed that those large circles in the center of the barkcloth are actually knees. Knees!

That experience still fascinates others in all the superficial ways: people find it so *exotic*, they love to hear the anecdotes we tell. And although we still find indulging this uncomfortable—although we still see these tales as reductive and self-serving—we know that they're entertaining, and we are amicably together in the telling. United. Allies. This experience is something that is *ours*.

But when we are alone in its deadly embrace, it is a source of deep resentment: *You ruined my work, and now I will ruin yours!*

It is a source of bitter guilt: *I ruined your work, and now I will ruin my own!*

And it is a source of extraordinary inanity as we slog through arguments as muddy as the forest floor:

Should Gregory have to sit at the table through dinner?

"Of course, he should sit at the table through dinner," I insist.

"Baining children don't have to sit at the table through dinner," Jeremy scoffs.

"The Baining have no tables!" I yell.

And we aren't Baining. We aren't Baining. This is surely the crux of it all.

We are so filled with anger. Still. We can fight about anything at all. We fight about my family and Jeremy's; we fight about work and housework; we fight about friends, his friends and mine, since we do not share many friends and we seldom go out with other couples. We seldom go out at all. Every night I have to cook dinner because we only eat at home, and we fight about this too. We fight about words and meanings as we once fought about phonemes. At the dinner table, a dictionary has a place setting of its own.

My own fighting style is rage: I break Jeremy's mother's set of china, hurling plates across the kitchen, one by one, while Jeremy looks on, stunned. My weapon is verbal: I talk and I talk, I analyze everything that is wrong, and I explain, in detail, exactly why. Jeremy's style is withdrawal; his weapon is silence. While I am arguing heatedly, he falls asleep. "Wake up!" I shout. "Wake up and fight!" But he just sleeps on, and wins.

We each have a modest fling, to get even.

Yet neither of us leaves. Indeed, we bought a house when we moved to Brookline, and we are just about to buy another. No one seems to be leaving. By now, so many friends have divorced—half of America has divorced. Why do we stay?

"It would take too much energy to divorce," says Jeremy absurdly, his very voice a shrug. It could be a Baining shrug: *I don't know, I won't say.*

"How would we divide things?" I say, just as absurdly, as if we had much of anything to divide. What I mean is, *"How could we divide?"* We are joined at the hip: Siamese twins who do not know where one leaves off and the other begins. How could we survive?

We married too young; we know this. We are siblings, competing. We are children playing house. We joke that we will never grow up. We joke a lot. This is one thing we still share: a sense of humor, generally dark.

Why do we stay? We do not discuss this. We do not really know. Part of it I'm sure is fear: my fear of being alone, Jeremy's of losing the battle. Part of it I'm sure is tenacity: the tenacity that kept us in the field. And part of it, I'm sure, although we cannot admit or understand it, is the love that so quickly drew us together at the start, in the primordial era of our youth.

But there is also, of course, the Baining: this experience that binds us together, that sits squarely between us, that somehow defines us. Who else would ever understand?

The resentment, the guilt, the inanity, the anger all bear down on me as I write about New Guinea. My life is a wreck, my marriage is a wreck, I have given up everything, I can hold on to nothing, I have to keep obsessively busy or sleep—these seem to be my only options—and it is all because of that trip. I focus my anger on the Baining, and I grow more hostile as I proceed. I have read that anthropologists often refrain from writing about unsuccessful field trips out of loyalty to the people they have lived with. I seem to have no such loyalty. I am shamelessly disloyal. I have nothing good to say about these people.

I write that this is a culture that has only five artifacts. Five! They have never looked to invent other ways to do things. Nor have they looked for other things to do. I write that this is a society that has no politics: there is nothing they want to achieve as a group. I write that they have no religion, no spiritual life: there is just the day-to-day living; what you see is what you get. I write that this is a society that has no wealth, a group that has no desire to move beyond subsistence.

I write that this is a people who have no curiosity, who have not bothered to name the stars, who have not even bothered to name the volcano that they can see erupting in the distance and that interests them so little that all they say of it—and only when asked—is, "Well, there must be a big fire there."

This is a people who look at eyes and see knees.

By now, fanning the embers of my scorn, I have worked myself into a fury. I have no room in my assessment to acknowledge the sane practicality of Baining life, its peacefulness and fairness, or the genius of their family setup: what wouldn't I have done to be able, like a Baining child, to leave my wretchedly unhappy family and—with everyone's approval—choose another?

And don't I share many of the Bainings' values? I have no high opinion of politics, I absolutely do not believe in religion, I oppose accumulated wealth, and I possess only selective curiosity—and none about the stars, which I certainly cannot name.

Why then the fury? If the Baining are not ambitious, what is it to me?

Apparently, it is everything. The Baining defy the very notion of ambition. As I see it, in their world nothing signifies, and it is this that so enrages and frightens and defeats me: that nothing signifies. Because they are right; they are right. Nothing on its own does signify. Politics, religion, art, thought itself—these signify only if we believe they do, they take on the virtues we attribute to them, they are what we make of them, they are our inventions and thus artificial, and without these phony inventions we create to distract us, we would see life as it is: you are born, you live out your paltry portion, and you die.

This is what the Baining have bequeathed us, this insight that our culture, with all its aspirations, is false. It is an insight that I believe has permeated our lives, numbing Jeremy, who has insisted on taking *just a job*, refusing to go where his talent will lead him, and who seems to me too unwilling ever to take a stand and assert that something *matters*, and forcing me to keep moving, to keep so busy that I do not think about this issue at all, and overwhelming me—once I come to a halt—with the pointlessness of my efforts, of any efforts at all.

I feel the Baining have ruined us by laying bare this fundamental void at the basis of our lives and life itself.

"There was nothing redeemable in this experience," my little book begins and proceeds to do its depressing best to prove it.

I send my miserable tract to only one publisher, who returns it with a long letter saying that this is anthropology, which is not a field they deal with.

But my book is most definitely not anthropology. I am not an anthropologist. I am not a social scientist. I have lived in New Britain with the Baining, but I have not done a study; I haven't measured anything. And though I do not believe in "measuring" aspects of life that cannot be measured—still, I have no evidence, no proof, nothing to show that anything I've said is true. Do I doubt that it's true? I don't know. But clearly, I must have doubts because at this point I realize that I cannot write this book as I have written it. I have to somehow show that my views are subjective—but also that they're right. I will have to try again.

The Story of a Lifetime: Part 2

I do not look forward to returning to this material—attacking an entire people has not in fact been very much fun—and I decide that I will take some time first and study our slides from the field. We have almost a thousand slides: the photographic essay that I never wrote. Jeremy and I look at them together, and we find as we browse intently through the images that the faces, the landscape, all of daily life in the bush seem extraordinarily vivid.

We study the portraits of people we knew well—Teingan, Tuvuan, Solmet—and the portraits of people whose names we never knew, or have long since forgotten, planting taro, cooking pig, clearing weeds from the earthen plaza, attending a meeting, or just hanging out. There are women returning from the garden, bent double under huge loads of firewood, one—perhaps Madeilas, we can only see her back—with a *bilum* of taro and a baby on top. There is Kyimkyim, holding some fronds for roof thatching—a good-looking man, I think, though I never noticed just how grungy his shirt and *laplap* are. There is a portrait of a woman chewing *buai*, her mouth and fingers daubed white with lime. And there is another woman sitting on the ground, her legs stretched out before her, naked except for her waistband and grass tuffet, who has the skin disease they call *pukpuk*—which is Pidgin for "crocodile"—because it turns the skin scaly. I remember being told that such people made good eating back in the day. I cannot say that she looks tasty.

And there, in full color, are the dances with the extraordinary masks.

We decide to invite friends to see these slides—we have never done this before. We have a party, a Baining party! We serve coffee, cookies, cake, wine, chips, and anecdotes. And people are amazed. They see the fire dance, with men dancing into the flames and sparks flying in the night. They see the spear dance, with men in their *bilas* running, those tall poles emerging from their backs. And those masks!

"What a fascinating life!" they exclaim.

A fascinating life? It's true the rituals are amazing. But that's one night in two months, I want to say. That's just one day in two years. You have no idea how empty the rest is! You have no idea how little happens! And look at these expressions of sadness! Look at Karigam sitting in a field of taro, embracing his son, his eyes cast mournfully down. No one can look sadder than a Baining. And of course, they are sad, I want to say. Who wouldn't be sad if nothing has meaning?

I do not say any of this, but I feel frustrated and desperate: I don't see how my book will ever get this across.

I try again to write my story. This time I decide to be inventive. This time I write the book in the form of a dialogue with myself: I ask questions and I answer them.

"So, did the Baining have curiosity?" I ask.

"Only the children," I reply.

"What did the Baining talk about?" I ask.

"They didn't," I reply.

"So, the Baining didn't answer questions because they themselves never posed questions?" I ask.

"Yes!" I reply.

"Do you think the Baining were unhappy?" I ask.

"Yes!" I reply—though as I put it, rather smarmily, "One felt they were."

I elaborate on each of my opinions. It is a one-man show.

But even I know this show is a flop. This version I do not send out to any publishers. This version I give to only one friend, who keeps it and keeps it and doesn't get back to me at all.

Finally, I call.

"It's so bleak," says this friend who by now is no longer a friend.

"Well, yes, it's bleak. It has to be bleak," I say. "The experience was bleak."

People want it all to be fine. They want anecdotes and charm. Above all, they want a happy ending. They want me to lie. Doesn't anyone want the truth? *No one seems to want my pain!*

Once my rage has subsided, I can see that my pain isn't much of a gift. Nor does it make much of a story. Of course, people want a happy ending—or at least a resolution; they don't want a wound that hasn't healed. But I can't see how to do it. The wound *hasn't* healed. And I don't even know that what I've written is true. I pack up my maps, my letters from the field, and my notebooks, and I haul them back down to the basement. The story of a lifetime, and I still do not know what that story is.

13

The Story of a Lifetime
Part 3

> Know thyself? If I knew myself I would run away.
>
> —Johann von Goethe

It is 1994, early summer in Cambridge, Massachusetts, Jeremy and I have just sat down to breakfast, and there on the front page of the *New York Times* is an article about New Guinea: "Last Rain Forest," reads the headline.

This is extraordinary. American newspapers seldom publish anything about New Guinea, our media in general pay almost no attention to the island, and when they do they tend to focus on World War II: the discovery of lost planes, the reunion of American soldiers with the villagers who helped them survive, Japanese tunnels.

Still more amazing, the caption on one of the photographs accompanying the article identifies the place that is pictured as Vunamarita, on the island of New Britain. Vunamarita! I can't believe it.

"Jeremy!" I cry out. "Look at this!"

And side by side, elbowing each other for space as vigorously, as competitively, as affectionately as ever, we struggle to read.

I skim down the page, trying to gulp it in, my eyes moving too fast to comprehend very much at all. I scroll quickly past the clichés: "The land that time forgot." I roll past the obligatory reference to a "Stone Age culture." I skip over the inevitable errors the journalist on quick assignment is bound to make: *Apinun*—the national greeting in Tok Pisin—most certainly does not mean "Happy noon," with its connotation of joyous New Guineans, but simply "Afternoon," an abbreviated "Good afternoon," as people say in the United States as well.

I take in the grim point of the story: logging is stripping the rain forest, making profits for the companies carrying out the enterprise and leaving the local population with a pittance—a few *kina* quickly spent on tinned meat and booze—and a bare landscape that can no longer serve their needs.

I cannot visualize the jungle denuded. It feels unseemly, like seeing your dog shaved or your grandmother naked. And Vunamarita had such a beautiful setting, overlooking Ataliklikun Bay, backing up against the lush Baining Mountains, and edged by the coconut palms of the New Masawa plantation, tall and graceful as giraffes.

I turn back to the photo, fearful of what I'll see. But I find that I cannot make it out. I do not recognize the place. Where is the dock? Where is the coconut plantation? Does it all look so different because there aren't trees? But why on earth would loggers want coconut trees?

"Can you make out this photo?" I ask Jeremy, who is so much better at anything geographical than I am.

But he can't. "It's pretty blurry," he says as he stares at it, trying to find what isn't there.

Rereading the article more slowly, we realize that this may not be the Vunamarita we know. Where are the Baining? The reporter does not mention the Baining at all, but this area, despite its Tolai name, was surely Baining land. I wonder if there could be another Vunamarita, also in New Britain. The word *Vunamarita*, in Tolai, means "Place of the Breadfruit Trees," and no doubt there are many such places; breadfruit trees are hardly rare. The name could be like "Springfield" or "Riverside" or "Oak Square" in America, a popular reference to many places.

That they have not ruined *our* Vunamarita—to use the Colonial Possessive—would come as a relief, although it doesn't make the situation any better for the people who live there. Nor do I know that our Vunamarita hasn't been ruined as well: we have not been in touch in twenty-five years.

But in a certain way I feel that I have never been out of touch with this place, and it has taken remarkably little—even this madeleine that has turned out to be a poppy seed muffin—to bring Vunamarita, Puktas, Wilaimbemki, and the entire journey flooding back.

We have been living in Cambridge since 1992—we bought a beautiful old Victorian house—and the move has worked out well. Jeremy has joined two partners in a software start-up nearby, I am teaching in a seminars program nearby, Cambridge is Cambridge, sui generis, and I have finally relinquished my dream of New York, or I have mostly relinquished my dream of New York—at any rate I have largely stopped complaining, and only when we fight.

We can still fight about anything at all, but these days we do not fight as violently or as often as we did. At almost fifty, we find it hard to keep up the pace. And we joke that after twenty-eight years, our fights have grown routine. We've had them all, and now they just repeat. "That's fight number 65," we will laugh, right in the middle of an argument, or "That's fight number 110—play the tape!" We still share a sense of humor, generally dark.

But almost fifty! I am finding this hard. To my surprise I have liked my forties, which have been so much better than my thirties or the dark age of my twenties that enveloped me before. But fifty is getting on. Fifty is getting mortal. Fifty, and I have yet to write a book. By now, I am desperate to write a book.

Part of the problem, I know, has been time. To write a book, I need time. For years I have kept myself so busy, writing columns, reviews, and essays, running book sections and teaching, seeing to my family, my house, and volunteer work, that I have not had an hour left over. By choice, I'm aware. A very good thing, I have thought. I have been wary of pausing; I know where that can lead. I have not forgotten the Slough of Despond and a year of Sundays. I have not forgotten electronic football: to this day I can hum the touchdown ring.

But I also know that more than time is involved. This past year, to make time, I boldly cut out my columns. I cut back reviews. But still I haven't done a book. I sit in my study—yes, by now I finally have a study—reading, searching, looking for a subject, which I never seem to find. I start on something and I stop: the subject doesn't seem right, and my research goes nowhere. It reminds me of my projects for New Guinea, my lazy Susan of possibility. It reminds me of being unable to cross the street. And I have come to think that I haven't written a book because I haven't been able to write the book that I need to write: that book about our lives among the Baining.

It isn't that I haven't thought of writing about the Baining since the last time I tried to write about the Baining. I have. They are always there. They are part of who we are. But clearly, my previous failures deter me—I am hesitant to go there again. Yet reading about Vunamarita this morning, I know that I will have to try. This extraordinary experience is out there; it lies within my grasp. This is truly a story: it is surely the story of a lifetime. If only, this time, I can figure out what the story is.

Once again I go to the basement and haul up the maps, the letters, and my journals, which by now are not only redolent of jungle rot but also pungent with cellar mold. Once again I am back in Puktas, in Wilaimbemki, waking to the cries of the *koki*, smelling the *kunai* grass, feeling the crusty taro in my ashy hand. Once again, I am poised to write.

But I am older now, by twenty-five years. Twenty-five years! It is hard to believe. The world has changed in this quarter of a century, the literary world as well as my own. When I first thought of writing about New Guinea, back when we had just returned, I thought of the work as an account. But no one these days thinks of writing an *account*. The very word sounds innocent, naive, antiquated, elementary: "What I Did on My Summer Vacation." We have entered the age of memoir. And this book, I realize, will be a memoir.

A memoir! But I loathe memoir. I dislike writing about myself—I seldom write anything about myself—and I dislike all this writing about selves that now permeates our literary world. The narcissism. The self-regard. The self-drama!

I too am filled with self-drama, I know this—twenty years of journals stand in evidence—but I don't assume that anyone cares. I certainly don't assume that *everyone* cares. How important people seem to think they are. How significant they seem to find their individual lives. This seems especially absurd in writing about the Baining, who are surely the least egotistical people on earth and who dramatize nothing, least of all their own lives.

For a while, avoiding the very notion of *memoir*, I try to think that what I write will be a travel book. Back in New Guinea, I had never read travel literature—I had never heard of travel literature—but by now I am fairly well read in the field. Indeed, for a couple of years, I wrote a newspaper column on travel books. I have read Patrick Leigh Fermor's luxuriant account of his ramble through central Europe. I have read Eric Newby's witty take on his trek in the Hindu Kush. I have read Isabella Bird's tale of traveling in Japan and have not forgotten how she tied an egg in a handkerchief and hard-boiled it in a hot spring. And most to the point, I have read Clifford Geertz, an anthropologist who believes that anthropological works are themselves related to travel literature.

A travel book definitely has a good sound to it. Much better than *memoir*. A travel book—or, better yet, a *travel narrative*—takes the work to another plane: a more literary, serious enterprise altogether, a work about something other than myself.

But really, I think, who am I kidding? Unless it is a guidebook, or a history, or a study of the flora and fauna of a region, what is a travel book, after all, but a memoir? "I went here," "I saw this," "I thought that," "I lived in the New Guinea jungle for sixteen months—aren't I the cassowary's tail!" No, there is no getting around it: this is a memoir, and it will have to be mostly about me.

But once I accept this premise, I hit another snag—a problem that I suddenly suspect has been central to this project from the start, so many years ago: how can this book be about me, when the story isn't mine? Surely, this is Jeremy's story. He was the anthropologist, this was his fieldwork, I would not even have been there if not for him.

"That's silly," Jeremy says, when I raise this. "You were there."

Yes, I was there. But I was *just the wife*, tagging along. Perhaps I cannot find my story because I haven't got one.

Now, Jeremy does have a story: The anthropologist who is a first-rate student sets out to do fieldwork. He is excited about anthropology, its theories, its ideas, its ethos; he is looking forward to contributing to the field; he has high, even grandiose hopes. When he ends up living with a people who not only seem to defy the field's theories and ideas, but are also shy and reserved, he finds himself in crisis: the theories and ideas he believed in now seem meaningless, and the questions he should ask feel like prying. Confused and upset, with no comfort or support from his single companion (me), he struggles on, until at last, disillusioned, he decides to leave anthropology.

Now that is a story. That story has an arc.

It is true Jeremy doesn't want to write about the experience, either personally or anthropologically. "I have no desire to write about New Guinea," he says so forcefully that it's pretty clear he would rather eat beetles.

As he sees it, he is very glad that he left anthropology. He has watched the field deconstruct amid a new anticolonialist awareness that questions intrusions, rights, and power and asks whose story is being told in ethnographies, the societies' or the ethnographers'? He too has read Geertz's critique of old classics in the field, and he has reconsidered the art and science of works he loved. He has long since had little use for theory: he is glad that he hasn't added any farfetched theories to the social science world. And he has watched anthropologist friends who did as brilliantly as he did in college end up teaching in unappealing places, wherever they could find a job.

He doesn't long for anthropology. He has no regrets about leaving academia with its petty politics and self-aggrandizing ambitions. He has loved his work, he loves the problem-solving aspect of programming, it has been years since he had *just a job*: he now has a company of his own. He likes his partners and the people he works with. He likes where he is living, and he will come to like it even more as his interest in antiquarian maps, just emerging, becomes a passion and he makes use of Harvard's extraordinary libraries. He *thanks* me for ruining his fieldwork!

All the same, I cannot get past the idea that the trip is his. I feel that the material itself belongs to him. I feel almost as though he holds the copyright on the experience. Do I have the right to appropriate it? Can I just take it and write it up as if it were my own? I think not. Especially when I consider what my sorry role in this venture was.

As I brood on this, I struggle to find a way into this experience, a framework to encompass the story. I have no trouble viewing the trip as "ours": that is how we have always spoken of it. "*We* lived in Puktas." "*We* lived in Wilaimbemki." "*We* ate taro." "*We* had a miserable time." Metaphorically conjoined twins: who can say where one's story leaves off and the other's begins?

And that is it, of course: "I think we should write this book together," I tell Jeremy. "A joint memoir!" I pounce on the idea once I have it, overwhelmed by its rightness. I see in it not just a solution to my problem but a chance to do fascinating work, something complex, original, and intriguing.

Jeremy finds the idea immensely amusing.

"Together?" he laughs. "In alternating chapters? With each chapter asserting that the previous chapter—*written by that other person who will go unnamed*—was entirely wrong?"

He reminds me about what happened when we prepared a talk on New Guinea for Gregory's ninth grade social studies class: sitting down to plan, we found ourselves back in the bush within minutes, locked in battle, ready to strangle each other. "*Nga!*" "No, *ngwa!*" "*Nga!*" "No, *ngwa!*" But we did settle down, I observe. We pulled ourselves together. We gave that talk.

"If you can find a way," he says.

But we both know that it won't happen. For one thing, Jeremy is right: we do not work well together, on New Guinea or, for that matter, on anything at all—house projects, cooking, social life, which we still seldom share. We remain in constant competition, for what I don't think either of us knows, and I can see that our dual memoir would be a duel memoir in the end.

In any case, it is obvious that Jeremy doesn't want to do this book, and a writer can't be passive; I cannot do it for him. He has never been particularly interested in "the story of his life": he doesn't see his life as a story. And this experience definitely isn't something he wants to explore. He believes that he has left it behind.

I know that I haven't left it behind. I cannot leave it behind. It may not haunt me as it did, but it still feels very central to my life.

"Some experiences are pivotal," I write: my opening sentence. At last I have begun. The summer sun shines in on my light and spacious study as I focus intently on the page.

But *pivotal*. This is not a word I like. It sounds mechanical, metallic—and, of course, it *is* mechanical and metallic. But for the moment I let it stand. The question is: what do I mean? That my life turned, was turned around by this experience? By now I wonder if this is true. Was I a different person when I emerged from who I was when I went in? Would I truly be different now if I hadn't gone to New Guinea?

I have thought of the Baining as forcing me to see through my culture. But as a child of the sixties, didn't I already see through my culture? Wouldn't I in any case have put quotation marks around "success"? Do I in any way believe I would have written ten books by now?

I have thought of the Baining as revealing to me the essential emptiness of life. But might I not have come to that on my own, with age? Don't many people perceive the emptiness of life—people who have not lived with the Baining? Isn't that also known as *depression*?

I have thought of the Baining as displacing me, making me a permanent outsider. But wasn't I always an outsider? Didn't I always feel that I was an observer looking on? Wasn't that why I thought that I would be a writer?

For Jeremy, I think, it is different: if he hadn't gone to the Baining, if he had done fieldwork in another culture—a culture that had a more typical social organization, a culture that was open to talking about their beliefs and customs, a culture that *had* more beliefs and customs, a culture that actually had *opposition between the sexes that they expressed in ritual*—he might well have stayed on in anthropology.

Though even there, he might have had a different life, but would he have been a different person? Might he not have come to loathe ambition in the cutthroat world of academia? He is not a cutthroat person. Might he not have cooled to theory as the cult of Levi-Strauss waned and cultural attitudes changed? He was always sensitive to charges of colonialism. Would he really have taken stronger stands or been less laconic? Can I honestly lay his reticence at the Bainings' door?

And if we hadn't done fieldwork among the Baining, would we have fought any less? Weren't we already fighting constantly even in London? Now that I think back, didn't we just briefly interrupt an argument on that summer trip in college to decide to get married in the first place?

I cannot answer for Jeremy, but looking back now, I don't feel that I can say what impact the Baining had on my life, how they changed me, or if they changed me at all. From here, the very experience looks flat. I was skeptical about anthropology when I went to New Guinea, and I was skeptical when I left; I was negative about going to New Guinea, and I was negative when I left; I had nothing I intended to achieve in New Guinea, and I achieved nothing. Did anything happen to me in New Guinea? Was I there? My story, I'm afraid, has no arc.

I try hard to shake myself out of this. "This is silly," Jeremy says again. "You were there." Of course I was there. I know how much this trip mattered: I have felt its impact since we returned. I feel that I only need to dig deeper, to understand why. I suspect there is too much I have forgotten, about what happened, or who I was at the time. How can I remember exactly? It was such a long time ago.

I decide that I need to reread my journals, and I need to read them with care. I feel that so far I have only skimmed them; I have to focus on what is there. If I don't plow through the dozens of letters, there isn't all that much to read: just two daily journals—though the early parts, in pencil, are so faint now, they are very hard to make out.

Still, I am eager to do this, and I tackle it all in one go. I sit at my desk, my legs curled under me, leaning into my past. Indeed, I lean so far that I can feel that I'm toppling in. Suddenly, I find myself down some awful rabbit hole, dark and overwhelmingly airless, observing things that I have never truly looked at before.

I'm appalled. I actually feel ill.

Who is this girl who whines and frets and argues? She is wildly ambitious, and extraordinarily petty, and her journal is a bore. "Bad day!" she moans. "What a miserable time!" "My god, why am I here?" I search in vain for descriptions of the landscape, the people, the living, for signs of intelligent life. She complains about her husband, she analyzes their fights in repetitious detail, and she talks about taro—the taro she has been given, the taro she has cooked, the taro she has eaten. One month she is collecting photos, the next she is collecting myths, and suddenly—right there in front of me!—she is writing poems. These poems bring me very low. Every other week she has decided to leave—she is going home or she is going to Rabaul—yet there she is, every day, droning on.

She mortifies me, this younger self, and as I read what she has written, I feel nothing but embarrassment and shame. What a waste she has made of it all. Who would want to read about her? Why would I want to write about her? If I disown her, I have no story, but maybe hers is not a story I want to tell.

By autumn, when New Britain is again in the news, when the Rabaul volcano has erupted, burying the beloved town in ash, I have already packed up my maps, my letters from the field, and my journals and stored away the Baining once again—this time, I am certain, for good.

14

The Story of a Lifetime
Part 4

> There is always something to be made of pain.
>
> —Louise Glück

It is 1998, an afternoon in April, and I am sitting in my study brooding on work. The question is what to write next. Now that I have given up my columns, this is always on my mind, and at this point I would like to do something new: I have written about books for many years, I wrote about magazines for many years, and I am tired of writing about writing.

A friend has recently published a travel essay in the *New York Times*, and I think perhaps I will do a travel essay too. As much as I have written about other people's travel writing, I have never undertaken my own—except for my efforts to write about New Guinea, which were not, as I saw it, exactly travel writing and which in any case did not succeed. But though I haven't thought about those efforts for ages—and though I'm sure, if asked, I would say that I had long since accepted defeat—I know at once, without thinking, that I'm about to try again.

The Story of a Lifetime: Part 4

This time I do not haul my journals, notes, and letters up from the basement: I am writing an essay, not a book, it will be only a thousand words, and I do not need to prepare. Is there any major point in this experience that I do not recall? I just write. And though I usually find writing slow, and though this subject has eluded me for decades, this essay—a comic view of two innocents abroad—comes together with remarkable speed. In two drafts I am essentially finished. I polish it, I send it to the *Times*, and they run it in their Sunday travel section.

I feel so chuffed. I feel as though I have aced my exams. I feel as though I have won a prize. I feel as though I have hiked to Wilaimbemki in three hours, crossing every log bridge on my own. I have published an article on the Baining. And it has taken me only thirty years!

Thirty years. It is hard to believe. I am fifty-two years old. I feel so distant from that girl in the bush, so far from who I was. Thirty years ago, I couldn't write about the Baining without weeping. Twenty years ago, I couldn't write about the Baining without raging. Four years ago, I couldn't even read my journals from the field without cringing. Despair, anger—shame!—all unfolding like stages of a peculiar grief. Yet now I have written about it all with wry humor, with self-deprecating edge, with esprit. I have transformed our painful experience into a journey that makes people laugh. I have made our tale of woe a delight.

But I have to wonder exactly what has happened here. I am glad, of course, that at last I have spun this straw into gold. But I find it unsettling as well. Where is the bleakness, the depression, the dark insight that was so much a part of the journey? Can this be the same trip? I haven't lied. I haven't invented. I am not one of those memoirists who play fast and loose with the facts. Thirty years ago I couldn't turn this story into fiction—and I couldn't turn it into fiction now—I am so deeply mired in the facts.

But what is the truth here? Is all of life just so much raw matter, to be kneaded into different shapes at different times? Is all memory subject to continuous revision? Clearly, it is. But how then do you ever settle on what really happened?

There is, of course, some reality check. Thirty years on, I cannot claim that the Baining ruined my life: my life does not feel ruined.

It's true, Jeremy and I can still fight about anything, large or small: Gregory, work, words, *the postage for my article on New Guinea! (Too little! Too much! Nga! No, ngwa!)* It's true I'm still prone to discontent. I'm still obsessed with all that I haven't written. I still lament daily in my journal: "Bad day!" "Bad to worse!" "Sharp pains in my head!" "What a terrible time!"

But in fact, things have been going pretty well. We are still living in Cambridge, both of us like it immensely, and when we leave our beautiful old Victorian next year, we will move to another, in Cambridge. I no longer whine about New York—I no longer even miss New York, which by now I know isn't home. Our son is getting married: we love his fiancée. I like the writing seminar that I am teaching. I have just edited an anthology of stories that will soon be published—my first book even if it isn't quite *my* book—and I see doors opening before me, or, at any rate, a door. I look forward to writing another—I hope I will write another—and if I do not feel absolutely sure, if I still obsess and anguish and do not understand, I would find it hard these days to blame the Baining for the books I didn't write.

Indeed, at this point, although it feels strange—even embarrassing—to admit it, I realize that I like the impact fieldwork has had on my life. I like the way it has set me apart. It may be true

The Story of a Lifetime: Part 4

that I have always been an outsider, but if I am honest, I used to be an outsider eager to get in. When I think of myself as a child, or in high school—even in college—I see a girl with her nose pressed up against the glass, yearning for entry, an invitation.

No more. Since New Guinea, I have loved to be outside. Since New Guinea, I am so outside, I feel that I have come from another country, another world. I am a visitor viewing everything through alien eyes. "Oh, is that how you do things here? How interesting!" At times, when Gregory was younger, he would grow exasperated with me. "Are those the kinds of cruises people take?" I might say, looking out at the huge boats in the harbor. "What?" he would say, annoyance mixing with disdain. "Are you from Pluto?" He would have liked a more conventional mother: a mother who went to the hairdresser, a mother who didn't smoke little cigars, a mother who would not only recognize a cruise ship but might even like to take a cruise. A mother who fit in.

But I have come to see how much I love this social and intellectual separation. This difference. This *distinction*. By now I understand that it defines me. And although it's possible that I would have come to this anyhow, I like to credit the Baining, a people who didn't fit in.

From this outside perspective, I am entirely a skeptic. There is little that I trust. I dismiss most psychology and sociology as *pop*; I call most intellectual theories *faux*. "Social science isn't science," I like to say. I put quotation marks around all "social research." I scoff when I read pronouncements about *human nature*, when certain patterns of parenting, or gender, or eating—even religion— are declared not only universal but apparently embedded in the human genome.

I know that I'm extreme. I'm aware I can be terribly annoying. I realize that I deny things that I know almost nothing about. But I feel that I know enough. I know how narrow our Western frame of reference is in America, where our studies seldom include data from European countries, let alone from Melanesia or Peru. I know how little is universal, how much is cultural, and that when people talk sweepingly about *human traits* and *human nature*, they are almost certainly wrong. "It can't be *universal*," I will respond to the latest theory. "The Baining wouldn't fit."

And how many others as well? How many societies do we know nothing about? How many cultural patterns have we missed? How many groups have we misunderstood? How much have we simply gotten wrong, our questions misdirected, the answers misinterpreted yet accepted as true? I have seen the Baining masks at our major museums, scrupulously mislabeled: "This mask is used in hunting rites," the reference card will say. Or "This mask is used in harvest rites." Or "This mask is used in initiation rites" or "commemorative rites for the dead." Yet the Baining have no weapons to hunt, they have no specific "harvest" time, they have no initiation ceremonies, and they do not commemorate their dead.

I know how little, from our limited viewpoint, we really know.

Writing my essay, I have grown aware of just how much I like this skeptical detachment that is so profoundly a part of who I am. It has long been a part of my writing, my teaching, my entire approach to life. I think back to that moment in Canberra so many years ago when I hoped that fieldwork, like Emily Dickinson's poetry, would make me "feel as if the top of my head were taken off." Surely, I got what I wished for—for better and for worse.

And there has certainly been a worse. I have not forgotten the downside of being blown away. If I now think differently about our trip, it is not because I have misremembered it. I haven't forgotten our unhappiness. Nor have I whitewashed the aftermath: the cultural disorientation that felt, at first, so deadly; the need to keep busy; my suspicion of success that I feel certain has limited my success; and the wedge between Jeremy and me that has made it so hard to be friends *as a couple* with others, the core of guilt and anger that has, even now, made it so hard to be friends with each other.

Jeremy and I do not talk about New Guinea. If we still share anecdotes with others, eyeing each other guiltily as we indulge, we do not discuss the experience in any depth—we have never discussed it in any depth—with each other.

Nonetheless, it is the centerpiece on our table: a huge rain forest with branches, roots, and vines, a canopy overhead and a muddy floor. We don't say, "What is this doing here, this diorama?" We pretend it isn't there.

But it blocks our view of each other. We are forced to peer around it: we see one another on a curious angle. We are forced to talk around it: our conversation takes circuitous routes. We are forced to fight around it: our battles are almost all indirect. Phonemes, as if the argument wasn't really about fieldwork. Gregory, as if the struggle wasn't really about fieldwork. Postage, as if even our fight about mailing my article on fieldwork wasn't really about fieldwork!

A code word has always been *ambition*. The subject arises by stealth, sneaking up at tense moments, and it always seems to take us by surprise. Yet the question is always the same: is ambition good or bad? The argument is always the same: we each have our stand. The Baining—unmentioned and unacknowledged—stand by silently, as referees.

Jeremy has never wavered from the view he took on returning from the field: ambition is bad; ambition requires stepping on other people's heads. Since this attitude dates from the field trip, I have to associate it with the field trip, but since we cannot discuss it, I do not know which jungle path led him to this point.

Is he like me, viewing our entire culture, including its version of "success," as phony? Is it the loss of his own ambition in the field, or the new critique of anthropology and his concern about using the Baining, about stepping on indigenous heads? Is it the Baining who made him believe that all a person can do is cultivate one's own garden (of taro)? How can I know? He refuses to say. Indeed, he has long since mastered the Baining shrug.

I find that I still can't accept this absolute view of ambition: it gnaws at me, and I cannot let the issue be. I feel that there is something personally askew in Jeremy's claims, since he himself is definitely successful. And I see this philosophy as terrible for me. I do not know how you can write anything at all without some form of ambition. I may not care about money or prizes, but is it best to write without wanting to be read? Should a writer long to be unknown? I find it trying enough to struggle with the belief that success is pointless; I cannot afford to see it as evil as well. I need to argue this down.

"Just why is striving bad?" I will say. "You aren't exactly *unambitious*," I point out. "You own your own company. Look at your work: you've developed a computer language. You're a perfectionist. How can you claim you don't care?"

Hypocrite! I want to shout.

He shrugs. His company isn't Microsoft, he says. Striving, working hard at something, isn't ambition, he says. "Once you take it there, then trying to do anything well—even cooking an excellent meal—becomes ambition," he says. He claims that I'm extending the word too far: I have diluted its meaning.

We have fought this out for so many years, I feel that we need to end the debate. I believe that this issue lies at the heart of our constant fighting, and if we could settle it, we would somehow be freed. I decide that I will look up the word in the online *Oxford English Dictionary*, which Jeremy has given me for my birthday.

Indeed, I look up both words, *ambitious* and *ambition*, and I print the definitions out.

"You see!" I say, waving around my pages. "You see!"

But I have already seen that I cannot claim victory. At best there is ambiguity. And really, he is right:

"Ambitious: 1. Full of ambition, thirsting after honour or advancement; aspiring to high position. 2. Strongly desirous (of something expected to bring credit or honour), eager."

This doesn't sound great. And the definition of *ambition* does not improve things:

"The ardent (in early usage, inordinate) desire to rise to high position, or to attain rank, influence, distinction or other preferment."

"Well," I say, grasping for something positive amid all of this "thirsting," and "high position," and "rank," "well, yes, ambition is about *getting on*. But it doesn't say you have to step on anyone's head to get there."

He shrugs again.

When my article appeared, Jeremy received an e-mail from someone he knew: "Well, how does it feel to have your life smeared across the pages of the *New York Times*, amidst the airfare discounts?"

I almost wept. We both know whose head was being stepped on. We both know who was being used. We both know who has taken whose story and turned it to her own *ambitious* ends.

At fifty-two, I am tired of this battle. I am tired of New Guinea and the Baining. But I feel that I am done with them now. I have written this essay, I have given people pleasure. At last I have made something of my pain.

What I have made, to be sure, isn't grand. It turns out that this wasn't the story of a lifetime after all; it was only a story. A thousand words. I have whittled it down to its barest bones. But I feel it is enough.

Indeed, I've found in recent years that I have grown increasingly laconic. I used to talk for hours with friends, analyzing our childhoods, our marriages, our choices, real and imagined. No more. Now I am amazed at how much people say that doesn't need to be said. The way people go on about their lives, about other people's lives. The lengthy profiles in magazines, the interminable biographies, the memoirs filled with intimate details. "*Sharing?* What's so great about *sharing?*" I say to a psychologist in my writing class, who stares at me dumbfounded. But all of this now seems to me *maus wara, agerapki mutki*—"full of spit." It is as if the Baining reticence that Jeremy innately understood has filtered down, its value at last taken hold.

Now that I have written my little essay, I feel that something has finished, and I am happy to leave this burden behind. I feel as if I have taken off my carrying strap, my *amalunga*, and set down the weight that I have carried on my back for thirty years. I have said all I need to say, and already I feel lighter, freer, ready to move on.

"Oh, we think there's more to say," says a friend after he has read my little piece. "We think there's more to say."

―
―

We are sitting in our living room, Jeremy, I, and this man, whom we haven't seen for months. His "we" in this statement isn't royal: it includes his wife, who isn't present but who has also read the essay. But he certainly looks haughty and self-pleased, if not regal, as he goes still further and amends what he has said:

"*We think you have more to say,*" he smiles.

At first I do not take this in. I can't believe that he has said it. I think that I may have misheard.

More to say?

And then the comment really hits me. It jabs me in the gut and winds me. It socks me in the eye and blinds me. Already I feel a tightening in my stomach, sharp needles in my head, a doughy wad of mixed emotions expanding in my chest.

More to say?

My God, I think, what a jerk! I wonder if I have ever liked this man. Or his wife. Or his children. That repugnant smile! How can he be doing this? What right does he have to intrude?

With everything roiling, I find that I can't reply. I feel so unprepared. It has been some time since this essay appeared, and by now it has settled. This article is past. Everyone seems to have enjoyed it: my editors, friends, people I don't know who have sent me notes. I've had nothing but praise. No one has found it insufficient or wanting. It's not a monograph. It's not a memoir. It's not some definitive work. *It's just a travel piece.* What is wrong with this man?

But I realize that he can't possibly know what he has done. No doubt he thinks that he is being intelligent—I know him; he always wants to be the smartest man in the room. No doubt he thinks that he is being empathic, perceiving the depth of the experience behind my facile piece, proud, as ever, of his *insight*. No doubt he even thinks that he is being helpful, encouraging me to do more, to be *ambitious*. No doubt I should just ignore what he has said.

But I can't. The words have already wormed their way inside me. They have already made themselves uncomfortably at home.

After all, they used to live here. After all, what he has said is merely true. He hasn't told me anything I don't know. Obviously, there is more to say. Obviously, I have more to say. And all of it is in my basement, a subterranean mass that I have hauled up and down so many times. Will I be hauling it up and down for the rest of my life? My God, is *that* my story of a lifetime?

It is surely a story that a Baining might love: A journey. A journey that doesn't leave home ground. A journey that always circles back. A journey that doesn't end.

PART 3

Well, This Is History

You could not step twice into the same river; for other waters are ever flowing on to you.

—Heraclitus of Ephesus

15

Testing the Water

I think it is only in the Port Moresby airport, while scanning the baggage regulations—*No spears! No arrows!*—that I truly believe we're going to New Guinea. But in fact, this trip has been planned for months. Our excuse for the journey is a map conference in New Zealand. But the Baining are the goal, New Britain the destination: San Francisco, Wellington, South Island, even Sydney are only stops along the way.

"We're going to New Guinea!" I tell everyone. Or better yet, "We're going back to New Guinea!" Going to New Guinea is an interesting trip; going *back* is a story.

This time I am determined to figure out just what that story is.

It is 2008, almost forty years since our trip to New Guinea. Half a lifetime. It is hard to believe. We still live in Cambridge, though we have moved to a larger house, for the garden I have missed and the space that Jeremy needs. He has sold his company and now works from home: his new field is antiquarian maps, his main interest the Arctic North. Maps of Spitsbergen and Novaya Zemlya adorn our walls; in our library, Barentz forever seeks the Northeast Passage and dies again and again; sea monsters frolic and threaten—one bears an uncanny resemblance to Uncle Hy.

Eight years back, I gave up teaching, I gave up journalism—I gave up *deadlines*—to write a book, and although I tripped at once into foreverland (Mulch the floors! Wash the weeds! *Avoid! Procrastinate! Delay!*), it has finally been published. My Northeast rite of passage.

We are grandparents now, and this has come as a shock. "We will never grow up," we have always joked, and suddenly it seems that we are growing old. Jeremy's hair has gone gray. He is slender but not the skinny youth he was. My hair is still long and wild, but there is less of it. There seems to be less of me. On the whole we are in very good shape: so far our joints have held fast. But if we're ever going to New Guinea, we know that it should be now: this could be a rugged trip.

Planning a trip to the Baining Mountains, we quickly learn, is still not like planning a trip to Italy or France. Indeed, finding out about the Baining proves no easier today than it was before. There are still no guides to the area, no travel tips about restaurants, or roads, or sights that are *vaut le détour*. There is no government information we can find.

Even the Web yields little beyond a few links to stagings of the Baining fire dance, which they now perform for tourists—exactly what that missionary in Moresby hoped for, so many years ago. Jeremy does turn up a video of a Puktas youth and his band singing and dancing in a riverbed. On YouTube! "Does this mean that everything has changed?" I ask. "Will the youngsters now have cell phones?" There is no way to tell. The band sings on, devoid of any context or, sadly, much of an audience. I join the very few fans who have "liked" it.

All we are looking for really are the basics: where people are living now and how to get there. Are the Puktas Baining still in Puktas? Have the Wilaimbemki Baining moved at last to Poiniara? Are there roads now to any of these villages? Can we cruise to Wilaimbemki in a jeep? Without roads, of course, I will not reach the mountain villages at all. I know this. I could barely manage the hike at twenty-two, and I am by no means either more fit or less acrophobic now. I have to hope for roads. But if there are roads, there will be traffic—outsiders, goods, news— and that without doubt will mean change.

We realize how little we know.

Jeremy writes to Father Hesse, the German missionary in Raunsepna who, we learn, is no longer in Raunsepna. Indeed, he is now archbishop of Rabaul. An archbishop! To me, this sounds extremely grand—though it is true *archbishop of Rabaul* hasn't quite the same ring to it as *archbishop of Canterbury*, and Rabaul, as it happens, is under ash. In any case, the archbishop does not reply. Ever.

Jeremy also writes to Jane Fajans, an anthropologist who lived with the Baining after we were there. She does reply, she is excited to hear that we are going back, and she would like to be helpful. But she herself hasn't been there for years, and she can tell us very little. She refers us to a colleague in Canberra, who can also tell us very little, though he sends a map and a paper written by another anthropologist back in the '80s. The '80s! This information, we realize, is twenty years old. Still, it's more current than what we know, and for us, it raises issues that are new. In 1969 logging and mining were not yet under way. Cash cropping had just begun. Bait fishing? I don't recall any fish.

From these meager sources, we piece out what we can. The Puktas Baining, it seems, are still in Puktas. Logging did some damage in the region, creating a large malarial swamp—so perhaps that was *our* Vunamarita in the *New York Times* after all. But logging there seems to have ended. There is a mining scheme afoot that will not benefit the people of Puktas, but at this point it is only a plan, and the colleague says he hopes to help defeat it. There is, he says, a road to Vunamarita, or close to, if you have four-wheel drive and can cope with some hairy river crossings.

As for the mountains, there may also be a road to Raunsepna, though this is somewhat doubtful, and it almost certainly does not go to Wilaimbemki. But the people of Wilaimbemki have indeed moved and are now living near the coast at Poiniara. At least they *were* living at Poiniara. As it happens, though, some Baining groups, after relocating, have moved back to their original villages, so we can't be sure that the Wilaimbemkina are still at Poiniara.

So nothing is certain, and there seems to be no way of reaching the Baining themselves to ask. Clearly, this is not a trip for people who need to know beforehand what they will find.

Still, if we cannot fully plan out the trip, we can prepare. To begin with there is the flight, with its length and extravagant cost. Friends warn about Economy Class. They feed us horror tales of trips to India and Japan. You will be squeezed, they say. Your back will go. Your neck will cramp. Your feet will swell. Didn't someone somewhere lose their toes? But though we hope for a Business Class deal with American Express—and though Jeremy swipes his Amex card with dedication—the fine print we somehow never noticed cuts us out: it will be steerage all the way.

Choosing where to stay proves emotional. We dream of being in Rabaul. We know—or think we know—that Rabaul is mostly gone, destroyed in 1994: we have seen photos of Tavurvur and Vulcan, the ash plumes sixty thousand feet high; we have read about the town half buried under six feet of ash; we know that almost everything, including government, has moved to Kokopo, some nineteen kilometers away. But Rabaul was our haven. Rabaul was our refuge. We do not pine for Kokopo.

Jeremy tours the Web: "The Hamamas Hotel," he says. "It's still in business."

The Hamamas! I remember the Hamamas, with its Chinese restaurant and expat clientele. In Tok Pisin—as Pidgin English is now known—*hamamas* means "happy." The inn's motto is "The Spirit of Rabaul." Clearly, this place is a survivor. But the white owner, it seems, has been accused of shooting a New Guinean. Not so much happiness, we figure. Not the spirit of Rabaul we really want. Jeremy signs us up for the Kokopo Village Resort, which is New Guinean owned and run.

A resort! My heart sinks. I picture a veranda and people sipping drinks with little colored umbrellas. I see them splashing in pools. I see beach balls, tennis balls, golf balls, racquet balls, balls of every persuasion and—whoever the owners—guests of one persuasion: white.

"A resort," I murmur glumly, shaking my head.

"Well," says Jeremy in consolation, "I wouldn't go that far. I think KVR is really just a hotel."

A hotel. My spirits do not rise. Indeed, at this point I realize that I haven't begun to think this trip through. When I see myself in New Guinea, I am living in a hut in the bush. I am squatting on the ground, smoking Baining tobacco, *brus*, wrapped in newsprint. My bed is a mat on the floor; running water is a nearby stream that isn't stagnant. The last thing I want is to be taken for a tourist in a country where I once lived. The last thing I want is to be seen as one of those people we mocked so long ago who want to "experience" the bush without getting dirty: people who cannot do without their comfort. What most stings, I know, is that I am of course a tourist, and at sixty-two I am not at all sure how much comfort I can do without.

"A hotel," I sigh. "It seems so soft."

"Soft?" laughs Jeremy. "Oh, I don't know about that. Better wait till you see the hotel."

The house fills up with lists. There are Jeremy's lists, my lists, and joint lists. There are lists for the dog. We find it satisfying to deal with necessities: passports and visas, cameras and clothes, shots and medications—though this last brings uneasy surprise. I discover that Enterovioform, which we took daily in the bush against stomach bugs, has now been banned throughout the world: it seems we're lucky that we aren't blind or dead. I also learn that the antimalarial Chloroquine, another of our daily pills, can cause serious anxiety and depression: "It drives you mad," warns a doctor friend from Australia. "Take some other medication this time 'round." Was this then what our fraught journey was really about? I joke. A pill and not fieldwork at all?

A major enterprise for weeks is refreshing our Tok Pisin, which we assume we will need to get by. We have forgotten most of what we knew, and what we knew will no longer suffice: the language has evolved, a lingua franca meeting the demands of an independent country and widespread use. Tok Pisin now has complexity and nuance. It also now has status: back in the sixties, there were merely Pidgin English phrase books and some language tapes at universities; today there is a set of CDs designed by Australians and native speakers to teach it.

This turns out to be an excellent course, and we follow the lessons diligently; we meet up afternoons to practice daily. We learn grammar, syntax, conversation, and the odd mix that is modern New Guinea: *kaukau* gardens and restaurants, oars and outboard motors, taboos and wireless, betel nut and Coca-Cola. We learn to compare the length of pythons (*"Dispela moran i longpela mo long dispela"*) and to express a longing for betel nut: "*E, poro, mi dai long buai ya*" ("Heh, friend, I'm dying for some betel nut"). We love it. We even enjoy the warning sessions about thieving *raskols* in Port Moresby since we by no means intend to stay in Port Moresby.

"Rea-*dy*?" asks the Australian instructor before each exercise set. "Rea-*dy*?" For weeks we go around the house saying, "Rea-*dy*?"

For Jeremy, *preparing* means making arrangements: it is solely a practical task—challenging, annoying, but not stressful. This time no fieldwork is involved: no grants to apply for, no thesis to design, no questions to devise for people who would rather not answer them. This time, without tension, he is getting ready for an adventure he is free to have.

For me, as usual, it isn't so clear: Exactly what, I keep wondering, am I preparing for? Do I want to make something of this journey? Do I want to write something when we return? What should I be thinking about? What should I be reading? Travel literature, anthropology, memoir? In some horror, I begin to sense a ghostly young presence yearning for a Project of Her Own.

It is hard not to think of using this trip as a peg to write about living with the Baining. But do I really want to go there? Again? Do I want to read those old journals? Again? By now, one journal has a brown and green growth across the top margin, a life form that narrows into the binding and has somehow seeped through all of the pages. The colors gleam, slightly phosphorescent. They look moist. They look toxic. I am not sure that I should touch the book. I hold it at arm's length and turn the pages only from the bottom. So far this fungus has thrived only in the margins, but it is obvious that in time it will eat away the words. Will the experience itself be lost? Do I care?

In truth, I have no desire to write something personal. I say this to myself, and I say it to others as well. I say it often. Our world is too full of the personal: all these memoirs—*How I Got to Be Me. Why I Like Being Me. Why I Hate Being Me. Me.* It is all so very un-Baining.

What I would most like is to write something *impersonal* about New Guinea. The field seems wide open: so little has been written—only academic monographs, books about World War II, a few adventure tales. I would especially like to write about Rabaul—though it is hard to think of Rabaul as anything but personal, being there seemed so much about us. Rabaul was where we had the comfort of a house: we could take real showers, sleep in a real bed, eat a meal with bread. It was where we had the pleasure of spending money, the luxury of closing doors. It was the only place in New Guinea where we made love. To be in Rabaul was to not be in the bush, and more than that, it was to be wonderfully suspended, free of ties, obligations, and responsibilities, a project that was going badly, a task always not yet accomplished.

But Rabaul was hardly only ours. People always talked about the charm, the magic of the town, with its slow pace, its friendly spirit, its luxuriant setting. Even now, when I search online, I discover a loquacious community of people who once lived in Rabaul, or worked in Rabaul, or grew up in Rabaul, or simply visited Rabaul and, like Jeremy and me, never forgot it. They send in anecdotes about their lives, queries about former friends, pictures of old Rabaul. They send in photos of Tavurvur and Vulcan erupting, gorgeous shots of fiery devastation. They mourn the loss of a town they loved.

Yet no one has written in any depth about this place. The only book relating to Rabaul that I have found is a brief photo essay in the anthropology library at Harvard, and it is hardly about the town at all. Surely, someone should write a history of Rabaul.

But even as I daydream, I realize that this will not be me. We will be in New Britain just ten days. Our whole trip with its conference and various stops will take more than a month, and we cannot manage more, but we will be in New Britain just ten days. *Ten days.* Such a puny length of time. A tourist length of time. An embarrassment. What on earth can you do in ten days?

Yet this isn't what we feel. For both of us, the trip feels outsize. It feels huge. Deep. Real. The journey of a lifetime. *Another chance.*

Will we blow it? Will those spectral youngsters seduce us? Will the Baining once again undo us? Will we find ourselves fighting the battles of the undead? Or will we find, as the ancient Greek proverb avows, that this river is a whole new place?

"Rea-*dy*?" we laugh, at once certain that we are, and just about equally unsure.

16

Wading In

Jackson International Airport, Port Moresby: we have been warned about the place. We have heard about the heat, the filth, the bugs, the stench of urine and vomit, the corruption, the muggings—even murder. This is an airport that one traveler rates online with skulls instead of stars: he gives it five. Another travel reviewer suggests that the airport was safer when the Americans and Japanese were bombing it in World War II.

Indeed, by the time we arrive we're on such high alert, it is almost disappointing to encounter nothing worse than chaos: crowds and long, unidentified lines, one of which is surely ours. Having landed late from Cairns, we fear that we'll miss the flight to Kokopo and face a night in the dreaded *Mosbi*. But a guardian angel from the Sepik guides us through: we run.

Running with us is a short, sturdy Chinese woman who, it is obvious, needs no help. She knows exactly where she is going; no doubt she has done this many times before. We nod to one another but cannot speak; we are huffing and puffing to the plane, which is small and packed and smells intensely of sweat. Once we are seated, we seek each other out—she is sitting three rows up on the left, but no matter: she stands and talks across the seats and aisle.

She asks where we are from and says that she was born in Rabaul, fourth generation: this is clearly a source of pride. She and her husband used to live in Rabaul—they run a business, she says, although she doesn't say what kind—but they have moved now, after Tavurvur, to Kokopo. *After Tavurvur*: this is a phrase we will hear many times in the coming days. Everything is Before or After Tavurvur: *After Tavurvur*, nothing has been the same.

"Where are you staying?" she asks, and when I tell her, I see at once that she disapproves.

"KVR is okay," she shrugs uncomfortably.

I ask if she thinks someplace else might be better.

"Rapopo would be better," she says.

I sigh. So we have made a mistake. I can imagine the dismal hole that we'll be staying in. Already I am planning to move, concerned about comfort, already I seem to have forgotten my longing for huts, for squatting on the ground and bathing in streams.

Only now does she ask what has brought us to New Britain, and what we plan to do here. I tell her our little tale about fieldwork and the Baining and our hopes now to reach the villages where we had lived. Here, too, she makes it plain she disapproves.

"To the bush?" she says. Her eyebrows rise. She obviously thinks we're out of our minds. "Well," she says, "you have a guide?"

A guide? "No," I shake my head. "We have no guide." I haven't even thought about a guide. I have pictured going on our own, just the two of us, as before, as always.

"You have to have a guide," she says sternly, as if talking to a slow or recalcitrant child. "How will you know where you are? In the bush? You'll get lost."

I sigh again. She is certainly right. We need a guide.

"Forty years," she shakes her head. "You'll find that things have changed. You'll find the natives are more cheeky now," she says.

Cheeky? *Cheeky!* We're surrounded by *natives*; the plane is full of *natives*—we are the only whites. Does she assume that they don't understand? But, of course, she doesn't care. And I don't know how to respond. Do I argue? Sneer? Pretend that I haven't heard? *Smile?* I had forgotten about this aspect of New Guinea, the bigotry even in Rabaul.

"We just lived here," I say. "We just lived here."

She stares at me, puzzled. She has no idea what I mean. Nor, for that matter, do I. But the comment seems to work: she sits down.

KVR has sent a van to meet us at Tokua airport. A good thing, since Kokopo has no taxi service, says our friend, as she rushes from the small terminal, relieved, I expect, that she needn't offer us a ride—as she would, I don't doubt. We are so plainly not her type; but we are white.

Our driver is KVR—not white. He is large and amiable and talks nonstop with gusto. But I hear only bits of what he says. I leave it to Jeremy to chat. As we drive along the flat, empty road, I struggle to make out the landscape as it dissolves in the dusk. Plantations. Palms. We're back, I think. We're really back.

At the small hotel office, we arrange for our unit. We ask about renting a car. We ask about dinner. We ask about the Internet connection that they have promised: I can hardly believe it: e-mail, Google in New Guinea! "Ah, the Internet," the clerk replies. "The Internet is down." The airport, we discover, is also down: an advisory note posted on the wall announces that volcano ash is so heavy, all outbound flights for the day have been canceled. No one leaves.

Volcano ash? I hadn't even known that Tavurvur was still active. Not that I'm afraid—not at all. Even in 1994, evacuation was so efficient that almost no one died. But might we be stuck here? Forced to stay on? For weeks? This is the great thing about New Guinea, I think: anything can happen. Already I feel a little high.

As we follow our driver, who has now become the porter, to our unit, I realize that Jeremy was right: Kokopo Village Resort, whatever its name and self-image, is not really a resort. It is all a minimalist affair.

The short path we are on winds along motel-like units on the right and landscaping on the left that has not yet been finished: much of it is simply earth. The room itself is bare necessities: two beds, a desk, a chair. Although the unit has a kitchenette—an extra we thought might be useful—it is hard to see how you could eat here: the kitchen is ill-equipped and hard to use; there is no table; the room has just the one chair. The porch has no chair at all. The bathroom has only one towel. It has the smallest sink I have ever seen. I stare in awe at this sink. It is only ten inches wide. It extends just six inches from the wall. It isn't four inches deep. An extraordinary sink! Our bathtub appears to be smeared with diarrhea. I stagger from the bathroom gagging.

"Shit in the tub?" says Jeremy. "Really?"

But it turns out the brown streaks are only soap: brown liquid soap, not the ideal color—the dispenser has leaked.

In fact, KVR turns out to be fine. They bring us more towels. They bring us another chair. Their restaurant serves breakfast with toast, and for dinner they offer something called Island Fish. I can order a glass of wine. The owners and their family are friendly; the staff is lovely.

At night when I smoke on the porch, large green crabs—drawn by the light or the warmth of my body or the scent of my cheap cigar—creep up to join me. We stand side by side, looking out at the dark. Amazingly, the room has no bugs. No six-inch grasshoppers, no giant beetles, no monster roaches. How do they do this, no bugs? I love the place.

The first day, our aim is to pull the trip together. We need the information we couldn't get back home, and Jeremy has made a plan.

"We'll start at Vunapope," he says, "where we'll try to see Father Hesse."

"The archbishop?" I scoff, remembering our letter. "You think he'll see us?"

"Who knows?" says Jeremy. "Maybe he never even got that letter. Why assume their postal system is better than ours?" he laughs. "Then we'll go to the government offices at Vunadidir and try to get in touch with James Tapele. I'm sure he can tell us pretty much all we need to know."

No doubt this is true: James Tapele is the acting district governor of the region—and he is Baining. It is rare for the Baining to hold office, any office other than councilor, and this is the highest post in the area. We are eager—and curious—to meet this unusual man.

We wake up early: a rooster provides the wake-up call. En route to breakfast we inquire about the Internet: still down. The planes too are still down. Indeed, the town is dusted in ash. Thick soot covers the paths and shrubs of KVR: we see caretakers hosing down the grounds.

After breakfast, our driver/porter from yesterday—the all-around man here, it seems—informs us that our car is ready and escorts us to the parking lot. He beams with pride as he waves us to a silver pickup truck so shiny it looks brand new. We make suitably appreciative sounds. Although Jeremy has never driven a pickup truck—and though driving here is on the left—he seems remarkably at ease as he hops in.

Vunapope isn't far. The road is well paved, and we have it to ourselves. When we arrive, it seems that we have the mission to ourselves as well. No one is about. The extensive grounds are well kept, but as we wander around, they feel deserted and unwelcoming. No signs direct us to an office. "Look, here's the priest's house," I say, pointing to the only sign in view, and at last, as we head for the cottage, a young woman appears, no doubt to stop us.

Following our guide to the office, we greet the woman at the main desk and ask for Father Hesse: "We knew him many years ago," Jeremy says, in Tok Pisin. "In the field."

"Oh," she says, "he died. A long time ago."

Died! My God! At once I forgive him for not getting back to us. Poor man, *dead*, and here I was being petty.

But wait: he died a long time ago?

"Oh, yes," she says, "many years," and she names some impossible date.

This can't be. He became archbishop not that long ago. And it turns out the father's demise is simply a misunderstanding: put it down to our first day of Tok Pisin. The dead missionary was someone else. Father Hesse is alive. No need to forgive him.

But the archbishop, it seems, is away at a conference, and the woman cannot tell us anything about the Baining. Nor can the other women in the room. They do not know about the villages. They are aware of Vunamarita, of course—St. Paul's is a mission station, after all, and a mission station with a history: the Massacre, the Graves of the Martyrs. But Puktas? Wilaimbemki? Poiniara? "We do not know these places," they say. A guide? "We cannot tell you about a guide," they say. "We do not know any Baining."

They don't know any Baining? This comes, I realize, as a double shock. For one thing, I thought they *were* Baining. Obviously, I would have known they were not if I had bothered to observe, because these women do not look anything like Baining—and I feel mortified that I didn't see, as if all New Guineans look the same! But Father Hesse has been so closely associated with the Baining, the people with whom he built his career, that I assumed his assistants would be Baining. Yet obviously this needn't be so. Vunapope is the Catholic mission headquarters for the region, Father Hesse is the archbishop of the region, and most people in the region are Tolai.

Tolai! This is the second shock. The Tolai are the archenemies of the Baining. And it now occurs to me that they are everywhere. Our hotel is run by Tolai. I realize that although I have never actually known any Tolai, I have always so identified with the Baining that I too took them for the enemy and disliked them on a strictly bias basis. I expected they would be aggressive and rude. Yet the Tolai we have met have been so friendly and kind.

These women too try to be helpful, although they cannot answer our questions. Is there a road to Vunamarita? They confer: "We aren't sure, but we think there is a road to Vunamarita," they say. Can we send word ahead to St. Paul's to say that we are coming? They confer again: "No," they say. "We know of no way to get in touch." Is there a road to the mountains? They confer yet again: "No," they say, "we do not believe such a road exists." As for a guide, someone to take us to the bush, they suggest that we ask at the *bung*, the large open market just down the street from our hotel, where the Baining come to sell their taro and peanuts. *Peanuts?* Apparently so.

We thank the women and ask them to tell the father we were here and to mention—or is it perhaps to warn him?—that we will return.

We realize as we leave Vunapope that we have learned almost nothing, but we are too excited for disappointment: we head for Vunadidir. This road, too, is paved, and at first, as we drive through the lush green landscape, the ride is fairly smooth. But soon the asphalt breaks up. Large fissures open before us, extraordinary fissures, earthquake-quality fissures. Jeremy drives slowly, but I fly about the cabin all the same. Ahead we see another pickup truck, and we stay just behind: if it disappears down some crevasse, we will be sure not to follow.

To our relief, we manage to arrive at Vunadidir, a complex of wooden houses that seems as deserted as Vunapope. There is not, we assume, much government here. But even as we're climbing the stairs, a compact, energetic young man emerges from his office and, in English, invites us in. "I am Dominic," he says, offering his hand. We recite the little tale of our return—our listener's surprise prevents this from becoming entirely tedious—and he tells us that James Tapele is at a meeting. "But you can wait," he says, offering in the meantime to assist and proving extremely helpful.

First off, he tells us that the Baining of Wilaimbemki are now indeed at Poiniara. This is something he seems to actually know. To get there, we should charter a boat at Lungalunga. And where is Lungalunga? "Ah," he says, "you drive along the coast, until you see a group of men sitting on the shore: that is Lungalunga, they are the boatmen, and you arrange with them for a ride."

As for Puktas, yes, there is a road. And as it happens, he says, he has a Baining *tambu*—an in-law—who can take us there. "If you are interested, Ignas can take you to Puktas tomorrow." *If we are interested!* We do not ask—we do not even wonder—how he knows so surely that his *tambu* will have time for this or agree to it. We just laugh with surprise: we have set up our trip!

At this point, James Tapele is still at his meeting, but Dominic mentions that a Baining happens to be visiting nearby; he leads us to the house so we can talk to him while we wait. The man seems willing—he climbs down the ladder from the house when Dominic shouts up—and we all exchange greetings, *Atlu!* We settle down on the ground.

This man is not from Puktas or Wilaimbemki, but when we ask about people we knew, he seems to know who we mean. Mlung? Mran? Tuvuan? Takiap? Kyimkyim? Teingan?

The man chews *buai* and studies the ground. "*Ah, em i dai pinis*," he says of Mlung. "He has died." "*Ah, em i dai pinis*," he says of Mran. "He has died." "*Ah, ol i dai pinis*," he says of Tuvuan, Takiap, Kyimkyim, and Teingan. "They have died." It is a roll call of the dead. Even Solmet? "*Ah, em i dai pinis*," he says of Solmet. "*Em tu.*"

Him too? Solmet? This is hard. The other people were older, but Solmet was so young. Just our age. I cannot imagine Solmet, so very vibrant, no longer alive. I picture him that first night in Poiniara, explaining to everyone why Jeremy and I had come. I see him looking cool in his sunglasses, sitting in our hut. I see him the day of the day dance, running with his spear. We say that we are *sori tru*.

By now we are all just staring at the ground, when James Tapele finally appears. He is a big, heavy man, with dark, liquid Baining eyes and a serious, brooding face. He remembers us, he says as we walk to his office. He even remembers our names: Iara and Kusaiki. He was only a child when we were there, and he lived in a nearby village. But, oh yes, he says, Iara and Kusaiki. He really does recall.

Wading In

James Tapele seems restless as we sit in the room, he on one couch, the two of us just opposite, on another: I sense that he is not a comfortable man. But he seems genuinely glad that we are here. He would like to meet with us, he says; he would like to get together and *stori*. We set up a time for the following week.

Driving back, we look back on our youthful disarray and reflect on how well we have done. We have one trip under way: tomorrow we will be in Puktas. We have a good sense of how to approach the other: we have only to reach Lungalunga. And next week we will *stori* with James Tapele. To *stori*: I didn't even know it was a verb. I wonder what any of us will say.

The rest of the day, although we can think of nothing but Puktas, there is little that we need to prepare. We spend the afternoon in Kokopo, wandering around. The town calls up no memories: if we drove through it on the way to Vunapope forty years ago, we don't recall. And in any case it would have changed *after Tavurvur*, expanding to replace Rabaul.

But Kokopo, we feel, cannot replace Rabaul. Kokopo is nothing like Rabaul, with its harbor and stunning bay, its majestic volcanoes, its exuberant encroachment of bush. Kokopo is a town without charm. It is a town of asphalt and shacks, cars and commerce: a gas station and garage, cheap restaurants, supermarkets, a bank, *an Internet Centre*, all looking makeshift and fairly rundown. Still, it is friendly. People stare—there are no other Europeans in the street, no whites, and they have surely seen no whites who look like me, someone as small as they are, with wild hair. They stare, but everyone smiles.

We stop in at the *bung*, with its surprising array of fruits and vegetables: tomatoes, cucumbers, corn, garlic, *muli*, coconuts, taro, greens, and, everywhere, great heaps of *buai*. I had no idea the economy was so majorly betel nut, and though I knew it was

Capitalism in Kokopo

popular—*E, poro, mi dai long buai ya!*—I didn't realize just how popular, and addictive, it is. I haven't yet seen all the signs forbidding chewing and spitting near buildings, and it seems I had forgotten the bright scarlet wads splashed around Baining huts. We cannot find any Baining in the *bung*, and vendors tell us that no Baining are around. We cannot tell whether they have already gone home or whether they didn't come in today.

Yu kam bek tumora, we are told. Early. But it will have to be another day: tomorrow we will be in Puktas.

We stop in at one of the supermarkets that have sprung up since we were here. Supermarkets: a whole new modern world, with Kleenex, paper towels, bottled water, and packaged bread, which we purchase for our trip. We stop in at the Internet Centre lined with computers just waiting to be used. Only one is

Wading In

in action, surrounded by a cluster of young men, playing some game, we assume—but not an Internet game: the Internet, we learn, is down.

In our room, we set up what we need for our trip. We pack up some extra shoes, the paper towels, bottled water, and bread that we bought, which is all the food we'll take—we are hoping to be offered taro. *Taro!*

Jeremy puts the finishing touches on the gift we will bring: an album of photos we took when we were here. We had trouble deciding on a gift: tobacco, the old standby, doesn't seem like much of a gift these days. Then a friend suggested this: a photo album for each village. As I look at the pictures of our house raising in Mlung's hamlet, I wonder if we will see our old hut. Would a house like that survive for forty years? Will anyone still be living in that hamlet? Will anyone we knew still be living?

Over Island Fish we decide to go to bed early: we want to be rested for this trip. We have arranged to meet Dominic and Ignas at nine, at Vunadidir. We don't really know how long it will take to reach Puktas; Dominic guessed two or three hours. I think back to our very first visit: four hours on the dock, all night on the boat, the time spent waiting for Maxie and his tractor, and then hiking in. A road to Puktas! I still can't quite believe it. I picture rolling into the village in a jeep. Clearly, my imaginary road is well paved if we are rolling, and I don't seem to have noticed that what we are driving is not a jeep.

17

Many Rivers to Cross

Puktas, Puktas, Puktas, I think, as we jolt and bump along the Great Fissured Way to Vunadidir. Will we really reach the village? The plans were so casually made. We speculate on the odds that our guide will even show. Pretty low, I suspect.

But I am wrong. He is already there when we arrive, and Dominic introduces us to Ignas, a short young man, with a long face, a bright-red mouth, black teeth, and a disconcerting way of looking down when he speaks. The trip will take "*tripela aua*"—"three hours"—he tells my knees when he has slid in beside Jeremy, who will be driving, and I have settled in the back. I cannot tell if this downward glance is just a tic, a misguided sign of respect, or an effort to look up my skirt.

We set off in high spirits. The road is well paved, and it is empty: no cars or trucks, no pedestrians in the road or even walking by the side of the road. Amazingly, there are bridges, real bridges. I can't recall seeing any bridges forty years ago. This doesn't feel like bush, and I suppose at this point it is suburb. As usual I do not know where we are; I leave this to Jeremy and now to Ignas, our guide.

At this stage in our journey, the road is straightforward—there is only one way to go—and we chat easily as we ride. Ignas tells us that he is from K—I do not catch the name—a village we will pass on the way. We tell him about our stay in Puktas and talk about the people we knew: Mran and Tuvuan, Takiap and Hapaluk, old Tulu, and, of course, Mlung. One by one we name them, and one by one Ignas tells us they are alive. All those people we heard only yesterday had died.

Mran? *"Ah, em i stap yet!"* says Ignas. "He is still alive!" Tuvuan? *"Ah, em i stap yet!"*—"She is still alive." Even Mlung? *"Ah, em i stap yet!"* he laughs, almost giddy. *"Em i lapun tru,"* he adds—"he is a very old man."

Well, of that I'm sure. If Mlung is alive, he is old. But could he be alive? It's true that in Wilaimbemki, old Sireigi remembered Bateson who had been there some forty years before. But Sireigi had been a child when Bateson visited the region, as James Tapele was a child when we were here; Mlung was probably close to forty. He would be eighty now. Does anyone here live that long?

But Mlung! Suddenly, it hits me. I would love to see Mlung. I have always felt so guilty that we didn't visit before leaving the country—I feel guilty now. I understand our exhaustion, our need to simply flee. But we had promised, and he must have felt abandoned. To see him now wouldn't alter that, but still it would make a difference. Something would be redeemed.

But if Mlung is there, we can't simply arrive, visit for an hour, and leave. Will we stay overnight? We aren't prepared. I haven't brought anything I would need—clean underwear, a towel, a toothbrush. No, if Mlung is alive, we will have to return.

While I am reflecting on this, the road has grown rough—it is no longer paved—and we arrive at the first river without a bridge. Jeremy comes to a halt at the water's edge. It isn't a wide river, but we have no idea of the depth. Do we just drive through?

Ignas gets out of the car and speaks to a woman who is standing on the bank. They gesture and point at the water. "*I orait,*" he says when he returns, "It's okay," and Jeremy floors the pedal and plows through. It's exhilarating, and Jeremy is thrilled.

"It's like the car ads on TV," he laughs, "where they tell you, *Do not try this at home.*"

While we are joking, Ignas remarks that the river now is low but later, when we return, it will be high from the afternoon rains. How high? I wonder. Will we be able to get home? Jeremy doesn't seem to hear, and I'm sure that he is feeling too bold and adventurous to worry; we let the comment pass.

As we proceed, the rivers get wider and deeper. Ignas jumps in and out of the truck. Sometimes he speaks with someone by the river who is fetching water or washing clothes; sometimes there is no one around, and he just peers into the water as if it were a crystal ball. Either way, he says, "*I orait,*" every time. I can't help wondering if he really knows. What if we get stuck in the mud? Do we just abandon the truck? We can't call the AAA. And what if the river gets deep in the middle? *What if we sink?* Shouldn't we make sure that our windows are open? Or is it closed? I'm certain there are rules for this.

By now we are deep in the bush. The road we are on is not really a road. It may once have been some kind of road—though none of it has ever been paved—but now it is just a path and very rough. I bounce wildly in my seat, clutching the hand grip firmly and staring out at the dense growth. All I can identify are the tall clumps of bamboo and the huge leaves of wild taro that suggest that there are gardens nearby. But no villages are visible, and apart from the people we meet at rivers, we see only one man, walking briskly, who does not even turn his head to look at

The "road" to Puktas

us, and one small child, who suddenly emerges from the bush, an apparition.

Now, as we drive, nothing is straightforward: the route has many forks with no clear main path. But Ignas seems to bear up well. He will pause for a moment to reflect and then gesture surely with his hand, a flat blade that gives us confidence: right, left, straight ahead.

We move on and on, higher into the Baining Mountains. None of us is talking now; we are fixed on the road, with its roots and stones and a steep drop to the side. Indeed, I am averting my eyes from this drop when suddenly Jeremy stops.

A fallen tree is blocking our path. The three of us get out and approach the tree, a small diplomatic delegation, but there is nothing to negotiate. This is not a little sapling; it is massive. This tree will not be moved. And as it turns out, to move it would be pointless: "No road," says Jeremy, standing on the trunk and peering over to the other side. Not even the kind of path we've been on, he says. Just uncleared bush. So here we are.

In fact, I realize, we have no idea where we are. Ignas hasn't a clue. Even Jeremy—Mr. Map, as I think of him—seems lost. The three of us hover around, staring out over the precipice, while Jeremy tries to gauge our location. "We're much too high," he says. He didn't notice the extent of our climb while he was driving—he was too intent on driving. But Puktas is not this high. Puktas is not a mountain village like Wilaimbemki; it's a subcoastal village, and we are a long way from the coast.

Gazing far down in the distance, Jeremy sees smoke. "You see those huts," he says, pointing to a brownish cluster in the forest. "That must be a village—that could be Puktas."

We have clearly overshot. We will have to go back to find the road.

I nod—but going back means turning around. Our truck, on its narrow path, is faced the wrong way, with a precipice on one side, the mountain on the other, and a tree straight ahead. Personally, I am ready to abandon the truck. But Jeremy, it seems, is in his element, unfazed.

"If I back up, I can turn around," he says, and it is true: there is a spot, some one hundred feet back, where there is a bit of room—but no room for error. I cannot even try to hide my cowardice as I leave the truck and walk down the road. Indeed, as Jeremy turns the truck around, with Ignas guiding from behind, I cannot even watch. I stare out over the precipice. I photograph a hawk, half afraid that I will also catch the truck careening down the mountain, bearing Jeremy straight down to Puktas.

But then, there he is, waving me in.

We resume our places now, a bit subdued. It's getting late, already one o'clock, our visit—if we ever get there—growing shorter by the minute. We do not know where we went wrong or how to right it, but we do know that we need to reach the shore: we need to go *nambis*—to the beach. As we retrace our route to the last river that we crossed, we hope we will find someone to ask, and luckily we do: a group of women watch us approach.

"You should ask the women," Jeremy says to Ignas. But Ignas, we find, will not ask. He shrugs, a Baining shrug: *Kwasik. Nogat.* He doesn't move. He could be Bartleby the Scrivener: *I would prefer not to.* Is he embarrassed? Is he shy? Or, as Jeremy will later joke, is it just that he's a guy and guys—even Baining guys—don't ask for directions? Finally, it is Jeremy who asks the women for the way to the road *nambis*, and we can only hope that those Tok Pisin lessons really took.

As we drive, I wonder how this could have happened. The Baining do not get lost. I cannot even imagine a Baining not knowing the way *nambis*. The Baining know the paths and rivers, the trees, the very rocks in their terrain, and we are not so very far from Ignas's own village. Is the problem that we are in a car, which makes everything look different? Or is Ignas perhaps a special Baining, with a sense of direction like mine?

At last, we reach the water. As we drive along the beach I find myself crying out *Yes!*, feeling the prickle of recognition even before I know where I am. This is New Masawa, and soon we see a group of Baining youngsters hanging out at what must be the mission school at Vunamarita. A few schoolboys rush over, jubilant—about the truck, about us, about the fact that we want to go to Puktas.

"We're from Puktas!" they cry, jumping into the truck. They direct us toward some high grass, which looks nothing at all like a road but does indeed flatten out as we drive, and fifteen minutes later there it is: the little church with the Graves of the Martyrs.

We are here.

For a moment I just stand still, trying to take it all in: the church we sat at so many times, in this same heat, in this same extravagant light, with this same intense, almost suffocating smell of vegetation. I am so back, it's visceral. Time travel. I am twenty-two years old, and I am wearing my little orange Marimekko shift, tied with a string. And what I want is just to sit down and remain here, just be here, in this pocket of memory.

But there isn't time for standing still; we're very late. If we are going to see anyone at all, we need to find some people now. We scramble up the rocks to the path that we took so many times, our young escorts leading the way—and as always, I promptly fall down. The boys pause, wondering no doubt what could be wrong with this curious person who cannot stay upright. Jeremy leans over to give me a hand. It is all slow motion, happening in two time zones at once: I am sixty-two and I am twenty-two, and I am holding everyone up, again.

"Maybe you should go on without me," I say.

Jeremy simply stares at me. "You've come halfway around the world for this," he says.

So I have. And half a lifetime as well.

The young men lead on, and we follow them to a hamlet where a woman is sitting in her *haus kuk*, her arm around a child. The child leans into the woman, the woman leans into the child; they look so sad they could be grieving.

The expression is so Baining I'm overwhelmed. We exchange greetings: *Amrs!* The woman's expression doesn't change. She shows no surprise at seeing us, two white strangers who have just appeared, out of the blue. We sit down and tell her who we are, why we have come. Her expression still doesn't change. She nods calmly. *So you have come. So you are here. Amrs! No big deal.*

It all feels so familiar. And indeed, the hamlet itself looks the same; it is the kind of hamlet we know. The little clearing, the bare ground without a blade of grass. The *haus kuk*. The house nearby: a true Baining house, it isn't even raised up on stilts. The thatched roofs, the sheets of corrugated tin. The woman with her melancholy air, her sad demeanor.

Yet as I watch her talking with the young men who have brought us, as I watch her glancing through the album of photos we have brought, I find myself wondering if this woman really is sad. Whatever her expression, when she speaks she doesn't sound sad. For the first time I question this idea we had of Baining sadness, whether it is only a facial expression that we have misread. A cultural gap. We share the expression—but why have I assumed that we share its meaning as well?

Jeremy asks about some of the people we knew. Mlung, first of all.

"*Ah, em i dai pinis,*" she says matter-of-factly.

So he has died, after all. Of course. And the others? Mran, Tuvuan, Tulu, Takiap, Hapaluk, Sil?

"*Ah, ol i dai pinis,*" she says. "*Ol i dai pinis.*"

Well, I think, by now this woman probably *is* sad, now that we have evoked this litany of death.

"*Ah,*" we say. "*Mitupela sori tru.*"

I feel that these deaths come even harder now because Ignas built up such hope, such expectations. What on earth was he thinking when he said that all these people were alive? Did he lie or didn't he know? And if he didn't know, why did he say anything? Perhaps he told us what he thought we would like to hear. Yet he had to know we'd learn the truth when we got to Puktas. Perhaps he thought, with him as guide, we would never get to Puktas!

He sits beside us now, his face, his eyes, completely blank, even as he hears about these deaths that he denied. A strange man, I think, perhaps the black sheep of the family, a ne'er-do-well: *his tambu Dominic has to find him work*.

But Kanga, the woman is saying, Kanga is alive. Kanga! How I would love to see Kanga. But it seems that we won't.

"*Em i stap antap*," the woman tells us—"he lives farther up in the mountains"—and we realize there won't be time. It is already past two.

The youngsters lead us on to another hamlet, where two young women are sitting in a *haus kuk*, each with an infant she is nursing, and two older children, the babies' siblings, I assume. Once again I am struck by how familiar everything is. The women are wearing *laplaps*; only one has a *meri* blouse. They are sitting under a corrugated tin roof, on a worn woven mat, splashes of betel juice around them on the hard cleared earth. A skinny dog sleeps behind them. There is little here, and almost nothing that wouldn't have been here before. It all seems just as it was.

We greet them—*Amrs!*—and tell them who we are. They show no surprise, of course, but they are welcoming; they smile. We sit down on some wood for a visit, and one of the young men we came with offers *buai*. Curiously, he offers some to Jeremy and me but hesitates before offering any to Ignas, the only one of our little party who would want it. When he does offer, belatedly, a bit stiffly, Ignas accepts, a bit stiffly. There is something unfriendly between them, but I can't begin to guess what it is.

We show the women the photos in the book, wondering who they will know. These women are very young; although they are mothers, they are still, I suspect, in their teens. One woman identifies Tomamia: her father, she says. Young Tomamia. I remember him well. The young man who made off with our bat!

We sit in silence. I try to find something to say. I ask about the small pig that has just trundled into the bush: I don't remember pigs in Puktas hamlets, only in the garden houses. "Oh, yes," the younger woman says. "There are many pigs in Puktas." So that is that.

Her baby catches my eye, and I smile. The baby gurgles and laughs. We continue to make eyes at each other. The mother smiles, and I smile back. I grow tense with this, saying nothing. I feel that I am boring these people, but I can't think of anything to say. Nor apparently can they. Or Jeremy. Is the problem just

Puktas hamlet (2008)

that all of us are shy? I raise my eyebrows at the baby, who gurgles some more. The mother smiles, and I smile again. My face begins to ache from all the smiling. There is so much goodwill here, but such a huge chasm of mutual reserve. It is all so uncomfortable and so familiar, so known.

"How did we do it?" Jeremy says, so quietly I almost miss it.

How did we do it. What an extraordinary thing for him to say. He says it almost casually, but at once I feel the warm shock of it ripple through me.

Looking back all these years, all I have seen is defeat, all I have focused on is what we failed to do—exactly as I have been doing now. Not once in all my efforts to describe, to explain, to understand have I acknowledged not just the difficulty of what we did but the fact that we did it.

In truth, I'm not sure exactly what Jeremy is referring to as he sits here, like me, I suspect, in two bodies at once, one of them young and skinny and wearing a forest green *laplap*. Does he mean life in the jungle? How we learned to navigate mud, how we waded through rivers and nonchalantly picked off the leeches, how we simply moved our sleeping mats when giant roaches fell on us, in mating pairs, from the beams? Or does he mean life in the village? Dealing with the lack of privacy, the children staring up through the floorboards, or the lack of cleanliness, the gobs of betel spit in the huts that we would inadvertently brush against or the dog shit on the paths that I seldom failed to step in?

Or does he mean this—and I think it must be this—the countless visits exactly like the one we are sitting through now: the niceness and politeness, the boredom and guilt, the blame and self-blame, the strain of seeing it through, so that whatever came of our sojourn at least there would be goodwill. Not once have I simply appreciated and forgiven those younger selves. And here is Jeremy, appreciating and forgiving us both—even me. We are here together, I feel, for the very first time.

By now it is time to leave. Already the rivers will be swollen, and it will be dark before we reach home. We say good-bye, *Amrs!* We tell the women we will give the book of photos to James Tapele—he will give it to the councilor from Puktas—and we follow the youngsters we came with back to the truck.

At St. Paul's we find some women tending the Graves of the Martyrs: the Bainings' eternal penance. The women do not know us; they have never heard of Lukun and Kuluga. But they are happy to see us, they are excited to see the photos, which they study, calling out faces they know, and they are pleased to find this ride across the river: they are done here for the day, and they are ready to go home. Suddenly, there are more of them—I cannot see where so many people have come from—and they all clamber into the truck.

Everyone is gay and noisy when we reach the river, where we see that another pickup truck is stopped at the bank. Jeremy pulls up behind it. Is there some reason these people won't cross? Some reason we shouldn't cross either?

Ignas scouts it out. The truck is simply broken. "*Em i bagarap,*" he reports. There is no need to worry.

But Ignas is wrong. By this time, since it has rained in the mountains, the water is deep, and our truck—now laden down with half a village—sags. Partway over, water streams through the cab. *Ay!* shout the people in the back. *Ay!* shouts the man beside me. *Ay!* I shout as I try to grab shoes, paper towels, bread off the floor. But we make it, if soggily, and our passengers descend and wave us farewell.

It is just the three of us now, and we are quiet as we ride. We realize that we are hungry. We had counted on taro that never appeared, and we have to make do with our sorry loaf of sliced bread. We plow on, bouncing on the road, slogging through the rivers, chewing spongy bread, until suddenly Ignas announces that here is where he is getting out.

Here? Is he really just abandoning us?

He is. His village is nearby.

"But how will we get back?" I ask.

Ignas doesn't think we'll have a problem. Nor does Jeremy, it seems. Perhaps by now Jeremy is just happy to see the back of Ignas. When he has left, I slide into his seat up front as though he never existed. We don't mention what a terrible guide he has been.

It is dark long before we reach the Great Fissured Way, and dark here is very dark: there are no lights on these roads. Jeremy drives cautiously, afraid of getting lost or dropping into some pit, but even more afraid of hitting one of the dozens of people walking, sitting, chatting in the road, oblivious, it seems, of any danger.

At last we reach Kokopo, and KVR: we are hungry and tired, but we have made it back in pretty good shape. This cannot be said of the truck. It is covered with mud. It smells rancid from river water. It is scratched. Although it is hard to see very much in the lights of the parking lot, we are pretty sure that we see dents.

Jeremy grabs some Kleenex and begins to wipe a window.

"Oh, Jer," I laugh, shaking my head.

We clean up quickly in our unit and just squeak into dinner before they close for the night. We have the dining room to ourselves and the very last portion of Island Fish. We're so tired, but so thoroughly awake, so alive, so lit up. Yet we sit in such silence we might be Baining. Neither of us talks. I think there is far too much to say.

18

The River of Death

Our fourth day in Kokopo and it is only now that we will see Rabaul—I can't believe it has taken this long. It's true we have been there once, but only in the evening, and though we saw a gorgeous sunset on the bay, it quickly grew too dark to see the town. Our goal that night was dinner at the Phoenix, the Hamamas restaurant known for its Chinese cuisine. If we could not, in good conscience, rent a room at the tainted inn, we could still, we decided, eat their food.

After dinner, our conscience had its doubts. The place, dark and formal, seemed a throwback to other days. The only other diners were two white men—Germans, maybe Dutch—talking business (mining or logging, no doubt) and a mixed-race couple with two children all dressed up as if for the Raj. The maître d', a handsome New Guinean woman with shrewd mocking eyes that couldn't place us, wasn't shy about asking who we were.

"The Baining?" she said, when we told her our little tale. She sounded proud that she had never heard of them. And she was amused that we were staying at KVR: she seemed to find this hilarious. "At KVR?" she laughed. "No, really—at *KVR*?"

I felt glad to be at KVR.

Whether KVR is glad to have us, however, I am not so sure. The day starts early with a call from our friendly porter-driver-man-of-all-trades.

"Good morning!" he says, all sprightly. "What did you do to the truck?"

He is polite. He does not say, "What the hell did you do to the truck?" or "What the fuck did you do to the truck?" And in fact, he is not so much angry as sad when Jeremy meets him in the parking lot and they examine the vehicle, only yesterday so shiny and proud, now filthy, nicked, dented, and reeking of river.

We will pay for the damage, we assure him, and it turns out it won't cost very much: there are advantages to living in the fourth world. Moreover, they will do repairs the next day, and do them fast: it will be only a matter of hours. But however they fix up this truck, we know they cannot restore it to its pristine beauty. Nor can we eradicate the stench: the aerosol we spray blends in to create a nauseating miasma. We open the windows and drive on.

Our plan for the day is to go to Lungalunga, to charter a boat to Poiniara—for tomorrow or the next day—and then circle back to Rabaul. Jeremy has mapped out a route. The road that he has chosen starts out well, as most roads here seem to do. We pass through a suburb filled with low, well-kept houses, bright ornamental gardens, and a vast array of missions, each with its church and its school. This, I think, must be middle-class life in Kokopo, though there is little evidence of life here: we see almost no one at all.

Soon, though, this road grows even worse than the Great Fissured Way. Massive roots invade the path already narrowed by a shallow ditch on either side, and great gobs of pavement have disappeared. I find it hard to believe that anyone uses this road; we haven't seen a single vehicle, and I suggest that we turn around. I don't think this can be right.

But it is. "*Em i stret*," we are assured by an elderly couple who flag us down for a ride to a clinic on the coast, which they promise lies just ahead. Once again, with this pair and the entourage that has suddenly appeared to accompany them, we seem to be carrying half a village: our poor truck, belly-down, crawls to the bay, where our passengers thank us cheerfully, depart right, and point us left.

As we follow the coast road, skirting potholes the size of small cars, I realize that I have no idea what we are looking for. There won't be a sign that says "Lungalunga": there aren't any signs.

"Men," says Jeremy. "We're looking for some men."

And there they are, a group of men sitting on the shore, just waiting: we have arrived.

"*Apinun*," we greet an older man who seems to be in charge: he at any rate commands a rock, while the others sit around him on the ground.

"*Apinun*," he replies.

The other men inch closer, while some women across the road, a few holding babies, approach to watch. As usual, everyone stares, but here, no one smiles. For the first time in New Britain, I do not feel that the atmosphere is friendly.

Jeremy says that we want to hire a boat to take us to Poiniara. Near Pondo plantation, he adds. The man takes this in, thinks it over, and states a price, which he proceeds to explain. He breaks down the cost of petrol, the cost for the boat, the cost of people and time. As he goes on, incomprehensibly for my limited Tok Pisin, I suspect depreciation may even figure in. The fellow is a CPA. But his price, although higher than we had expected, sounds fair. We settle on a day.

But it turns out—and I should have known—that it is not this man who will be taking us: he is the boss. He invites us to shake hands with the fellow who will steer the boat. This is a young man, very young, a youngster really, though he is missing all his front teeth.

As we finish our negotiations and say good-bye, I realize that I do not feel at ease with this at all. But I cannot say exactly why. Is it the unfriendliness? Do I feel some threat in the air? Do I fear that once aboard we will be mugged? Is it just our boatman's youth? *Is it his teeth?*

I'm not sure, so I say nothing, but as we drive to Rabaul, my discomfort does not abate: it deepens. I find that worries swirl. Does this youth truly know the way? Can he handle a boat, even in a storm? If we capsize, will he know what to do? I can barely swim, no matter that I "passed" my college swim test. I am hardly able to tread water. And are there sharks here? *Giant squid?*

"You know, I really don't like it," I finally say. "This boat trip makes me nervous."

"But why didn't you say?" Jeremy asks.

"My qualms were so vague," I say. "It was only a feeling. It wasn't something I could name." And I still can't. I truly hope it wasn't just the teeth!

I expect that Jeremy will be annoyed: after all, we have already made these plans. But he isn't. To my surprise, he takes it up. Perhaps because this fear is so unlike me: this is not my kind of worry, safety, mere life and death—it isn't like work, or getting fat. Perhaps he himself feels uneasy as well. And perhaps something has changed between us: amazingly, it suddenly occurs to me, we haven't argued once on this trip.

"Why don't we stop by the Kulau Lodge," he says. "It's on the way. They might recommend someone else to take us. They might even charter boats themselves."

The Kulau Lodge! I didn't realize that this inn was still around. Forty years ago, for the Europeans of Rabaul, this was very much the place to be. A beautiful setting on the water. A fancy dining room. I remember we dressed up and came for dinner once—a splurge—and met the *kiap* here. An expat fairyland, but we enjoyed it all the same.

"But why aren't we staying *here*?" I ask as we walk through the grounds to the office, remembering what a special place this was. "Too colonialistic? Did they shoot a New Guinean too?"

"No, no," Jeremy says. "It was the online reviews. Broken toilets. Rats. Bugs the size of birds."

Others too must have read those reviews. No one is here. The doors on all the cabins are closed; the main building is locked. The place seems abandoned, devoid not only of guests but of owners, caretakers, signs of life. I wonder if they are even in business.

We have just decided to leave when a young woman appears—out of nowhere, it seems—and asks if she can help. She is lovely, slender and graceful, Eurasian I think, and well dressed. She seems professional; she speaks English. I wonder what she can be doing in this deserted resort. Surely, I think, she could do better.

We ask if they charter boats, but as by now we expect, they do not, although she says that at one time they did. But she can recommend someone who does, and she will give us his telephone number. We follow her inside.

While she is searching through files, I study the large open dining room, flipping through my own files of memory, trying to picture how it was. I think I can recall exactly where we sat that night for dinner. But I am inventing: the room, she says, has been redone since then, many times.

Forty years! She is too young to imagine forty years. For her, the crucial number is fourteen, the year that matters, 1994. *Before* and *after Tavurvur*, she says: before, things were good; and after, they weren't. There are few tourists in Rabaul these days. The businessmen are mostly gone. And then, she adds, it is just her and her mother now, since her father left. I am sure there is that "before" and "after" as well.

This explains who she is, or at any rate why she is here, and by now I am framing a story: how her white father abandoned her Asian mother and left them in the lurch with this hotel. But where does this story go? Will this stunning girl, who seems so intelligent and competent, just stay on here? Will she hang in for her mother's sake? Will she give her life to this empty, dying inn?

"Actually," she says, interrupting my reverie, "the men at Lungalunga would be fine, you know." It seems the trip to Poiniara isn't difficult; the boatmen just follow the coast. People here, she says, view the Lungalunga fellows as a taxi service.

"But you can call Stephen Woolcott," she adds, handing us a card. "Stephen will take care of you."

Stephen Woolcott. I feel guilty just hearing the name—so white, so very English. So is it race that is the issue here? *This is even worse than the teeth.*

In Rabaul we need a phone, we need a restroom, we need lunch, and to our dismay we end up at Hamamas again: a white person's place for white people's needs. The woman at reception remembers us and lets us use the phone, but Stephen isn't in. The maître d' remembers us as well. "Still at KVR?" she laughs mockingly, shaking her head.

Today the dining room is entirely empty except for one woman in the corner who we think must be the owner. She is reading a book about Vietnam, and we wonder, meanly, if she and her husband are planning another colonial-style inn. This one hasn't much of a future.

And now at last we can see Rabaul. We wander around the port and then head to the market, the famous Rabaul *bung*, still busy, though now just a fraction of what it once was. We don't see any Baining here, selling their taro and peanuts, but we buy two woven handbags from a woman who says that she is from the Sepik. The streets around the *bung* are bustling with people, all New Guineans, and all locally owned shops. Steamships and BP's, the white people's stores where we once bought everything, have closed.

There is not so very much to see right here, and we drive to the Vulcanological Observatory, which is just outside the town, atop a hill. We pass a checkpoint along the way, but we have no sense of what they are checking: the guards smile broadly and reach into the cab to shake our hands. It turns out that we cannot

Ash cloud of Tavurvur, seen from Mango Ave. in Rabaul

Tavurvur and the scrub growth where downtown Rabaul used to be

tour the observatory itself without an appointment, but from the summit the view is spectacular. We watch Tavurvur billow. Jeremy photographs Rabaul, a panorama of ruins.

So far we have been only in the area of the town that has been restored, although it seems that I haven't fully understood this. When we drive down from the observatory, I am still expecting to see Mango Ave. But this is it, Jeremy says, as we pull up at the end of the much-loved street. The end of the road. I still do not really understand. How can this be it? I had expected to see remains—not nothing. But straight ahead there is only ash.

"Did you know?" I ask Jeremy. But, of course, he knew. The question is why I didn't. Every report said the town had been destroyed. I have read this myself many times. Indeed, I know the facts by heart. I could write the report.

The River of Death

On September 19, 1994, the eruption of Tavurvur and Vulcan triggered heavy rain that mixed with ash plumes to form mud—falling mud that crushed the houses of Rabaul. In the months that followed, as ash continued to fall, it covered the remnants of the town. Soon after the first eruption—before much information could even be obtained—the Hawaiian Volcano Observatory could report with assurance that Rabaul had been "nearly totally destroyed."

What part of *destroyed* had I failed to understand?

I leave the car and gaze down what had been Mango Ave. and is now just a stub. As I stare straight ahead, along a line of telephone poles, I finally get it. Perhaps I had to see. Or not see. There is no Mango Ave. It's gone. The ANU house where we stayed is gone. The newsagent where I bought my newspapers

Mango Ave. in Rabaul—after the volcano

and Penguins and trashy books is gone. The movie theater, the restaurants, the mysterious Chinese trade stores, the house where we picked up Loki—all gone, everything crushed and buried.

My eyes fill up with ash. They burn with it.

As we drive back to Kokopo, it is hot in the truck, but there is no point in turning on the air: the stench of river seems even stronger than before, and if we close the windows we will choke. We move slowly leaving town, caught in traffic—workmen are repairing the road—and I can see the heavy soot that has settled on the plants and shrubs that line the way. A green and black decor. It is hard to understand how they can breathe. I am amazed that they survive.

I feel tired when we get back to KVR. Deeply tired. I dislike napping in this heat: I tend to wake up feeling drugged and groggy, lost, I don't know where I am. But now I have to sleep: my eyes are closing on their own. Jeremy and I lie down close together, our legs entwined despite the heat.

In my dream I am standing alone on a road and looking down a long, narrow path. Everything is dark, a greeny dark, and I know that this path ahead is the river of death. "The river of death," I murmur, waking up. "I was standing at the river of death." I feel drugged and lost, just as I had feared, and for a moment I don't know where I am. But as we lie very still, our legs still entwined despite the heat, we both know exactly where I was.

19

Back Eddy

By midweek we are restless to get to Poiniara: we see this as the focus of our journey. It is not, like Puktas, a return to *place*: after all, we never lived in Poiniara; we spent only one night in the village, which wasn't yet completely a village when we were here. But Poiniara, in our minds, is Wilaimbemki: the Wilaimbemkina we knew built this village, they lived there, their children live there now. The connection runs deep. And we have no idea what we will find. They grow cash crops now: Will there be money? Will they have goods? Will the Baining now be *consumers*? I think back to that store they wanted us to run. Are they running a store themselves these days? And who are *they*: will anyone we knew still be alive?

But although we are anxious to just get there—although we would like to go the very next day—Stephen Woolcott cannot manage it until Sunday. "That could be best," Jeremy says, reluctant as we are to wait. If we cannot let the Baining know that we are coming—and so far we haven't found a way—church, at least, will bring everyone together in one place.

We wait, using skills that we learned right here in New Guinea to fill up time.

First off, we have to return to Lungalunga, to tell the young boatman that we have changed our plans: we can't simply fail to appear. This is a task I would truly like to skip. I feel bad that we are deserting him and anxious as well: Lungalunga did not feel friendly to start with—just how angry will he be? And his companions? As we ride I picture the two of us standing on the shore and the group of boatmen closing in. But as it turns out, the young man is alone, and though taken aback he does not appear to be angry. Indeed, in his surprise he looks vulnerable. But that, of course, could be the teeth.

In any case, I have no regrets. Stephen Woolcott seems eminently competent; he is nothing like Ignas. His boat, he has told us, has life vests: I will be safe. It has a canopy: I will be dry. And I do not even have to feel too guilty: Stephen is not the whitebread expat I had expected. Like the young woman at the Kulau Lodge, and just as beautiful, he appears to be Eurasian, and for him, as for her, this is home. He grew up here; he is married to a New Guinean woman. "I can't imagine living anywhere else," he says. Though he adds that as a diving guide, he is finding things hard these days: diving tours no longer flourish as they did. *After Tavurvur* is understood: its ashes have fallen everywhere.

With time to explore the area, we drive our rancid truck wherever there are roads. We visit plantations, making our way along rows of cacao: sometimes we see workers, but no one objects to our intrusion. We visit places we would have judged too "touristy" to bother with forty years ago: a small museum with dusty relics, broken masks, faded maps, and rusting World War II aircraft on the lawn; the peaceful Bita Paka War Cemetery, with graves of those who died in that war, fighting here in New Britain. We return to the Vulcanological Observatory—this time, by appointment—and watch them track volcanic activity around the world as well as right outside their door. From on high we watch Tavurvur smoke. "At night," says the guide, "you can see the fire."

We drop in on the Kokopo *bung* and talk with some Southern Baining women who are sitting under a large umbrella selling taro. The tubers are beautiful, and huge: I don't remember taros this size. How long would it take to cook them? I wonder. I can hear Mlung whining, *Lukun, ating i no tan*. And I'm sure he would be right, it wouldn't be done.

The women seem happy to meet us and to hear about Puktas and Wilaimbemki, Northern Baining villages they do not know. "Where do you come from?" they ask. "How long did it take you to get here?" Journey questions, of course.

We stop in at the Internet Café, as we jokingly call the Internet Centre, for the amusement of hearing, yet again, that the Internet is down. And we finally eat dinner at Rapopo—so highly recommended by the Chinese lady on the plane. It is filled with tourists and businesspeople, whites who have come for diving and deals. We are so glad that we aren't staying here. And their Island Fish, I note with satisfaction, is not as good as the Island Fish at KVR.

But although we enjoy our wandering about, we can't help feeling that we are wasting time—until we visit the Agmark office in Kokopo. Agmark is a company that buys cocoa from the plantations along the coast of East New Britain, and their office isn't far from KVR. We drop in casually: we hope to get some useful information, perhaps some way of contacting the Baining before we arrive, but we have no great expectations for this visit. We do not expect the man we meet.

"Ah, the Baining," smiles Graham McNally as he greets us warmly. An agricultural worker somewhat younger than us, a Scotsman, I think, he arrived in the area years ago with a Peace

Corps kind of organization and stayed on. As we sit in his tiny office, we tell him our well-worn little tale and chat about Wilaimbemki, a village he never saw, and he talks about how much has changed since he first came, since independence, and *after Tavurvur.*

For one thing, he says, the Europeans have moved out, abandoning the plantations that were only marginally profitable. Marginally profitable? This comes as a surprise. I had always thought those plantations were not just exploitative but lucrative, rolling in dough. Apparently not. And then, he says, the Baining at Poiniara now own the land. This too comes as a surprise, and good news. The Pondo plantation would now be theirs.

But the Baining, it seems, do not want to manage it. "They want us—they want Agmark—to stay on," he says. "'We're farmers,' they insist, 'not businessmen.'" He seems bemused by this but also impressed. "These people know so clearly who they are and what they want—I really admire them," he says. "I admire their humility, and their shrewdness."

Shrewdness! I have never heard the Baining called shrewd before: neighboring people, missionaries, government officials have tended to see them as somewhat "slow." And who has seen their humility as a virtue? It has generally been held against them, judged as a tribal inferiority complex in relation to the Tolai, or as depression.

Yet he is right. It is as if this rare perceptive man has cleared the bush and opened up this other view. I think about how measured the Baining are, how calmly they deal with life as it comes, and how very strong the Baining identity actually is. And if they insist on claiming ignorance, how refreshing in this world of arrogant peoples and people—all laying claim to superior ethnic or personal wisdom—to find one people ready to acknowledge how much they don't know.

"I'm so glad you like the Baining too," he says as I am reflecting on all of this—and I nearly blush. He is referring, I feel sure, to the many people he has met—those *other* people—who do not like the Baining, who find them enigmatic, unfriendly, "uncooperative," even mockable. But I hardly deserve his implicit accolade: *I* was one of those people.

Yet, thinking back to my journals, the wretched accounts I tried to write, I realize how much those feelings have changed. I do like the Baining now, enormously. I too appreciate their humility, their reticence, their sane reductiveness, their ability to accept life without undue fuss. When did this happen, this total shift? I can't say. But I do not believe that the cause is forgetfulness: I haven't forgotten. Not at all. I would like to think of it as age and recognition. Distance, of course: I'm not living with the Baining now. And acceptance: I am not a Baining after all.

"Let me know how they're doing," he says as we leave, and we promise that we'll return with news. But as for getting in touch with them beforehand, he tells us that there isn't a way: we will simply have to appear.

At last it is Saturday. We are more than ready for this trip. We think about preparing, but there isn't anything to do: Stephen has even said he'll pack a lunch. Our only task is to get a good night's sleep and arrive early at his house. He has warned us that it is rainy season where we are headed, across the peninsula, and the water will get rougher by the hour: in the morning we should get out fast.

I'm so excited, I'm afraid that I may not sleep at all, but I drift off at once. At midnight, though, we are jolted awake by cries. "Please. Open the door. I beg of you," a man is shouting over and over. "Please. Open the door. I beg of you."

At first, still groggy, I think that he's at our door, but then I realize he's at the next unit over. Has someone locked him in? Or out? Is he in trouble? I get up and knock on the adjoining wall.

"Are you all right?" I call. "Are you okay?"

This seems a bit foolish, since it's fairly evident he isn't "okay." There is no reply.

"*Yu laik mi kolim polis?*" I say, switching to Tok Pisin, which seems even more foolish, since he himself has been yelling in English, and whatever is happening there, it isn't likely that he wants the police. Again, there is no reply.

"Give it up," says Jeremy, watching from the bed, and I do. But the plaintive cries persist through the night, and I lie awake, fretting: I will never wake up on time, I'll collapse the next day, this precious journey will be ruined.

But although we do not sleep for more than three hours, we are so psyched for this trip that we're up before dawn and we reach Stephen's house on time. He urges us to leave at once. The water, he says, is already rough, and his diving boat, although sturdy, isn't large. Indeed, with a bench on either side, two rows of seats set low between, and no cabin, it seems that eight more people would fill it up.

I think I know about rough: I remember that knockabout voyage from Pondo with our truant plantation managers in a speedboat far smaller than this. But in fact this is worse than I recall. And I am not as fit as I was. Sitting on the bench, clutching a pole, the vibrations piercing my spine, I am shaken so violently that I rise in the air. Jeremy takes me around, afraid that I'll fly overboard. The canopy I so admired turns out to be mere ornament: a horizontal wind blows rain in my face, soaking and tangling my hair. My little jacket hood is useless: I will look like Medusa when we arrive.

Back Eddy

We follow the coast, passing Ataliklikun Bay and Vunamarita. From here we can see the large bald area where logging must have taken place. We pass Lassul Bay and *Wara Pukpuk*, "Crocodile River," says Stephen. "But there aren't any crocodiles," he smiles. The three of us agree that probably at some time there were.

Mostly, though, we do not talk. It's too difficult to hear above the noise of the motor and the wind, and we don't seem to have much to say. We have told Stephen why we are here, but I cannot gauge his response. He doesn't seem to have one. It may be that he finds us so weird, living in the bush, *returning* to the bush, that he has muted his response. He is very polite, and we are clients after all. Or it may be that as a guide in New Guinea, he has met so many eccentrics that we barely warrant notice. In any case Jeremy and I are distracted by the shifting elements: the intermittent rain, the intermittent sun, the change in the wind as we move from open to protected spaces, the spectacular reefs—and by whatever lies ahead.

"Poiniara!" says Jeremy, gesturing toward the beach. It has been just three hours, precisely as Stephen said.

We arrange to meet up with Stephen in a few hours' time and wade to shore, where we see several youngsters walking on the beach. I cannot imagine what we look like, two white foreigners, wild-haired and disheveled, emerging from the sea, half hopping as we struggle barefoot through the sharply pebbled mud.

But the youngsters do not seem perturbed; they take us in stride. Clearly, they are Baining.

"Which way is Poiniara?" Jeremy asks them, while I am putting on my shoes. He explains who we are, how we once lived in Wilaimbemki and are returning now to visit.

"Iara and Kusaiki," he says.

"Iara and Kusaiki!" they call out. "Iara and Kusaiki!"

The call echoes back to the bush, and a group of young men gathers around.

We smile at each other: incredibly, they know who we are.

As we leave the shore heading inland to the village, the young men call out words, the names of plants or birds. "*Angalip*," they say, pointing to a huge nut tree. "*Angwatium*," they cry when we see a crow. It is as if they are reteaching us Baining, reintroducing us to the terrain.

I hear Jeremy talking to the youngsters as they walk just ahead, but I do not join in; I am focused on the hike. I am not afraid of this hike. I know that it is brief. I know it isn't steep. We aren't even walking quickly. And it isn't raining now: the sun is broiling down. But I have to work to keep up, I'm still dazed from the vibration of the boat, and my head feels oppressed by my wet and tangled hair.

One young man walks beside me as we reach the bush, offering his arm to assist at any rock or root that might trip me. He's so gallant: he reminds me of the *komitiman* such a long time ago. (What committee? If I knew, I can no longer recall.) Indeed, he is so gallant that when we come to a river—I am just removing my shoes—he and another fellow start to pick me up. As if I were a *misis*! I have never been carried anywhere, my whole body stiffens, set to refuse—but I'm surprised at how easily I give in. We really have no time for my pride. I will only slow us down. And no one cares.

As the path winds through the bush, we cross this river three times before we reach the first of the village huts. One of our escorts beats on the bamboo wall.

"Iara and Kusaiki!" he says to the man who appears at the door. This man seems old enough for us to know him, but I can't place who he is, though he certainly seems to know us.

"*Atlu!*" we greet him. "*Atlu!*" he replies, casually, as if we had left not forty years ago but just the other day. "*Iara*," he says to Jeremy, "*wannem bilong yu, em i dai pinis.*"—"Your namesake has died." Gentle Iara. But my *wannem*, Solmet's wife, Kusaiki, is still alive, he says, although she does not live here in Poiniara.

We trudge on to the village clearing, pausing only once, when I stop to braid my hair, which is blocking my vision and clogging up my brain. Our young friends knock on houses as we go, calling out our names and gathering followers, mostly other youngsters who dance and swarm, surrounding us with bodies

Poiniara (2008)

and noise. They are not blasé: they may take us in stride, but they are excited to see us.

We seek out older faces, people we might have known. And a few, a very few, are there. We meet Young Teingan—as we used to call him, to distinguish him from our older friend—though he is no longer young but a thin old man with rheumy eyes. And two of Kyimkyim's daughters! Sawilki, who looks sturdy and handsome, hugs me with such strength I nearly tumble. Memories stream back of her sitting next door, a young girl, helping her mother, Madeilas, who has yet another baby at her breast. We stare at each other, reconfiguring what we see, finding familiar features through the years, our eyes tearing up. We are really back.

In the clearing, it grows chaotic as everyone presses to see the book of photos we have brought. Jeremy holds it out in front of him, but this method is clumsy and doesn't work. Unless he lets it go, they can't see; if he lets it go, with so many grasping hands, it will be ruined.

Things are feeling out of control when a slender young man appears and calmly takes charge. "My name is Edward," he tells us in English. "I am a teacher," he adds. Addressing the villagers in rapid Baining, he has everyone sit down. People form a large mass in front of us, older folk in the back, youngsters closer in, and the youngest—the children and babies—with the women in the middle, under a tree. When everyone is quiet, Edward asks us questions and translates our answers into Baining.

"They are Americans," he says. "They are from Boston. They lived in Wilaimbemki long ago—*foti yia!*—to learn Baining customs. And now they have returned. They have come a very long way. They have brought a 'memory book,'" he says, holding the photograph album aloft. "This memory book will remain here with us, in the village."

It's an excellent performance. He explains everything lucidly and succinctly, far better than we could have ourselves, and everyone listens. I love the term he has invented: a "memory book." He seems so intelligent, so fast, so very capable. We can't help thinking of Solmet that night in Poiniara so many years before.

Jeremy speaks next. "My wife and I came to Wilaimbemki a long time ago," he says. "Forty years. We came to learn the Baining ways, and we lived as the Baining lived. We were very young. And the Baining of Wilaimbemki took care of us. They gave us taro, they gave us wood, they taught us their language." Standing beside him I watch the audience as he speaks: they nod but sit very still. "We have come back now to thank the Baining for taking such good care of us," he says. "We are happy to be here, and happy to find the village doing so well."

He goes on a bit more but keeps it brief, and it's a good speech, warm and real. People look pleased. I know that I too should speak, but I am shy. And as I look on, as I watch Jeremy now, so easy and assured, so like and unlike that nervous young man first greeting the Baining in Puktas, I realize that it's okay if I don't speak: this is *his*. I just smile and smile.

At some point I realize that I am dizzy. The heat, the crowd, the emotion—*all the smiling*—have gone to my head; I need to sit down. Jeremy tells Edward, and soon someone brings a board that he sets down under a tree.

"They call this a *lapun sit*," says Edward, "a seat for old folks."

Old folks! It takes a moment for this to settle in. But it is true. I am old folks now. This is why they can carry me across the river: not because I'm a *misis*, but because I'm old. This is why I can sit here: not because I'm a *misis*, but because I'm old. And it feels all right, being old. I feel enormous relief.

As I sit under the tree, below the level of the crowd, I can pull into myself for a moment. Looking around, I realize that as in Puktas there is little here and nothing that wouldn't have been here before. There are houses around the clearing, the same kind of houses the Baining used to live in. But nothing else. Just bush, the clearing, and these houses. The village still feels so distant from everything, so isolated, so remote.

Of course, I know there have been changes, changes I cannot see. People grow cacao now; they live on allotments; they own the plantation. The women no longer wear grass tuffets, they all wear *laplaps* and *meri* blouses. The youngsters sport T-shirts, with pictures of Bob Marley, or Mike Lee, or Mickey Mouse. Still, from my perspective, sitting here, now could almost be then.

While I am time wandering, Edward comes over to introduce me, with pride, to his mother. She is a lovely woman, slender and fragile looking for a Baining. "My father," he tells me, "was Langi." Langi! Kyimkyim's son. But Langi, he says, has died. As with Solmet, I have trouble believing that he has died. Such a young man, even younger than we were, a boy when we knew him. I remember him bringing me grubs when Jeremy was away. I see him dressed in his *bilas* for the spear dance, his parents, Kyimkyim and Madeilas, hovering over him. I am unable to age him in my mind.

"We live *hariap* here," Edward says to us later, when we mention all the people we knew who have died. *Hurry-up*. An inventive phrase I don't immediately grasp. People here do not live long. In this view, they live fast.

Indeed, as I look around, it strikes me that almost everyone here is young. It's wonderful to see so many children in what once seemed to be a dying people, the numbers steadily declining after World War II. Most of the people here were born after the early '70s, when the village moved to Poiniara.

"They have never been to Wilaimbemki," says Edward. "They do not visit the old village—no one goes back."

Very soon, I realize, Jeremy and I alone will have witnessed that part of their heritage. We alone may remember it.

I would love to see Wilaimbemki now, if a helicopter could drop me in the bush, but I can't imagine that much of it remains. In moving, people would have taken anything that lasts: the corrugated tin, the metal pots, Solmet's cupboard where Loki's kittens were born. By now, the jungle will have moved in, covering the plaza, sprawling over the rotting houses, overgrowing the old gardens. Wild taro will be everywhere.

Poiniara (2008)

Poiniara (2008)

Taro: we have almost forgotten.

"Is it possible that we could have some taro?" we ask Edward, who clearly finds the question strange. No one is cooking now; no one is eating. We explain, to him and the people around us, how much we have missed Baining taro: where we live they do not have taro like theirs.

Word passes through the crowd, and someone finds us a taro that was cooked many hours before. We each take a bite, and though it is stale now, and dry, it is *taro tru*, and the very smell of it transports me back. Edward takes our camera and photographs the two of us holding the taro together. Taro, just everyday taro: the Baining must find us very odd.

While Jeremy talks to Edward, I wander around taking photos. I am not good at this, working so quickly and worrying that

Poiniara (2008)

my intrusion may not be welcome. And as I peer around the camera, I do not think it is. The older youngsters fool around and strike poses, but some of the children—and even their mothers—appear frightened. I am an alien, a creature from another world. I smile and I smile.

We realize that it will rain soon—it is starting already—and we should move on. We haven't been here long, yet if we aren't staying three weeks, or three months, three hours is enough: there isn't more to say or do in this setting, and people need to get back to their lives—and out of the rain.

We thank Edward and exchange addresses. Then we say our farewells. It is just as it was before: people approach us, singly and in pairs, to shake our hands. Everyone shakes our hands. They have us shake their babies' hands. "*Atlu,*" they say solemnly. "*Atlu,*" we nod solemnly in return. Such an earnest people, I think. So serious. So polite. So civilized.

Trekking back to the shore, with the rain gaining strength, we take a different path and cross the river only once. Our escorts stop at the plantation and ask the manager—a New Guinean though not a Baining—to drive us to the beach in his jeep. We wave good-bye to Edward, to the youngsters who met us on the beach, to Young Teingan who now looks so old.

On the boat trip back, the water is even rougher than when we came. "Did it go well?" Stephen asks, and we tell him that it went well, very well.

"They knew us," we say, still amazed.

But with the wind, the rain, the din of the motor, and the lurching about, we speak even less than before, so little can be heard. Again Jeremy sits close on the bench, to hold me fast on the boat, and we lean into one another, almost dreamily.

"Edward must be Solmet's son," he murmurs.

"No," I say, "he told me that his father was Langi, Kyimkyim's son. I met his mother, who was married to Langi. But Langi," I say, "has died."

But Jeremy shakes his head. "He looks so much like Solmet," he says. "He acts so much like Solmet."

And, of course, Jeremy is right: Edward is Solmet's son, as James Tapele tells us when we see him. How had I forgotten? The Baining adopt. Edward is Solmet's son, and at Poiniara it seems that history has eerily, poignantly, *elegantly* repeated, forty years on.

20

Unexpected Currents

With only a few days left, we are closing in on the last of our projects: to *stori* with James Tapele. We have been very curious about this man, the rare Baining who has entered the wider world. And our curiosity has only grown now that we have seen just how isolated Baining villages are even today, how insular the Baining have remained. I think of Edward and how many things he might do in this new country. Yet there he is, choosing to stay within the fold: the Baining way. James Tapele has somehow resisted that homeward, inward pull. Will he talk about this path he has taken?

"What will we *stori* about?" I ask Jeremy.

"I have no idea," he smiles.

We certainly do not foresee the way our meeting will go.

While we are waiting for James Tapele's visit, we spend a day winding up. We leave a message for our friend at Agmark, who is tied up in meetings, telling him that the Baining of Poiniara are thriving. We try to have dinner at the Kulau Lodge to thank the young woman for her help but get so lost on the lightless roads that we are forced to give it up. With equal parts hunger and distaste, we return to Hamamas instead. The maître d', when she hears that we will soon be going home, no longer bothers even to tease. After all, we never did leave KVR; we never learned: *we never came to Hamamas!* And now it is too late. She is pure disdain.

The heaviest ash we have yet seen falls on Kokopo, coating the town. At KVR, they hose and they hose. As I stand on our little porch, I greet the woman who is washing down the shrubs, a small child at her side. "M— Pidi," she says—I do not quite get her first name—as she extends her hand. She is the hotel's founder, I discover, with her husband, although she tells me that they have passed the business on to their children now. I make sure not to mention the furtive lunatic in our neighboring unit, she is so clearly proud of the hotel. She shows me how much they have expanded since the start.

"Those," she points to several units, "were our earliest rooms. This weekend we will celebrate ten years," she smiles. "But I worry," she adds, no longer smiling. "All this ash."

I nod but keep to myself how very right I think she is to be concerned. I cannot understand why people have chosen to expand here in Kokopo. It is true they seem safe from volcanic destruction. But they know that Tavurvur continues to fume, that seasonal winds will carry ash their way. How can they live here? What will this do to their lungs? And who will travel here to stay at this family's hotel, I wonder, as I watch people pass, shoulders hunched, heads down, their faces covered by scarves. The children wear little white masks. In fact, ash has closed the schools early for the day, says Father Hesse.

Father Hesse! We have caught up with him at last.

At Vunapope they have told us once again that the archbishop is at a meeting. But this time we wait. And as we sit in the outer room, skimming German magazines starring the German pope, Jeremy just happens to glance out the window—and there is Hesse, rushing across the lawn. He is a tall man and he moves fast, almost loping, but there is no way that we are letting him escape. We catch up at the site of the new church he is building. Still building, I think, after all these years.

We introduce ourselves politely. But he knows exactly who we are. Jeremy wrote him that letter. We have left messages at his office, twice. No one else looks like me.

He stares at us for a moment: I feel the chill coming off him in the heat of the day.

"Ah, the Baining," he says. "Yes, it was a trying time, wasn't it?"

A trying time. All at once I think I understand why he has been avoiding us. Here he is, archbishop of Rabaul, honored for the work he did with the Baining. But that work had a darker side, and we are the ones who know it: we are the ones to whom he confessed his problems and frustrations; we are witnesses to the less successful story that the public tale—perhaps even his own private version—omits. As with Bateson so many years ago, here we are, wafting in like an ill wind, stirring up bad memories.

But we have no desire to discuss the trials of that trying time. We do not want to pin him down, or expose him, or even refer to the difficulties. Indeed, we have nothing bad to say about the Baining. We tell him how thrilled we were to return, after all this time.

I watch his expression as he tries to piece this out. Has he really nothing to fear here? No unwelcome truths?

"Yes," he says at length, cautiously. "It must have felt like a real homecoming."

"It did," we smile. "It really did."

We talk briefly about Tavurvur, the air, the schools, but we cannot draw him out. Father Hesse has no time for us. He keeps looking at his watch. He has to get back to his site: the church that he is building, not on rock, not even on sand, but on ash.

At last the day of James Tapele's visit arrives. He is supposed to come at four and stay for dinner, but he turns up at KVR early—actually, while we are napping—mainly to tell us that he cannot stay. "*Ol i protes*," he says, somewhat vaguely: there is some labor protest that he needs to attend to. We arrange to have dinner the following night instead.

Still, since he is here and since it seems that he has a little time, Jeremy suggests that he might like to see some photos of Wilaimbemki. He explains about the photograph albums we have compiled for each village, the "memory books," as Edward so aptly called them—in fact, we still have the Puktas album, which we hope that James will deliver to the councilor there.

"But we have more photos," Jeremy says, "many more—almost a thousand more." He tries to explain that these photographs are on the computer, but in the end it is easier just to bring the computer from our room. The three of us head for a table on the veranda, which we have to ourselves. A waiter brings iced tea.

To us, this feels exciting. We love these photos: the dramatic pictures of the dances at Wilaimbemki, Raunsepna, and Alakasam and, even more, the portraits of Baining at work, or at meetings, or just hanging around, the essence of that photo essay I never did. If neither of us wrote about the experience, still, here is a record of the people: a selective record, to be sure, but honest. No Photoshop in 1969! These photographs, we think, are the best thing we took from New Guinea, and we feel delighted, almost proud, to show them to James. "Here are the Baining," we feel. "Right here."

But I notice as we scroll through the pictures that James seems restless and uneasy. I suspect that he has the labor protest on his mind—both whatever it is about and also the pressure to get there. I suspect too, from our first brief meeting, that he may be a restless and uneasy man.

But it soon becomes clear that the photographs themselves are disturbing him. He keeps looking at the screen and then turning away. He stares at the pictures of women bent double under huge loads of wood and taro; he does not seem amused at the baby sitting, like a cherry, on top. He shakes his head. It seems that the strength that so impresses us somehow upsets him. But he appears most distressed at the photos of the woman chewing *buai*, her mouth and fingers daubed with lime, and the woman with *pukpuk* sitting on the ground, her legs stretched out before her, her grass tuffet tucked under her. He pauses at these pictures; he looks pained.

"*Olsem Aprika*," he says, shaking his head sadly. "*Olsem Aprika*."—"It is just like Africa," he has said.

I take this in slowly. It seems like a world to absorb. It is just like Africa, and Africa, it seems, isn't good. To James, Africa must represent the *primitive*, the uncivilized. But how then does he see New Guinea? How does he see the Baining? Not, apparently, like this. I believe that these photos embarrass him. They shame him. He doesn't want them around. Indeed, he doesn't want them to exist.

I look again at these photos, forced now to see them through James's eyes. And, of course, I see, and though we do not look at each other, I can tell that Jeremy does as well. Those women bent double under their loads: *we* see enormous strength; *he* sees women almost naked serving as pack animals. That woman chewing *buai*: *we* see someone entirely unself-conscious, entirely *other*; *he* sees someone backward—and not nearly *other* enough.

All of this is churning in my head when James raises a more disquieting question.

"What are these for?" he wants to know. "For whose benefit?" He asks if we will sell them.

Sell them? "No, no," we tell him, both of us speaking at once. "We took these photos for ourselves. We have brought them now to share, to show. We don't intend to sell them." It is our turn now to be horrified: as if we were the *National Enquirer*!

Yet even as we are denying this, small sparks begin to fire in my brain, pinpricks of shame. After all, we did intend to sell them, didn't we? Not as he meant, to be sure, although I am not entirely certain what he did mean, but wouldn't these photographs be part of a book? A book that would be sold? And as he asked—as they ask in crime novels, in *murder mysteries!*—who would benefit: cui bono? Not the Baining, certainly. Even in showing the photos to friends—who find the people so "exotic"—don't *we* get the credit, aren't *we* made more interesting, enlarged?

By now I am overwhelmed. I am so taken by surprise, which in itself is a surprise. I had thought we were aware. I had thought we were self-aware. Even forty years ago, weren't we sensitive to racism and postcolonial issues? We never used the word *primitive*. We didn't think of the Baining as *primitive*. *I* thought their philosophy was stronger than ours. And haven't we long been aware of the issues of anthropology, the new awakening on both sides: anthropologists questioning the West's arrogant study of the *other* and the *other* nowadays questioning back?

Yet it's clear that we never worked it all through. It is as if, alongside the pictures of Baining that a Baining would rather not see, we have found a picture of ourselves that we too would rather not see.

"Well," James sighs, gesturing toward the screen, "this is history," he says. He sounds resigned.

———

Unexpected Currents

After this, I find that I am anxious about meeting James for dinner the next night. I am afraid that he was disturbed not only by our photos but also by the sense that we, Iara and Kusaiki, are not who he thought we were. It is unsettling to think that we aren't even who *we* thought we were.

In addition, KVR's kitchen was closed the night before—brought down, it seems, by its drains—and we are worried that there won't be any dinner. Where will we go? *Rapopo?* But it turns out that the restaurant is open and surprisingly busy. Although usually there are only a few of us for dinner, eating quietly in the dimly lit dining room, this evening most tables are full. For the first time we eat out on the veranda.

James seems a bit more comfortable tonight. But by now it is clear that he is not an easy man. He carries his restlessness with him. It is as if he cannot settle. Our conversation cannot settle either. It skitters about, from topic to topic, from Tok Pisin to English, from one dangling sentence to another, and I find that I cannot keep up. Jeremy seems to be doing better. To me, the conversation feels like a ball of loose ends.

Overall he seems worried and very negative. At Poiniara, he says the Baining aren't doing quite as well as we have been led to believe, even if they do own the land. Apparently, there are debts, complications. I cannot follow the details.

He talks about some murders. Witchcraft was involved. Suga was also involved, he says, and he insists that it's the Suga we knew, eccentric Suga, so this must have been some time ago: Suga, even when we knew him, was an older man. But I cannot tell if Suga was the victim or the killer, I cannot make sense of why the murder occurred, and in any case I'm certain that I'm mishearing. The Baining, I thought, had little to do with witchcraft. Was I wrong? And does James believe in witchcraft? I find it hard to believe that he would tell us if he did.

Toward the end of the meal, James says that he has been gathering Baining history, and he would like to write it down. A history! We tell him we think this is a wonderful idea, and he opens up a bit.

"*Rabaul* and *Kokopo*," he observes, "these are both Baining words: the Baining were here first," he says, "before the Tolai."

"Yes," Jeremy agrees. "We have heard people say the Baining were here before the Tolai. But I had no idea that *Rabaul* and *Kokopo* were Baining words. People know so little about the Baining. We hope you will write this history—it's needed."

James talks a bit more about his project, but he seems to see it as a struggle, perhaps too difficult to do.

"If you like," I say, hesitant, cautious, unsure that I should be saying this at all, "if you like, we could help with the writing."

"Yes," he says without commitment. "I could send it." I can see that he is mulling this over. "I could do that," he says. "I trust you."

And there it is, *trust*: he doesn't trust us at all. Exactly as I feared. It feels strange. I see the two of us as utterly trustworthy. Who could be more trustworthy than us? But we are Europeans, we are whites, even if we are Iara and Kusaiki—and Iara and Kusaiki aren't what they were: he has seen those photos.

He will never send us this work, I feel certain, even if he writes it, and I truly hope that he does. Not much has been written about the Baining, but what is out there is so often incorrect or distorted. I think of those Baining masks we have seen in museums that link them to initiation rites, and hunting rites, and harvest rites, and commemorations of the dead, none of which the Baining have. I think of the missionary writings that give religious import to Baining rituals that those rituals do not have. I think of the academic writings that find abstract dichotomies and parallels and meanings in Baining culture that the Baining themselves would find alien. I think of the New Guinea stamp we have bought depicting a spectacular Baining mask that has been misidentified as Tolai—*Tolai!*—surely, the ultimate error and insult, here in the Bainings' very own land. Can't someone get the facts straight? Can't someone write the truth about these people?

James Tapele could. Apart from the intelligence and drive he must possess to have gotten where he is, this man is an insider who has stepped outside what is so entirely an inside world. He has the distance to take in the whole and the closeness to understand what he is describing. But he has to be willing to look. Can he shed his embarrassment and shame to acknowledge the story of his people? Can he bring himself to see the Baining naked?

As we shake hands and say good-bye, I feel doubtful that he will try. But only a Baining, I am sure, could get the story of the Baining right.

21

Across

The night before our last in New Guinea, I stand on the porch of our unit, smoking my little cigar. As I lean against the rail, a large crab sidles up to me, as usual, stopping just below the step, which I assume—and hope—he cannot mount. Together we look out past the chain-link fence where people are still walking in the street. The grounds around me are empty, but I hear laughter and singing not far away: staff relaxing after work, perhaps rehearsing for the weekend fete.

The trip, I realize, is over. Tomorrow we will just be marking time. I am not in any rush to get home. Going back I know will be difficult: crossing time zones and climate zones, culture zones and age zones. Just leaving will be hard when I have been so intensely *here*: driving through rivers, getting lost in the bush, the two of us as foolish, as blithely oblivious to danger as when we were twenty-three and immortal. And back home will be real life, which will feel burdensome and daily and dull and much less real than here, where everything feels so alive, so immediate, so physical, every moment in play. I love this place. Already I feel a longing, a yearning to be here: I miss it even before I have left.

All the same, I am ready to leave. It isn't just the trip that is over: I feel as though the journey itself has come to a close. Ten days should not have been enough, such a thimble of time. And what, after all, have we done here? Who have we seen? A few hours in Puktas, a few hours in Poiniara, a few people we knew who knew us, Rabaul itself under ash.

Yet the trip has felt enormous. Huge. Deep. I feel as though we have made a journey to the underworld: as though we have actually been to Wilaimbemki, as it was; visited our house in Mlung's hamlet, as it was; met with our Baining friends, as they were—Mlung, Mran, Tuvuan, Kyimkyim, Madeilas, Teingan, Solmet, Iara, all of them hovering, nodding in greeting, smiling. *Amrs! Atlu! So you are back. We always knew you would return.*

And of course, it hasn't been only ten days, just the last ten days of forty years, the final stretch to a finish line we didn't believe we would ever reach and weren't even certain existed.

"Will we be able to talk about New Guinea now? Finally?" I ask Jeremy.

"Probably not," he says, and both of us laugh.

Still, we have hacked our way through a jungle of memory, and here it is: the other side.

From here, I can see it whole. There we are in London, arm in arm, joined at the hip, Siamese twins who don't know where one leaves off and the other begins. There we are traveling to New Guinea, alternately doing battle and making love. At each stop—after family, and Bateson, and Canberra—we think: at last we're alone! As if we didn't still have the other to contend with, as if—despite all experience and reason—we still believe that two can be one.

And there we are trundling into Puktas, the Baining youngsters carrying our gear. We think we are traveling light, but from here I can see all the baggage: the personal needs, the desires and ambitions, the hang-ups, the rivalry, the possessive, demanding love.

And my God, right there in that duffel, all of Western Civ! We think we are so sophisticated, but look at us—so young, mere fledglings. We are here to ask: *How do you live?* But we also find ourselves asking: *How does one live? How should we live?* We keep rifling through that duffel for answers, but we find that over time, the contents have gone moldy from the moisture, or they have melted in the heat, or they have been chewed and shredded and mauled by a wonderland of bugs.

Even the ideas we still recognize look different, absurdly, almost comically distorted, as if seen through a series of funhouse mirrors. Of course! Here among the Baining, they are inflected by shape: some have grown long and transparently thin, some have grown round and fat and seem unnaturally inflated, some have diminished and seem tiny. Most are now simply flat; they have no dimension at all. How could we have thought the theories of Freud or Levi-Strauss, the philosophies of Hardy or Thoreau, the doctrines of Adam Smith or Karl Marx—each so much a product of *terroir*—could withstand every culture and climate? Needy, lost, we look to the Baining for answers to questions they have surely never asked.

From here, I see the Baining looking on. They seem kindly: they take us into their village; they feed us. Do they have any idea really who we are? Have we any idea really who they are? I cannot imagine what they are thinking. I cannot imagine even what they are thinking about. But why should this come as a surprise? I barely know what Jeremy is thinking, his mind works so differently from mine: we see and know such different things. How then could I ever get inside the head of a Baining? And which Baining? Mlung? Kyimkyim? Suga? How can we assume that all of these people share the same thoughts and attitudes, that they—unlike us, so individual, so singular—are all much the same?

From here, I see our field trip as a Rorschach test, brought to life: the assignment is to look around and find the story. But what could we see but what we had learned to see, what we were able to see? What kind of story could we tell but the kind of story we had learned to tell? What meaning could we find but the sort of things we had learned to comprehend as *meanings*? What lexicon could we use but our own index of untranslatables: religion, god, and ritual; incest and taboo; ambitious, intellectual, curious; happy, sad, shy, bored—*doomed*.

And the story we came up with—the story we wrote but could have sworn that we had read—clearly gripped us. A powerful, frightening, yet seductive view of life stripped down to its essence—of life devoid of meaning—it connected to something we knew. Indeed, we read it back into our lives. As if the Baining way of life was more *real*, more *true* than ours. As if we felt that we ought to be Baining. As if we believed that at heart—stripped down—we already were.

"To me, they never really seemed foreign," Jeremy has said. "From the first, they didn't seem all that different."

"Yes," I agreed. "I know." But we were wrong: surely they were.

From here, it seems to me that I understand the Baining even less than I thought I did, which is just as it should be: I have set aside the assumptions I didn't even realize I had. From here it seems to me that the Baining like being Baining. I do not think that they are sad. I have no idea if they are bored. I certainly do not think that they see themselves as doomed. They always come home. They keep to themselves, and they remain so much themselves, holding fast to their Bainingness. As anthropologist Jane Fajans has observed, the Baining have willingly accepted some changes—from the missions or the government—but none that conflict with their traditional culture, which persists. National independence, Tavurvur, commerce, huge eruptions have occurred in the past forty years, and here are the Baining, still Baining: still farmers, still pragmatic, still reserved, a people with no use of their own for rank, or power, or wealth. Or the outside world, if the world would let them be.

And so far—almost incredibly—the world has mostly let them be. From here, I can only wonder what will happen to the Baining now: now that they have some form of wealth to inherit, cacao lots to leave their children, trade and markets to determine the value of their produce, which is no longer only taro. Will they change? Will they grow greedy? *Ambitious*? Will they think about *getting on*? Will some company move their mountains for minerals and overturn their world? Will loggers strip their forests and denude their lives?

Or will Tavurvur in some sense continue to preserve them, daunting intruders with fire and ash? Will the cacao market prove shaky, as our Agmark friend feared, and the Baining return to their gardens? Seeing the Baining in these mountains where so little appears to have changed in forty years—in eighty years!—it is easy to imagine and hope that it never will.

But I realize as I come to the end of my little cigar, the smoke curling into the night, that I have no way to forecast the future, and I am here to revisit the past. What a mark these quiet people made on our lives. How they awed and angered and frightened us with how little they seemed to need, threatening everything we thought, even thinking itself. There was before and after the Baining, and after, nothing felt the same. There we are at the end of our field trip, running in fear and anger from what the Baining seemed to have revealed about life and ourselves. There we are forever after, running in place. "Never reaching home," admits Jeremy, now, at last, after all these years.

We can't change that past, but we have given it a different ending, which has changed the story itself. We are no longer

Yes, we will say. We came by plane.

Na yutupela stap long Australia? Long Pot Mosbi? How many hours in the plane?

We stayed in Australia, but not Port Moresby, we will say—and altogether, from home, it was twenty-five hours in the plane.

Ah, tupela ten faiv aua! they will say. *Tupela ten faiv aua! Yutupela kam longwe tru!* they will say. And they will smile at us and one another, taking pleasure in the satisfying length of this very long journey.

Yes, we will say, *longwe tru*. And standing close—so close that we can feel each other's warmth—we will smile at them and one another, taking pleasure in the close of this extraordinary journey. A long, long way.

afraid, we are no longer angry, and we are no longer running. We see no need for judgments—one culture against another—and no choice between them that we ever could have made.

From here, we no longer blame our young selves for not being who we thought we should be. From here, we no longer blame one another for not being what a partner, we thought, should be. From here, we no longer blame the Baining for not being who anthropologists thought they should be. And from here, we no longer blame this journey for leaving us in exile, which now feels like a place of our own.

We aren't Baining. We have never quite come home. But our battles—with the Baining and one another—have ended. And somehow everyone has won.

Tomorrow we will go to the market to bid farewell to the Baining. We will find them sitting by themselves, under an umbrella, surrounded by bundles of taro.

Atlu, we will say.

Atlu, they will smile.

These will not be Baining from villages we know, and we will tell them our little story: how we lived in Puktas and Wilaimbemki a long time ago. They will nod, and smile again, and they will talk about what interests them most: journey questions, of course.

Yutupela kam long we? they will ask, by now getting up and coming over, the group of us standing in a huddle. Where are you from?

We come from America, we will say. Boston is our hometown—*asples bilong mitupela*—we will add, thinking that this is something they will like to know and enjoying the colorful Tok Pisin—*asples!*—which we will miss.

Ah, they will reply. *Na yutupela kam hia long balus?* they will ask.